# The Light of Nature and the Law of God

## Antislavery in Ontario 1833–1877

ALLEN P. STOUFFER

Louisiana State University Press
Baton Rouge

First published in the United States 1992 by
Louisiana State University Press

Printed in Canada on acid-free paper

This book has been published with the help of a grant from the
Canadian Federation for the Humanities, using funds provided by the
Social Sciences and Humanities Research Council of Canada. Publication
has also been supported by the Canada Council through its block grant
program.

---

**Library of Congress Cataloguing-in-Publication Data**

Stouffer, Allen P., 1937–
  The light of nature and the law of God: antislavery in Ontario,
  1833–1877 / Allen P. Stouffer.
    p. cm.
  Includes bibliographical references and index.
  ISBN 0-8071-1791-9 (alk. paper)
    1. Slavery — Ontario — Anti-slavery movements — History — 19th
  century.   2. Abolitionists — Ontario — History — 19th century.
  HT1052.S76     1992
  326'.09713'09034 — dc20
                                                            92-10289
                                                                 CIP

---

Published simultaneously in Canada by McGill-Queen's University Press.

This book was typeset by Typo Litho composition inc. in 10/12 Palatino.

*For Sarah, always the first reader,*
*and for Scott and Kirk*

*In memory of my parents,*
*Lambert and Alma Valentine Stouffer*

# Contents

# Tables

# Abbreviations

AAS    American Anti-Slavery Society
ACS    American Colonization Society
AFAS    American and Foreign Anti-Slavery Society
ASC    Anti-Slavery Society of Canada
BFAS    British and Foreign Anti-Slavery Society
CHR    *Canadian Historical Review*
DCB    *Dictionary of Canadian Biography*
EES    Edinburgh Emancipation Society
FCAS    Free Church Anti-Slavery Society
GES    Glasgow Emancipation Society
NAC    National Archives of Canada
UCAS    Upper Canada Anti-Slavery Society

# Preface

A respected mentor once told me that determining the direction of one's research was largely a matter of turning one's head to the wind and continually sniffing the breeze. As a young graduate student I was puzzled by the comment, but this study's tortuous path from inception to completion corroborates the perceptiveness of that statement. Some two decades ago, while preparing a dissertation on Canadian-American relations at the close of the American Civil War, I casually noted the remarkable curiosity that Ontario editors displayed about the future of the American freedmen. The topic was only tangentially related to my main interest at the time and I gave it little more than a passing nod. However, it lingered in the back of my mind as an enticing subject for future consideration. A sabbatical leave provided the opportunity. The outcome was an essay on Ontario's perception of the freedmen which revealed a good deal about British North American racial attitudes in the period following the Civil War. Inevitably, this raised questions about racial attitudes before 1860. Were British North Americans' impressions of American blacks as slaves similar to their image of them as freedmen? Had the Civil War and emancipation made a difference?

Since an analysis of Ontario newspaper attitudes on Reconstruction had been productive for the postwar years, I felt that a similar approach might work for the prewar era. For example, what had provincial editors written about John Brown's raid on Harper's Ferry and his subsequent execution? What had they written about the Dred Scott decision, or "Bleeding Kansas," or the 1850 Fugitive Slave

Law? Would the editorials unwittingly reveal British North American views on African Americans, as in the case of Reconstruction?

The Fugitive Slave Law seemed to be a promising departure point, and I began reading Ontario newspapers for late 1850. To my surprise, this led to accounts in the Toronto press of the formation of the Anti-Slavery Society of Canada. This was a pulse-quickening find, for the society's leaders would have been certain to discuss the slaves. The quest for their comments led the research through their abolitionist writings and activities in British North America and then across the Atlantic, revealing a deep involvement in the British antislavery movement. This trek through the labyrinth of British abolitionism combined with the provincial abolitionists' virulent attack on slavery to divert my interest from the original topic. Thereafter, the object of the quest was the antislavery movement in British North America.

The strong religious affiliation of virtually all the actors in the story thus far unmistakably pointed to the next phase of the research. How had the various Ontario denominations responded to slavery? Answering this question unexpectedly led down another corridor to the discovery of an earlier stage of the provincial movement in the 1830s. And so it went; pursuing one subtopic led serendipitously to the next, until the feasibility of a book-length study became clear. In retrospect, it was a matter of "continually sniffing the breeze."

Several people made important contributions to this study. Jason H. Silverman of Winthrop College was an inspiration from the beginning, with his enthusiastic support and his generous contributions from his own research files. Robin Winks of Yale University, C. Peter Ripley, editor of the Black Abolitionist Papers project at Florida State University, and George Shepperson, now retired from Edinburgh University's Department of History, offered warm encouragement and wise counsel in the formative stage of the project. C. Duncan Rice, dean of New York University, and Neil MacKinnon and A.A. MacKenzie, my colleagues in the Department of History at St Francis Xavier University, read parts of the manuscript at various stages. Dr Neil Semple, formerly a senior archivist at the United Church of Canada Archives and now an independent historian preparing a study of Canadian Methodism, read the entire piece and saved me from several pitfalls in Canadian church history. John Webster Grant guided me to sources that illuminated Canadian Methodists' response to slavery. John McKivigan, an associate editor of the Frederic Douglass Papers at Yale, obligingly permitted me to adapt his codebook for use in the quantified section on Canadian antislavery leaders in chapter 8, while Muhammad Fiaz, then chair of the St Francis Xavier University's Department of Sociology, gave unsparingly of his time to help analyse the data.

Numerous institutions and people associated with them facilitated my access to sources. At the head of the list stands the indispensable assistance of the Angus L. Macdonald Library's Interlibrary Loan Department at my home university. *Slavery and Abolition* and *Ontario History* generously granted permission to quote extensively in chapters 2 and 9, respectively, from my two previously published articles, "Michael Willis and the British Roots of Canadian Antislavery" and "A 'Restless Child of Change and Accident': The Black Image in Nineteenth Century Ontario." Leon Warmski drew on his specialized knowledge of collections at the Ontario Archives to accommodate numerous requests in person and by mail, as did Kim Arnold at the Presbyterian Church in Canada Archives, and the staff of the United Church of Canada Archives. I am equally indebted to Christine Mosser and her assistants in the Baldwin Room at the Metropolitan Toronto Central Library. Other Canadian institutions that I frequently drew on include the National Library and the National Archives of Canada, the Anglican Archives at Church House in Toronto, the Robarts Library at the University of Toronto, the Douglas Library at Queen's University, the Weldon Library at the University of Western Ontario, the public libraries in Chatham and London, and the Raleigh Township Centennial Museum.

American libraries supplied much material that was vitally important. The Boston Public Library's periodical collection was an unmatched source of abolitionist journals. Oberlin College Library and Archives, the William L. Clements Library at the University of Michigan, the Beinecke Rare Book and Manuscript Library at Yale, the Houghton Library at Harvard, the Morris Library at the University of Southern Illinois, Howard University Library, and the New York Public Library all either accommodated my visits or generously provided copies of rare items.

In Britain, where sources were critically important in establishing ties between Canadian and British antislavery, I am particularly indebted to the following people: Dr Fiona Spiers of Leeds for advice on locating material and for warm hospitality; Mr Alan S. Bell, librarian at Rhodes House, Oxford, for typed copies of letters too fragile to be reproduced otherwise; Miss Katherine Davidson and Mr Ian F. Maciver of the National Library of Scotland, who helped me to obtain copies of rare pamphlets at an early stage in the research; Dr B.L.H. Horn, assistant keeper of the records at the Scottish Record Office, for reading minutes of the Renfield Street church in Glasgow during the pastorate of Michael Willis and for commenting on their prospective usefulness; and John and Sheila Bain of Kincardine-on-Forth for their cheerful hearth and comfortable bed. The following institutions made their records available: Dr Williams's Library, London; the British Newspaper Library, Colindale; Rhodes House Library, Oxford; Wolverhampton Borough Archives; the William Salt Library, Stafford, and Staffordshire Record Office; John Rylands Library, University of Manchester; Mitchell Library, Glasgow; Renfrew District Library, Paisley; the Scottish Record Office, National Library of Scotland, Edinburgh Central Library, and New College Library, all in Edinburgh; and the Linen Hall Library and the Wesley Historical Society (Irish Branch), Aldersgate House, both in Belfast.

I am very grateful to Margaret Dalrymple, editor-in-chief of Louisiana State University Press, and especially to Philip Cercone, executive director and editor of McGill-Queen's University Press, the primary publisher. Each handled the initial review process with professional grace and sensitivity, and both extended to me every courtesy in cooperating to see the manuscript through to publication.

Two other people deserve special mention. Deborah Murphy, the Department of History's industrious secretary, earned my enduring gratitude. No one could have asked for more than her cheery disposition and loyal, efficient work as she typed the manuscript's numerous drafts. Carlotta Lemieux's keen editorial talents helped me to avoid many mechanical errors and improved the prose immeasurably.

Finally, I must express my appreciation to the St Francis Xavier University Council for Research and to the Social Sciences and Humanities Research Council of Canada for several grants, without which the research for this volume would have been impossible.

*The Light of Nature and the Law of God*

# Introduction

Few historians would claim that antislavery has received its full due in Canadian historiography. In retrospect this is surprising, for antislavery was one of the great nineteenth-century reform movements, and it became an important theme in Anglo-American history. With a steady flow of fugitive slaves across the border in search of freedom, British North America's proximity to the United States meant that the provinces could scarcely avoid some involvement. Moreover, continuing immigration from the British Isles at mid-century increased the likelihood of provincial participation, for with the numerous immigrants came antislavery convictions. Yet investigation of Canada's role in ending slavery in the United States has been quite limited, and some studies are outdated. C. Peter Ripley's recent work on Canada in the *Black Abolitionist Papers*, which comprehensively details the work of black abolitionists in British North America, is a notable exception. However, in both perspective and method, research on the activities of white provincial abolitionists lags far behind the increasing number of innovative studies on American and British antislavery.

Scholarly analysis of the field began with Fred Landon's 1919 master's thesis, "The Relation of Canada to the Anti-Slavery and Abolition Movements in the United States." Unfortunately, this pioneering work skirted significant analysis of important sub-themes, such as the Anti-Slavery Society of Canada and the role of the churches. Nor did Landon's numerous later articles weave the various strands of the antislavery story he uncovered into an integrated account. "The Anti-Slavery Society of Canada," Ian C. Pemberton's 1967 master's thesis, enlarged the picture of Canadian antislavery somewhat. In following the society's development from 1851 through the early 1860s, it identified several social and religious forces that influenced the organization. Both studies recognized that Canadian antislavery was part of a larger North Atlantic abolitionist triangle but did not enlarge on the topic. Their lasting contribution was to establish that there had been an antislavery movement in Canada.

A 1960 dissertation by Alexander L. Murray, entitled "Canada and the Anglo-American Anti-Slavery Movement: A Study in International Philanthropy," examined the subject more broadly and moved the study of British North American antislavery from a largely Canadian framework to an international setting. Foreshadowing the comparative approach that students of black history used after the 1960s, Murray found that the agitation against slavery was an Anglo-American phenomenon in which Canada participated mainly because it was a haven for fugitive slaves.

The most incisive analysis of Canadian antislavery to date, however, is Robin Winks's "'A Sacred Animosity': Abolitionism in Canada," an essay that appeared in 1965. Its findings echoed through his ground-breaking *Blacks in Canada: A History*. Drawing on a rich variety of sources, this wide-ranging and perceptive piece established the general contours of the field. It found that Canada's participation in the abolition movement was mainly the result of proximity to the United States, rather than the result of concern for the rights and equality of the fugitives who fled to Canada, a conclusion that was also implicit in Murray's work.

By more realistically assessing the nature of British North America's commitment to black rights and equality, these studies performed an important function. They dealt a blow to the popular myth that the provinces were a prejudice-free haven at the end of the Underground Railroad, empathetically waiting to receive slavery's oppressed victims. The mid-nineteenth-century reports of Benjamin Drew and Samuel Gridley Howe, American abolitionists who investigated Canada West's reception of fugitive slaves, revealed the existence of much prejudice. Jason H. Silverman's judicious *Unwelcome Guests: The White Canadian Response to American Fugitive Slaves, 1800–1865* (1985) corroborated this finding.

However, in attributing British North America's antislavery participation to the proximity factor so fully, there is reason to question whether some studies attached enough importance to the threads of idealism interwoven in its antislavery tapestry. For example, during the later 1830s, well before the rising number of fugitive slaves allegedly forced British North Americans into the antislavery stream, there was substantial evidence of antislavery sentiment in Upper Canada. This early wave of hostility was strong enough to foster the region's first antislavery society. The Upper Canada Anti-Slavery Society proved to be short-lived, but the abolitionist writings of publicist Peter Brown showed that the antislavery sentiment in which it was rooted did not entirely disappear in the following decade. The British North American colonies were still closely tied to the mother country, which remained the chief source of settlers in the pre–Civil War era. Inevitably, the values and institutions of the homeland retained a powerful hold on immigrant behaviour patterns. British North Americans, therefore, were likely to be influenced by the antislavery movement that was currently thriving in Britain. Earlier works recognized that British North American antislavery was one side of the abolitionist triangle which the North Atlantic partners shared; but they underestimated the flow along the antislavery axis from mother country to colony, a theme that this study explores at some length.

In the antislavery campaign that reached maturity at midcentury, Canadian abolitionists relied mainly on the Elgin Association and the Anti-Slavery Society of Canada to achieve the twofold task of aiding fugitive slaves and bringing public opinion to full-voiced condemnation of slavery. The churches seemed a likely ally in this benevolent mission, for they were an important influence in the lives of nineteenth-century British North Americans, and historians have noted the extensive involvement of evangelicals in antislavery. However, studies such as C. Duncan Rice's *The Scots Abolitionists, 1833–1861* and John R. McKivigan's *The War against Proslavery Religion: Abolitionism and the Northern Churches, 1830–1865* reveal the churches' surprisingly ambivalent role in British and American antislavery. The Canadian churches were no different; some abolitionists succeeded in committing their denominations to forthright support of antislavery, but other bodies remained aloof. At first glance, this diverse response seems attributable to the differences between traditionalists and evangelicals, but this explanation breaks down when applied to Canada West's numerous Methodists, and it therefore requires fuller examination.

In addition to proximity to the United States, the British connection, and the church, a broad range of socio-economic factors undoubtedly influenced the Ontario antislavery movement. This study seeks to identify them by employing an innovative quantitative approach that is characteristic of much recent Anglo-American slavery and abolition scholarship, applying it to the analysis of the leader-ship as well as the rank and file of Canadian antislavery. The re-sulting group profiles yield a more sharply defined image of those involved and thus enhance our understanding of the movement's character.

While the Civil War and the Thirteenth Amendment ended slav-ery, they left unfinished business for the abolitionists. Through the turmoil of Reconstruction, Americans laboured to define the role that the liberated slaves would play in their society. Only with the compromise of 1877 did the great crusade at last end. No organized antislavery movement continued in Canada West, but British North Americans displayed much interest in this process and their jour-nalists extensively discussed the freedman's destiny. Analysing their comments reveals much about underlying Ontario attitudes towards blacks and, interestingly enough, makes the region's earlier reluc-tance to adopt abolition more comprehensible.

This study is not an exhaustive examination of antislavery in Can-ada. Relying on existing scholarship to trace the decline of slavery in the British North American provinces early in the nineteenth century, it focuses on the movement among whites in present-day Ontario (the region previously known as Upper Canada and, later, Canada West) to end slavery in the United States between 1833 and 1877. The Ripley study obviated the necessity of dealing with black abolitionists' activities except where they overlapped with the work of other abolitionists. The analysis of Canadian antislavery will not be complete until it has also been explored in francophone and Atlantic Canada, as well as in the work of independent abolitionists such as John J.E. Linton, Alexander Milton Ross, and William Som-merville.

# 1 The Loyalists and Slavery

A feeling of satisfaction, tinged with expectation, animated the people awaiting the speakers in Music Hall at the new Mechanics' Institute. Despite the harsh weather that swept across Toronto that February night, a near-capacity crowd had gathered for a meeting of the Anti-Slavery Society of Canada. An evening of speeches usually drew numbers in this provincial town where there was little excitement, but this was a special occasion. It was 1863, the midpoint of the American Civil War, and Abraham Lincoln's long-awaited Emancipation Proclamation, implemented the previous month, was a promising step towards freeing American slaves. Some society members had been pursuing this goal for decades, but the whole audience shared the sense of accomplishment. Before the meeting ended, speaker after speaker had praised England for liberating the 800,000 slaves once held in the British Empire and had given thanks that freedom was now in sight for the 4 million American slaves. Curiously, although the speakers were generally well informed about the long history of the Anglo-American antislavery struggle, none of them mentioned Upper Canada's experience with slavery or thought to praise the generation of settlers who had eliminated this evil from British North America early in the nineteenth century.[1]

The reason for this anomaly was that the people gathered in the hall that night, like many of their twentieth-century descendants, collectively had forgotten that slavery ever existed in Canada. In fact, nineteenth-century British North Americans prided themselves on having escaped the loathsome institution which shamed their freedom-canting republican neighbours. The Canadian historian François-Xavier Garneau, writing in the 1840s and perhaps seeking to contrast New France favourably with Quebec after the British conquest, encouraged the growth of this complacent self-image. While almost certainly knowing otherwise, he intimated that New France had been saved from the scourge of slavery by wise colonial authorities, who had discouraged the introduction of Negro slaves. The French crown shared credit for this virtuous policy, according to Garneau, for it had rebuffed local requests to secure slaves. Some writers accepted Garneau's account uncritically, and the legend of a slavery-free Canada quickly took root. In 1849, when the Toronto *Globe*, ironically the province's leading antislavery newspaper, extended this to the post-conquest era by claiming that "slavery never had an existence in Canada," the statement went unchallenged.

Fortunately, twentieth-century scholars such as jurist William Renwick Riddell and, more recently, the historians Marcel Trudel and Robin Winks have revealed the full dimensions of the development and eventual demise of slavery in Canada; yet the myth still has deep roots in the popular mind. A full re-examination of how slavery ended in Canada is not intended here. Yet it must be the point of departure, for it helps to explain why Upper Canadians, the focus of this study, responded so lethargically to the call for immediate abolition of slavery that surged so powerfully through Britain and the United States in the late 1820s and early 1830s.[2]

ALTHOUGH SLAVERY EXISTED in seventeenth-century New France, it never became very extensive and it lacked firm legal sanction until the late 1680s, for the colony's economy had little use for slaves. Until 1663, the province was a seigneury of the Compagnie des Cent-Associés, whose purpose was to reap quick profits from furs. Since fur trading did not require gang labour, there was no need for a large-scale slave system. Indians themselves held aboriginal slaves – "panis" – whom they had captured in battle or obtained by trading with other tribes, and French settlers occasionally purchased these captives to serve as field hands or domestics. However, Negro bondage was not common. The first black slave for whom there is a clear record was a man named Olivier Le Jeune. The English sold him in Quebec in 1628, but evidently he was freed later, for on his death in 1654 he was listed as a domestic rather than a slave. It is doubtful if there was another black slave in the colony until late in the century.[3]

When New France came under royal control in 1663, Louis XIV's minister of marine, Jean-Jacques Colbert, implemented a policy that envisioned intensive colonial development. Jean Talon, the new intendant, and his successors worked assiduously to strengthen the colony by diversifying its economic life. In 1677 the Sieur des Bringandières received permission to develop mines in the province, but a labour shortage hampered the enterprise. He appealed for help to Governor Denonville and Intendant Champigny, who in 1688 convinced the crown to allow the importation of slaves. Permission was granted the following year, but uncertainty created by the immediate outbreak of King William's War virtually nullified the royal assent. Approval was renewed in 1701, but implementation of the scheme was interrupted again when the War of the Spanish Succession began the next year. Unfortunately for New France, Paris abandoned its colonial development policy in 1704 in order to avoid risking economic competition with the mother country, and thereafter the colony was left on its own to obtain slaves. As a result, New France reverted to dependence on the fur trade, and slaves lost their appeal.[4]

Without the wars that enveloped the turn of the century, slavery might have become more deeply interwoven with the socioeconomic fabric of eighteenth-century New France. Even so, it did take root, for wealthier families sought slaves as household servants and field labourers. The previously obtained royal approval to import slaves afforded a legal basis for the institution, and the final steps in defining its legal status were soon taken. In 1709, Intendant Jacques Raudot issued an ordinance that removed all doubt about the condition of purchased labourers by declaring that "all panis and Negroes who had been purchased and who will be purchased, shall be the property of those who have purchased them and will be their slaves." Thirty years later, a second directive specified the procedure for freeing slaves by voiding verbal manumissions and requiring a notary's certificate recorded at a royal registry to validate the transaction. To govern slave behaviour, New France's officials relied on the *Code Noir*, a body of law developed in 1685 for French West Indian slaves, even though it did not officially apply to the Canadian colony. A careful analysis has found that by 1759, just before Britain seized New France, there were 3604 slaves in the colony, 1132 of whom were blacks, and that 77.2 per cent of the total resided in towns. Thus, while slavery was present in New France, it never became a dominant feature of economic and social life.[5]

Initially, Britain's conquest of France's North American colonies in 1763 strengthened slavery. Clause 47 of the Articles of Capitulation, which were completed in 1760 when the Marquis de Vaudreuil surrendered Montreal to General Jeffery Amherst, stated that "Negroes and Panis of both Sexes shall remain in the possession of the French and Canadians to whom they belong; they shall be at liberty to keep them in their service in the Colony or sell them: and they may also continue to bring them up in the Roman religion." These provisions, which were reaffirmed in the Royal Proclamation of 1763, were included virtually without change in the peace treaty of 1763 when France ceded to Britain her mainland North American empire east of the Mississippi River. The treaty also replaced French civil law (under which slaves had informally received minimal protection from the *Code Noir*) with English civil and criminal law. This obliterated the slaves' rights, for in the latter system of jurisprudence a slave was treated as an item of property entirely without rights. French civil law was reinstated in 1774 by the Quebec Act, but when the Province of Quebec was divided into Upper and Lower Canada in 1791, English civil law was instituted in Upper Canada (today's Ontario), but the English criminal law code became the law of both. Much to the disappointment of the newly awakened antislavery forces in Britain, the famous case of *Somerset v. Stewart* in 1772, which found that slavery could not exist in England, had no effect in British North America. When Granville Sharp, the British abolitionist who had initiated the *Somerset* suit, tried to end all British slavery by applying the decision to the entire British Empire, he quickly found that British common law did not extend to imperial regions in which colonial statutes recognized slavery. In fact, the imperial parliament soon extended further protection to slavery in British North America by a 1790 measure designed to encourage immigration into the colonies. It permitted free entry of "Negroes, household furniture, utensils of husbandry or cloathing [*sic*]," provided the items were not sold for one year.[6]

Buttressed by these new legal sanctions, slavery continued in Quebec during the early British period. General James Murray, the first British governor, in 1763 requested a New York friend to purchase, for his own personal use, two sturdy young slaves together with suitable wives. He also harboured the aspiration of using slavery in the development of Quebec agriculture. Despairing of finding suitable farm labourers among ex-soldiers or the French population (the French, he believed, would only work for themselves), Murray wanted to import black slaves, preferably from the northern colonies, since they would already be adapted to the severe Canadian climate. Parish documents of the time record slave marriages and baptisms, and newspapers carry advertisements requesting assistance in locating runaways. Slavery was also a continuing theme in the official correspondence of the period.[7]

Farther east, in the colony of Nova Scotia, slavery was slower to make its appearance. Although there was the occasional exception

– for instance, there may have been a slave at Port Royal in 1606, and Isaac Louis de Forant, governor of Louisbourg, owned one in 1739–40 – the Acadians on the whole seem not to have held slaves. However, slaves arrived soon after the English settled Halifax in 1749. In 1752 there was a reference to a "Negro servant" in a Halifax will, and the same year Joshua Mauger, a navy victualler, offered black slaves for sale in the new town. Within a decade, slaves had been introduced in Liverpool, and then in New Glasgow, Bridgetown, and several other communities. The usual notices of sale and offers of reward for returning fugitives soon appeared. An act of the general assembly extended indirect legal sanction to slavery in 1762. It provided that if anyone, including a "Negro slave," left a pawn or pledge worth more than five shillings with a liquor vendor, that person or his owner could initiate proceedings to reclaim it, and the vendor would be liable for a fine.[8]

Although the British conquest perpetuated slavery, reducing the already minuscule rights of the slaves to the point of extinction, in reality it caused no fundamental changes to the institution as it had existed in New France. Within twenty years, however, another event brought with it influences that were to have fateful consequences for slavery in both Quebec and Nova Scotia. For although the American Revolution initially strengthened slavery in these two colonies, in the long run it released forces that placed slavery on the road to elimination in British North America three decades before the institution was ended in the British Empire and a half century before it disappeared in the United States.

At the close of the American Revolution, substantial numbers of people who wished to retain their ties with the crown fled to British North America. Some of these Loyalists, as they were called, were slaveowners whose bondsmen accompanied them. Moreover, late in the war, in an effort to weaken the rebels, Sir Guy Carleton, who was commander-in-chief of British forces on the continent, offered freedom to slaves who joined the British cause. After the fighting ended, those who had done so were transported, along with the white Loyalists and their slaves, to various British colonies, including Nova Scotia. Although Carleton kept full records of the former slaves he embarked, in case their owners made future claims for compensation, it is impossible to determine how many of the several thousand blacks in Nova Scotia after the Revolution were slaves and how many were free. On the other hand, most of the blacks who went to Quebec entered as slaves of fleeing Loyalists, but there is no clear record of the numbers involved. The first census to record slaves, taken in 1784, counted 304 in the region that would shortly become Lower Canada. However, this figure is probably too low, for some slaves had been liberated and more were arriving regularly. The Loyalists spread quickly into the fertile Eastern Townships and westward along the shore of Lake Ontario, and there were slaves in most communities. In the Niagara region alone, for example, there were estimated to be 300 in 1791.[9]

In these conditions, slavery, a relatively stable feature of early British North American life, underwent several changes. The number of black slaves increased rapidly, effectively replacing the panis. Slaves performed a larger variety of tasks, for they brought a multiplicity of skills from their differing backgrounds, and no longer did they reside mainly in the urban areas of New France. But if slavery initially drew fresh impetus from the Loyalist migration, this proved to be short-lived. Since freedmen also were part of the influx, slaves must have seen that a dark skin did not necessarily dictate hereditary bondage and they must have begun to think about their own freedom. Some white Loyalists found that they could not profitably maintain a large body of slaves after the heavy work of field clearing was done, and manumissions occurred. Moreover, since the immigrants came from areas with differing slave codes and customs, they applied a mixture of the familiar practices. The least harsh practices tended to become dominant among those who came from colonies that did not have well-developed slave codes, and the operation of slavery was thus moderated. Slave families were maintained intact, slaves were baptized, and some even received rudimentary education. Most important, some Loyalists came from areas like New York and New England where slavery was weakening and where there was already a move towards an antislavery position. Once settled in British North America, these Loyalists were likely to view slavery as a remnant of America's corrupt republican institutions from which they wanted to distance themselves. For these underlying reasons, the Loyalists virtually ended slavery in Canada within two decades of their arrival.[10]

The new colony of Upper Canada led the way with legislation that mortally wounded slavery. The driving force behind this step was John Graves Simcoe, the lieutenant-governor of the colony. Simcoe had shown a special interest in blacks during the American Revolution when, as a young British officer in New England, he had unsuccessfully proposed forming a corps among the free blacks of Boston for service in the conflict. On his return to England after the war, he briefly represented St Mawes, Cornwall, in Parliament in 1790, and from that position he reportedly spoke out against slavery. Before entering office in Upper Canada, he wrote privately that in his view slavery violated both the spirit of Christianity and the British constitution, and he declared that he would approve no legislation that treated descendants of Africans differently from Europeans. Although Simcoe was zealous for Upper Canada's growth, he entertained doubts about the 1790 imperial statute that was intended to promote immigration to British North America; he feared that the law, by allowing slaveholders to import their slaves duty free with other property, would expand provincial slavery, and he even considered issuing a proclamation freeing the slaves. Thus, Simcoe brought to his post a deep-seated abhorrence of slavery. Fortunately, a convenient opportunity to strike a blow against it soon appeared. [11]

In March 1793, Peter Martin, a free black, informed the executive council of Upper Canada of the case of Chloe Cooley. Chloe, a young female slave belonging to William Vroomans of Queenston, had been bound and forcibly taken screaming across the Niagara River under cover of darkness, and then sold. Martin and a witness to the incident, William Grisley, warned that many such sales were likely to occur. The council, in which Simcoe was joined in his desire to end slavery by Chief Justice William Osgoode, immediately resolved to prevent the repetition of such a callous act and directed Attorney General John White to prosecute Vroomans. As Simcoe must have known, since Osgoode and White had conferred previously, this would not have succeeded in the courts, for Vroomans had full right to sell Chloe, since he was her owner. It is therefore likely that the council hoped that threatening to prosecute Vroomans would arouse public opinion against future transborder sales and even against slavery itself. [12]

The event offered Simcoe a welcome excuse to take action on this subject. He had White and Osgoode prepare a bill calling for the gradual abolition of slavery, and this was introduced into the legislative assembly on 18 June. But since at least six of the sixteen members were slaveholders, the bill awakened, as White claimed, "much opposition but little argument." Simcoe attributed the resistance in part to the high price of labour and the scarcity of farm workers, but he also knew that there were some Upper Canadians who already possessed slaves and had recently purchased more at low rates from Indians; doubtful that the existing law adequately protected their investment, they strongly opposed White's bill, since it added a new element of uncertainty. There was also a farm bloc which, while sympathetic to the restriction of slavery, wanted additional slaves and therefore pressed for a two-year grace period in which to acquire them. Surprisingly, the skilful attorney general was able to harmonize these conflicting interests, and he succeeded in steering a measure through the house by 28 June. The legislative council, three of whose seven members were slaveholders, approved it with some minor amendments, and it became law on 9 July 1793. [13]

The law that emerged was a compromise measure and less thoroughgoing than Simcoe desired; in his view, slavery was a practice that "social policy and humanity unite[d] to condemn." Yet he welcomed the new legislation for the considerable victory it doubtless was. The law declared that it was "unjust that a people who enjoy freedom by the law should encourage the introduction of slavery" and that it was therefore "highly expedient to abolish slavery in this province, so far as it may be done gradually without violating private property." The law ended the importation of slaves and freed their children at age twenty-five, but it partially accommodated slaveholders by continuing for life the servitude of those already enslaved. There could, however, be no new enslavement, since future indentured servitude had to be limited to nine-year contracts, and owners who freed slaves were required to guarantee that the freedmen would not become public charges. [14]

Shortly after Simcoe left the province, proslavery forces rallied briefly. They were strong enough in 1798 to carry, by a vote of eight to four, a bill that called for renewing the importation of slaves; but the legislative council shelved the measure and it was never reintroduced. Thus, while the 1793 law freed no slaves, it dried up the source of new recruits both from natural increase and from foreign sources, and it placed slavery on the road to extinction. Thereafter, slavery declined steadily in Upper Canada. [15]

In Lower Canada the attack on slavery followed a different course. The legislative council received a bill to abolish slavery in early 1793, but it was tabled by the large majority of thirty-one to three and was never revived. Nevertheless, opponents of slavery still had the resources of the press and courts which they could summon to their cause, and the former already had offered some support. William Brown, the proprietor of the Quebec *Gazette*, and his nephew and successor at the newspaper, John Neilson, both were sometime slaveowners who evidently had experienced a change of heart, for from 1790 the *Gazette* published antislavery poetry, stories of slave-ship atrocities, and other material likely to sway public opinion. [16]

However, it was the court, under the leadership of Chief Justice James Monk, that played the key role in restricting slavery in Lower Canada by interpreting the law in such a way as to make slavery untenable. In 1798 Monk caused a considerable stir by releasing two slaves who appeared in the Montreal Court of King's Bench. Charlotte had left her owner and, because she refused to return, had been jailed by the magistrates. She sued for her freedom on a writ of habeas corpus, and Monk released her. The news spread quickly and other slaves in the city became restive. One, a woman named Jude, was imprisoned under circumstances similar to Charlotte's and also appeared before Monk. He ruled that although an imperial statute of 1562 allowed a magistrate to sentence slaves, apprentices, and servants to houses of correction for punishment, there was no authority for committing them to common jails or prisons, as had occurred in the case of Charlotte and Jude. Despite the mitigating consideration that no house of correction existed in Montreal, Monk found that Jude had been jailed improperly, and he freed her on this technicality. In handing down his decision, the chief justice surprisingly announced that slavery did not exist in the province and warned that this was how he would interpret the law in future.[17]

Understandably, this turn of events alarmed slaveholders, who now feared unrest among their slaves and faced the prospect of losing their investment. They petitioned the assembly with a lengthy statement explaining why, in their view, Raudot's ordinance of 1709 and the imperial statutes of 1790 and 1732 sanctioned slavery in Quebec. (The latter permitted the sale of slaves and other property to cover debts against estates in British North America, but unbeknown to the petitioners, the slave clause had been repealed by an imperial act in 1797.) The petition led to the introduction of a bill in the assembly, similar to the 1793 Upper Canada statute, that would have recognized slavery but would have regulated and limited its life, and ended the importation of slaves. After receiving second reading, it went no further; neither those advocating the complete abolition of slavery nor those wanting no restrictions on slavery could support the bill, and it was tabled. Similar measures fared no better in 1801 and 1803. Meanwhile, in 1799, the government had opened houses of correction, a step that seemed to provide a means of circumventing the technicality that Monk had used in releasing Jude; but the law establishing the houses of correction did not specifically require that fugitive slaves be committed to them, and Monk in any case soon made it clear that he had no intention of permitting the measure to protect slavery.

In early 1800 the case of the fugitive slave Robin, or Robert, came before the court. He had left his owner's farm and taken up residence with a Montreal tavernkeeper. The owner, James Fraser, had Robin seized and lodged in Montreal's newly established house of correction, whence he was brought to court. In a tortured reading of the law, Monk released Robin, arguing that the 1797 act had repealed not only the provisions of the act of 1732 pertaining to the sale of slaves but also all laws concerning slavery in the province. This was a gross distortion of the 1797 statute that effectively deprived slave-holders of legal recourse when slaves sought their freedom. Yet the assembly enacted no new legislation to protect slavery, and in 1829 the executive council indirectly gave legitimacy to Monk's decision by claiming, when requested by the American government to return a fugitive slave, that slavery was not recognized by Canadian law.[18]

The decline of slavery in the Maritimes followed a mixed pattern. In Nova Scotia, the Presbyterian minister at Pictou, James McGregor, aroused public opinion on slavery in the late 1780s when, in a pamphlet, he sharply attacked Daniel Cock, a fellow Presbyterian cleric in the neighbouring presbytery of Truro, for owning two slaves. But it was Thomas Andrew Strange and his successor Sampson Salter Blowers (the two chief justices whose tenures spanned the years 1791–1833) who most effectively attacked slavery by a series of decisions in Nova Scotia's highest court around the turn of the century. When cases arose involving the return of fugitive slaves, they avoided making a decision, if possible, for they knew that slavery was legal and did not want to reinforce it. Usually, they tried to get the parties to sign an agreement by which the slave would be freed after serving for a specified period. If that failed, they required the case to be tried by a jury, which frequently found for the slave. These tactics effectively smothered slavery in Nova Scotia, much as Monk had done in Lower Canada. When slaves began to abandon their owners, a group of slaveholders in Annapolis County in 1807 petitioned the assembly either to protect slavery, so that their property would be secure, or to abolish it with just compensation. A bill reflecting these wishes was introduced but failed to pass, and within three years a missionary who came to the area reported that all blacks were free.

In the remaining Maritime colonies of Prince Edward Island, Cape Breton, and New Brunswick, all of which had been newly organized after the American Revolution, slavery took firm root only in the latter. No local laws restrained it, and the chief justice, George Duncan Ludlow, defended it, insisting that the long-established practice of slaveholding throughout the British Empire sanctioned it in New Brunswick. When Solicitor General Ward Chipman challenged its legality in 1800, in the case of Nancy Morton who was suing for her freedom, he failed. The court divided, with two judges favouring her release and two opposing it, and she was returned to her owner. Nevertheless, although neither legislative enactment nor judicial restrictions were applied to slavery in New Brunswick, there, as elsewhere, owners were soon paying their slaves and freeing them on limited time indentures.[19]

In these conditions, slavery was soon suffocated throughout British North America. The latest known sale of slaves occurred in 1806 in Upper Canada and in 1807 and 1809 in Nova Scotia and New Brunswick, respectively, and the last reward for returning a fugitive slave appeared in New Brunswick in 1816. There were no further advertisements for slaves in Halifax and Quebec beyond 1820 and 1821. In practice, slavery in Canada had virtually disappeared by the 1820s – only two decades before mid-nineteenth-century British North Americans would deny that it had ever existed – although it did not legally end until 1 August 1834, when the British Emancipation Act of the previous year took effect. [20]

ANTISLAVERY IN THE HANDS OF the Loyalist generation was the work of individuals – Lieutenant-Governor Simcoe, Chief Justice Osgoode, and Attorney General White in Upper Canada; Chief Justice Monk in Lower Canada; and Chief Justices Strange and Blowers and Solicitor General Chipman in the Maritimes – who used their official positions to do what they could to restrict slavery. In this era, antislavery was never a mass movement in the classic sense, employing the techniques of organization and public education through large meetings and propaganda distribution to marshall public opinion, as was characteristic of the later phases of the abolitionist movement.

Another feature of the early-nineteenth-century British North American antislavery thrust was its essentially negative and anti-American cast. After the initial shock of resettlement was over, Loyalists came to see slavery as a residual vestige of the republican society which represented so much that they despised. Eventually, they became vaguely embarrassed for having retained it, so they threw it off with relative ease and quickly erased the disagreeable fact from the national memory.

Above all, the Loyalists' response to slavery reflected a pervasive pragmatism, for freeing their slaves was a practical act. Once situated on the land, the new settlers found that they could no longer profitably maintain a large workforce. The economy of colonial British North America – where general farming based on family labour was the order of the day – was not conducive to slavery. After the courts called slavery's legality into question, the value of slaves began to drop and owners saw their investment evaporating; in these circumstances, financial prudence dictated that it was wiser to negotiate a contract with a slave, which would at least ensure that he would continue to give service for a specified period, than to retain a slave of diminishing value and risk his flight. Individuals like

Simcoe, who denounced slavery because it violated the rights of the individual under the British constitution, or like James McGregor who shared Simcoe's moral aversion to slavery, were relatively few. Even Strange and Blowers, despite their important contribution towards ending slavery, accepted the functional alternative of permitting slaveholders and slaves to conclude limited time indentures. This avoided the crucial issue of whether slavery was morally acceptable, and hence it skirted the question of whether the owner morally had *any* further right to the slave's labour. In fact, Loyalist antislavery appears almost devoid of concern for the slave and his rights as a human being. Loyalists never defined slavery as a poignant issue freighted with a moral imperative; slavery for them was simply an unfortunate and disadvantageous practice whose absence would improve their circumstances and their society.

These considerations – the absence of an organizational base and slavery's amoral character – are important, for they distinguish Loyalist antislavery from the movement's later phases and afford insight into the ensuing course of Canadian abolition. British North Americans, after bringing an end to slavery so early, virtually ignored the awakening British campaign of the late 1820s to end slavery throughout the empire (which climaxed in the 1833 Emancipation Act), and they also ignored the Garrisonian crusade that arose in the United States in the early 1830s. Several figures who rose to prominence in Canadian abolitionism at mid-century were deeply involved in the British struggle, but the average British North American remained uninterested. If the effort to eliminate slavery in Canada had been construed in moral rather than pragmatic and anti-American terms, it would have been difficult to disregard the moral challenge implicit in the continuation of slavery in the British Empire and the American South. And if there had been an organization in place, there would have been no difficulty in redirecting its efforts, as the British antislavery societies were to learn. Instead, British North Americans sat on the sidelines until 1837, by which time the immediatist Anglo-American antislavery crusade was well underway.

# 2 Roots: The British Connection

By the late 1830s, slavery had been dead in Britain for more than half a century, but its demise throughout the empire was more recent. In 1823 the Liverpool cabinet sought to ease the slaves' harsh existence in the West Indies, but it left colonies that had legislative assemblies to implement the "ameliorative policy" on their own. Predictably, they procrastinated until public opinion demanded not merely amelioration but immediate emancipation. This wave of public indignation first stirred in 1826, but it gathered force after 1830 until it crested in the 1833 Emancipation Act. Several future Canadian abolitionists participated in these momentous events; John Roaf and Robert Burns laboured in the Midlands and western Scotland, while Charles Stuart carried the torch on the national scene. After 1833, when concern focused on the apprenticeship system and on ending American slavery, Michael Willis and Peter Brown joined the ranks. Eventually, they migrated to the Canadian frontier, carrying with them the ideals and techniques they had learned in the British antislavery struggle.

SLAVERY ENDED IN BRITAIN IN 1772 with the James Somerset case. This Virginia slave, brought to England by his owner, escaped, and was freed when the court decided that slavery violated the common law and therefore could not exist in Britain. Some ten thousand British slaves were liberated. Granville Sharp, Somerset's champion, hoped to end all British slavery by applying the decision throughout the empire, but he quickly learned that the common law did not supersede colonial statutes that recognized slavery.[1]

British Quakers, who had long been troubled by the immorality of slavery, renewed the struggle a decade later when they petitioned Parliament to end the slave trade. Ignored, they cooperated with like-minded reformers to establish the Society for the Abolition of the Slave Trade. This organization brought together forceful young men such as Thomas Clarkson and William Wilberforce. Under Sharp's leadership, it fostered numerous auxiliary groups that raised funds and circulated the antislavery publications of the London-based committee.

This effort to choke the slave trade might have succeeded had it not been for the French Revolution. In the tense atmosphere of the day, the blood-soaked excesses of the Paris revolutionaries cast suspicion on all reform impulses and temporarily checked the movement's growth. Nevertheless, the ensuing Anglo-French war unexpectedly advanced antislavery by adding several French sugar-producing islands to the empire's Caribbean holdings. Financially pressed British West Indian planters feared there would be competition from these fertile islands, which now enjoyed full trading privileges within the empire. The planters withdrew their opposition to terminating the slave trade, believing that without a fresh supply of slaves, the former French colonies would not be a threat. Dormant through the war, the antislavery movement now stirred into life. In 1807 it secured legislation that outlawed the carrying of slaves in British ships and their importation into any colony.[2]

Some now believed that slavery's days were numbered; fewer slaves would mean that their value would increase, and this would ensure better treatment by owners. Eventually, people would see that free labour was more efficient than bond labour. A new organization, the African Institution, redirected the movement's energies to achieving strict enforcement of the antislave trade laws, encouraging legitimate forms of trade with Africa, and inducing other nations to emulate Britain. Generally, the laws were rigorously enforced, but experience with Sierra Leone – a colony for free blacks that had been established on the west coast of Africa – fell far short of the African Institution's humanitarian and commercial aspirations. This decreased interest in Africa, and after 1814 the institution concentrated on restricting the slave trade through international agreement, a slow and often disappointing process.[3]

In the meantime, it had become apparent that ending the slave trade was neither hastening the decline of slavery nor improving conditions for the slaves. Lower survival rates for slaves in the West

Indies than in the American South conclusively proved that British planters were still working their slaves to death. Moreover, colonial courts offered slaves little protection from their masters. Dismayed antislavery leaders resolved to intervene, and in 1823 they formed the Society for the Mitigation and Gradual Abolition of Slavery throughout the British Dominions, generally called the Anti-Slavery Society. Many veterans of the earlier struggles filled its ranks, but there were energetic young newcomers such as Thomas Fowell Buxton, who took over from the aging Wilberforce the role of leader and parliamentary spokesman. The society's goal was to alleviate the slaves' harsh working conditions immediately and to secure their freedom at some unspecified future time.[4]

The society lost little time in pressing its modest objectives. In May 1823, Buxton offered motions in Parliament that condemned slavery for violating both the British constitution and the precepts of Christianity, and called for its abandonment as soon as the public good permitted. His statement also demanded the early liberation of slave children and their education at public expense, checks on masters' punitive authority, access of slaves to the courts, and the right of slaves to purchase their own freedom.[5]

The Liverpool cabinet responded sympathetically to these proposals, rejecting some, such as freedom for slave children, supporting others, and even surpassing them in one instance by opposing whipping in the field or as a punishment for females. In place of Buxton's reforms, Foreign Secretary George Canning won Parliament's acceptance of resolutions calling for "decisive measures" to improve the slaves' lot. The government accepted responsibility for implementing this "policy of amelioration," as it was called, in both crown and legislative colonies. If the latter proved recalcitrant, Canning promised to seek Parliament's advice, but he was confident that "through determined and persevering" but "judicious and temperate enforcement of such measures," the slaves would be freed as soon as was compatible with their own welfare, the safety of the colonies, and the rights of private property. Although sceptical of the outcome, Buxton and his associates grudgingly gave their support.[6]

Whatever the real intent of the Liverpool cabinet, the amelioration policy produced disappointing results. A year later, the only evidence of improvement that the government could cite was the founding of bishoprics in Jamaica and Barbados to advance religious education. Amelioration had met "reluctance and even positive refusal" in the crown colonies, and its reception was even worse where there were legislative assemblies. In 1826 the Anti-Slavery Society concluded that the evidence rendered desperate "the hope of [slavery's] extinction, or even its effectual mitigation, without the direct and authoritative interference of the Imperial Legislature," and it petitioned Parliament "to take the great work of Colonial Reformation into their own hands" in order to end slavery at the earliest practical point. London supporters quickly circulated these sentiments in a petition, and when Buxton presented it in Parliament he demanded that "either the House must renounce their pledge to the public on behalf of the negro or at once take the question into their own hands."[7]

This awakening of public opinion in 1826 – London was not the only city to petition Parliament – forced the government to pressure the colonies with the "Trinidad Order." The authorities had used this model in implementing the amelioration policy in the crown colony of Trinidad, and after two years it undeniably had resulted in improved conditions for the slaves. The legislation was to be circulated to the colonial assemblies to compel them either to accept or reject the plan in their forthcoming sessions. However, Parliament was dissolved in mid-1826 before the scheme was fully implemented. What followed until 1830 was a series of governments that were either too short-lived or too preoccupied with other issues to do anything but follow what one historian has called the Liverpool cabinet's "discredited policy of admonition and rebuke." This, combined with the occurrence of an industrial depression, retarded the antislavery movement in the late 1820s.[8]

The year 1830 saw fresh signs of interest in antislavery. Parliament received petitions from numerous antislavery meetings in widely scattered parts of the country. This new concern was forcefully expressed at the Anti-Slavery Society's spring meeting in resolutions asserting that since the colonial legislatures had introduced no amelioration in the seven years since 1823, slavery must now be abolished as quickly as possible; and Parliament must fix a date for freeing slave children. The public was urged to petition legislators to secure these ends. While this moderate stance was satisfactory to the rank and file, it left younger and more radical society members dissatisfied. They believed that halfway measures were pointless; the time had come to insist on an immediate end to slavery. Parliament must at the very least fix the end of 1830 as the time to free slave children. This group soon gained sufficient strength to form the Agency Committee, a virtually autonomous affiliate that pursued immediatism by sending speakers throughout the country to organize like-minded societies and to sponsor petitions.[9]

The new government elected in 1830 continued the ameliorative policy but accomplished little, for resolving the larger issue of parliamentary reform was its main concern. It had no success in its efforts to entice the colonies to implement the 1823 resolutions by rewarding them with reductions in the sugar duty. When the Reform Bill of 1832 finally passed, parliament was dissolved and the country prepared for an election. Eager to capitalize on the enthusiasm generated by the Reform Bill's success, the Agency Committee campaigned vigorously to gain the newly enfranchised electors' support by using committees of correspondence and organizing a national poster drive, and by extracting antislavery pledges from candidates. It continued the pressure after the election until the new government introduced the proposals in 1833 that resulted in the Emancipation Act. This measure freed slave children after 1 August 1834 and placed adult slaves in an apprenticeship, during which they would earn their freedom while receiving food and shelter. The legislation also restricted the punishments that planters could give their slaves, but it awarded owners £20 million to compensate them for property loss. [10]

John Roaf was the first future Canadian to appear in this long struggle to liberate British slaves. With the colonies stonewalling on amelioration, the Liverpool Quaker merchant James Cropper, a founder of the Anti-Slavery Society, addressed a meeting in 1826 in Wolverhampton, where Roaf pastored the Queen Street Congregational church. Cropper told the people of Wolverhampton that they could daily foil slavery by substituting free-labour East Indian sugar for the slave-grown West Indian product; but, above all, they must support the government's "noble and liberal" amelioration principles. Roaf "spoke at length," offering a resolution that was combined with several others in a petition that the meeting endorsed and sent to Westminster. The petition condemned slavery and shamed the obstructionist colonies, but it praised the government's ameliorative initiative and encouraged it to press on with "systematic efforts to induce general Exertions in behalf of this ill-fated race." [11]

It is impossible to know precisely the full extent of Roaf's participation in the emancipation struggle between 1830 and 1833. The numerous brief reports of antislavery meetings in Wolverhampton during the period usually mention only the names of visiting speakers. Yet it would have been decidedly out of character for this enthusiastic, warm-hearted man, who had a gift for speaking, to have remained on the sidelines. In Wolverhampton he backed the Friends of Religious Liberty, organized the Mechanics' Institute, and at great personal risk fought a deadly cholera epidemic as secretary of the City Board of Health. He was "minister of power and salvation," fired with an evangelical zeal that was shared by his working-class parishioners, who enjoyed "loud and vigorous" singing accompanied by a "strong band" and a "double bass viol." Such a man was likely to remain at the forefront of the battle in his Midlands city, for in the election of 1832 he begged Staffordshire voters to elect no one "who would not promise to use every exertion to wipe away that foul stain from the land – negro slavery."[12]

Although the evidence is frustratingly incomplete in Roaf's case, Robert Burns's antislavery record is clearer. Burns was a Church of Scotland minister, and in 1830 he aroused interest in the slavery question in his Paisley parish and the west of Scotland with an overture in the Synod of Glasgow and Ayr declaring slavery to be anti-Christian. He said that the synod must petition Parliament to remedy the dreadful circumstances of West Indian slaves and to win their eventual admission to full rights as British subjects. This brought a "full discussion" on the synod floor, and after speaking at "great length," Burns was charged with preparing the parliamentary appeal. Synod was "extremely anxious," declared the petition, for the government to implement the 1823 resolutions. It expressed deep concern over the moral condition of the bondsmen, which was unlikely to improve without emancipation; therefore, facilities for the slaves' religious instruction were imperative. The petition implored Parliament to adopt measures immediately that would promote the slaves' best interests and bring emancipation at an early date.[13]

Burns's caution may have stemmed from doubts that the synod was ready to take a stronger position, or perhaps he was not yet an immediatist himself. But he shortly abandoned gradualism, probably because of events in Edinburgh. On 8 October the Edinburgh Society for Promoting the Abolition of Negro Slavery held a meeting that had great significance for British antislavery. Gradualists presented resolutions calling for slave children born after January 1831 to be free, and many felt that this was a considerable step forward. However, it dismayed radicals, and Andrew Thomson, the respected minister of St George's Church in Edinburgh, shocked the meeting's leaders by unexpectedly denouncing the resolutions for their moderation. Freeing slave children but postponing general emancipation seemingly legitimized some men holding others as property. The time had come, he boldly declared, for immediate emancipation, even if some blood was spilled. An amendment embracing these sentiments passed, stunning the moderates, and they nearly lost control of the meeting when the Lord Provost of Edinburgh suddenly left the chair, refusing to preside over such proceedings any longer. The meeting reconvened a week later, when Thomson eloquently defended his plea for immediatism, and sent a petition to Parliament demanding "immediate and total" abolition of slavery. These meetings, some of the "largest and most respectable assemblages" ever held in the city, drew great publicity, and the petition garnered 22,000 signatures. Historians generally acknowledge that this was the turning point when British antislavery swung to immediatism. [14]

Thomson's prominence in these events no doubt allayed any lingering qualms that Burns had about immediatism, for the two were close friends. Years later, Burns still loved to recount the thrilling story of Thomson's dramatic intervention at the Edinburgh meeting. This news would have sped to Paisley, for full reports soon appeared in the Edinburgh press. [15] Within days, Burns was leading a Paisley meeting [16] which erased all doubt that he stood on the threshold of immediatism. [17]

While Burns's contribution to arousing interest in slavery in western Scotland probably outstripped Roaf's work in the Midlands, Captain Charles Stuart's role in British antislavery before 1833 eclipsed the activities of both. After a tour of duty in the East India Company's army, this colourful British-born eccentric had settled briefly in Upper Canada before relocating in upstate New York in 1822 to teach school in Utica. The students idolized his youthful ways; before school opened in the morning, he exuberantly participated in their boisterous games, and on a Saturday afternoon he might be found at "mimic war," leading them in an imaginary charge across the village common with blasts from his French horn. Yet this pious "children's friend," who was capable of displaying the "tenderness of a woman," lived a strangely Spartan life. He preferred simple foods and occupied monkish quarters, sleeping on a pallet that was placed outside in summer months. He always dressed in a "Scottish plaid frock," and his brisk stride must have turned heads on his usual four to five mile morning walk into the countryside to get breakfast.

While Stuart was in New York, he established an intimate friendship with youthful Theodore Dwight Weld, the future American abolitionist. So deeply affected were the two by Charles G. Finney's revival that Weld trained for the ministry under Stuart's sponsorship, and together they engaged in revival campaigns with Finney's Holy Band. When Weld's sister Cornelia rejected Stuart's marriage proposal, he returned to England in 1829 and renewed his acquaintance with William Blair, an associate from East India Company days. Residents of Bristol, Blair and his wife Mary were convinced abolitionists of the immediatist stripe; and by the time Stuart arrived, Blair was already conducting antislavery meetings in the West Country. Although earlier accounts assumed that Stuart had absorbed abolitionism while in New York, Anthony Barker's recent study convincingly argues that Stuart became an avid abolitionist and adopted immediatism as a result of the Blair contact. [18]

Beginning in 1830, Stuart played a central part in the events leading to the Emancipation Act in his role as an evengelist of the immediatist gospel. This commitment, bringing close contact and moral support from other ardent abolitionists, doubtless helped fill the emotional vacuum left by his matrimonial disappointment, while his experience as a revivalist gave him a tool that would be "demonstrably innovative and forceful" in antislavery. [19]

His first task was to write an antislavery pamphlet entitled *Petitions Respecting Negro Slavery*. This pamphlet attacked the Anti-Slavery Society's 1830 petition (which many regarded as a hopeful departure) for being too conservative. It was not enough, wrote Stuart, for the friends of antislavery to ask that slave children be freed; abolitionists must demand "*complete and immediate emancipation* of the negroes," for slavery was sinful, and Britain had to escape from its clutches. He called on the nation to unite in an effort to destroy slavery, convinced that Britons were ready for the task. [20]

Stuart then went to Ireland and began a vigorous campaign to spread his principles there. His Dublin host was Charles Orpen, a founder of the immediatist Hibernian Negro's Friend Society. Travelling extensively, Stuart held meetings, organized societies, promoted petitions, and distributed his writings, which the Dublin society published. Everywhere he dramatically displayed a West Indian slave whip as a graphic demonstration of the cruelty of slavery. He returned to England in the spring of 1831 as an agent of the Hibernian Negro's Friend Society, and under the auspices of the Birmingham Ladies Negro's Friend Society, he spent a month lecturing in the towns of Staffordshire and Warwickshire. [21]

These tours in Ireland and the Midlands enabled Stuart to shape an antislavery philosophy that formed the basis of his abolitionism for the next quarter century. Contact with the Hibernian Negro's Friend Society stimulated him to write, and the society to publish, at least thirteen pamphlets in Ireland alone. The society's position, that slavery transgressed God's law and was therefore sinful, coincided with Stuart's conclusion in *On the Prospective Emancipation of Slaves' Unborn Children*. Man was bound by all God's laws, he asserted, and could not randomly select portions of them to respect; the excuse of expediency, because of slavery's profitability, was not acceptable. This tract also claimed that the record of blacks in Haiti, Sierra Leone, and Canada proved that slaves were ready for immediate freedom. Stuart borrowed two other ideas from the Dublin abolitionists: the contention that the sinfulness of slavery made the struggle a global task rather than one limited to the British Empire; and the Quaker proscription of slave-grown produce. *Can West Indian Slavery Be Justified from Scripture?* and *Is Slavery Defensible from Scripture?* found fundamental differences between plantation slavery and Old Testament slavery, destroying the argument that the latter justified the former. Stuart's best-known work, *The West India Question*, emphatically rejected the idea of compensating planters for liberating their slaves.[22]

At the cutting edge of antislavery thought in late 1830, Stuart's immediatism was a key factor in energizing the wave of public opinion that now began to surge. Blair had urged the reluctant London Anti-Slavery Society to establish lecture agencies; but, except for considering the possibility of issuing a circular asking the public to lobby their MPs, and advocating petition-sponsoring meetings in support of Buxton's parliamentary initiatives, little had been accomplished. A timely letter from Charles Orpen describing Stuart's success in Ireland, however, had a telling effect. Let abolitionists flood Parliament with petitions and secure antislavery pledges from political candidates, he urged. Stuart's "most gratifying results" in Ireland through "deputation" showed what revivalist techniques in the hands of a skilful practitioner could accomplish for antislavery. These considerations evidently strengthened the hands of the younger radicals on the committee, for the Agency Committee was established in mid-1831. It soon employed several agents, who toured the nation, ardently spreading the immediatist message. Stuart, who had contributed so much to pioneering the agency method, was a co-founder of the Agency Committee; but, driven by the zealot's passion, he was not content as a policy maker. The fall of 1831 found him back in the field as an agent on a second tour of the Midlands, where he visited twenty-five towns, sometimes speaking as many as three times in the same location.[23]

Over the next two years the Agency Committee waged an effective campaign to secure emancipation. Soon it boasted 1200 local committees and a large enough treasury to secure independence from the Anti-Slavery Society. The Agency Committee concentrated on converting public opinion to see the need for immediate emancipation, while the parent organization focused on Parliament. After the Reform Bill passed, the Agency Committee sought support from the newly enfranchised voters and extracted immediatist commitments from parliamentary candidates, as well as garnering support through a national poster campaign and through a network of committees in London, Edinburgh, and Dublin that coordinated local efforts. When the newly elected parliament faltered over introducing abolitionist legislation, the Agency Committee renewed the pressure until victory came with the Emancipation Act in August 1833. Thus, the Agency Committee, whose philosophy, methods, and campaign Stuart was so influential in shaping, played a decisive role in the final thrust for emancipation.[24]

But Stuart had more to contribute to British antislavery during this era. In the early 1830s, American abolitionists, like their British counterparts, were turning to immediatism, but gradualism still had an influential exponent in the American Colonization Society (ACS). Founded in 1817, this organization sought to deal with slavery by freeing slaves through either purchase or moral suasion and by colonizing them outside the United States. This was necessary, according to the ACS, because deep-seated prejudice inevitably generated social conflict, preventing blacks and whites from living together harmoniously. Hence, it was in the free black minority's interest to live elsewhere, and the society was willing to help them. With this in mind, the ACS had established the colony of Liberia on the west coast of Africa, and it undertook to relocate as many blacks as the society's resources would permit. By 1830, the numbers actually transported were small; so, to promote its cause and raise funds, the ACS sent Elliot Cresson to tour Britain in mid-1831, which was just when the Agency Committee was organizing.

Stuart evidently had little previous knowledge of the ACS, but Weld, who now also was an immediatist, supplied information about the society, as well as other news of the progress of American antislavery. Shortly after Cresson arrived in England, he and Stuart had the first of several interviews. Stuart quickly concluded that "the principles and system of the society upon the whole, were so decidedly criminal and cruel, that it ought to be strenuously reprobated and opposed. This I stated upon the spot to Mr Cresson without reserve." Convinced that the ACS's accommodationist stance would perpetuate slavery long into the future, Stuart quickly moved to check Cresson. The speed of the attack surprised the American; in less than a month, Stuart published *Letter on the American Colonization Society*, a sharp attack on Cresson's sponsors. Emphasizing the similarity of the antislavery struggle in the two countries, Stuart wrote that America's obligation to its blacks was identical to Britain's duties to its slaves: "To obey God by letting them go free, by placing them beneath wise and equitable laws, and by loving them all, and treating them like brothers." The ACS blatantly denied this responsibility by deporting freed slaves, he maintained, and he called on Americans and Britons to cooperate in solving their common problem.

This was only the first of several anti-ACS pamphlets (replete with supporting information drawn from Weld's material) that were distributed widely in Britain and frequently reproduced in the *Liberator* and other American antislavery periodicals in Stuart's effort to sandbag Cresson. Stuart dogged the footsteps of the exasperated Cresson throughout the British Isles for two years of "sustained harassment ... exploiting the connection and goodwill he had established with antislavery workers in many parts of Britain." The contest extended to periodicals and provincial newspapers, and even to lecture halls, where the tenacious Stuart often appeared a few days ahead of Cresson to warn the audience against the American, or where Stuart's supporters heckled the ACS agent with poignant questions. By the spring of 1833, Cresson's mission was a failure; the goal of the tour had been to net £100,000, but it had landed barely a few hundred.[25]

Stuart actually had conducted two antislavery campaigns simultaneously between 1831 and 1833: one to commit British public opinion to immediatism, and the other to discredit the ACS. Both succeeded, but the latter produced results that no one had anticipated: by acquainting the British public with current issues in American antislavery, Stuart's anti-ACS drive opened the door for William Lloyd Garrison's successful tour of Britain in 1833 and laid the foundation for Anglo-American antislavery cooperation. This transformed the struggle into a transatlantic movement. British abolitionists, who might otherwise have laid down their arms, now identified slavery in the American South as the new enemy, and British abolitionism entered a new phase, in which Canadian abolitionists would again play a role.

The first signal that British antislavery was entering another phase was the appearance of new provincial abolition societies in Scotland in 1833. At an October meeting in Edinburgh, George Thompson, one of Stuart's most gifted agency lecturers, acknowledged that British emancipation was a great achievement but reminded his listeners of the immense task that remained: freeing the millions across the Atlantic who were still bound. Thompson announced that Garrison's New England Anti-Slavery Society had invited him to tour America and renew the struggle there, and he asked for Scotland's help. The meeting responded to his challenge by forming the Edinburgh Emancipation Society (EES), whose purpose was to combat slavery around the world and assist Thompson on his American mission.[26]

Among the people named to the committee was the future Canadian abolitionist, Peter Brown, an Edinburgh linen merchant with rising prospects and a taste for the city's public life. Brown had probably been involved in both the Edinburgh Society for the Abolition of Negro Slavery and its predecessor, the Edinburgh Society for Promoting the Abolition of Negro Slavery, whose existence extended back to Andrew Thomson's immediatist speech in 1830. But this cannot be confirmed; nor, with one exception, are the details of his activities in the EES known, for these organizations' records have not come to light. However, the one surviving glimpse of Brown in the EES reveals an eager committee member busily shouldering his responsibilities. When Thompson returned from America in early 1836, the society greeted him with a soirée. Brown worked on the committee that was responsible for the arrangements. To help with the occasion, forty "stewards" were drafted, mostly young men from EES families. Among them were George Brown (Peter's older son) and Daniel Wilson, classmates at Edinburgh Commercial School who years later would rejoin forces in a celebrated Toronto fugitive slave case. Since Mrs Brown belonged to the EES ladies' committee, antislavery obviously was a family concern, just as it would continue to be in the Brown household decades later in Canada. [27]

Meanwhile, a second group had formed in Glasgow, the Glasgow Emancipation Society (GES). Several figures from this influential and long-lived organization were to resurface in Canadian antislavery. James Johnston, a Glasgow woollen and carpet merchant, had been active in the pre–1833 era, most notably as a deputy of the Glasgow Anti-Slavery Society (the GES's predecessor) to the London Anti-Slavery Society. He was one of a small group that met late in 1833 to consider organizing a new body, and he worked on the subcommittee that finalized arrangements. The organizational meeting occurred a few days later in the church of Ralph Wardlaw, a noted Congregational minister and abolitionist, with Johnston presiding. Elected treasurer, Johnston filled an influential position in the society which occasionally included chairing executive meetings. In one instance, he wrote to the colonial secretary urging the government to investigate the illegal presence of numerous slaves on Mauritius. Johnston, whose wife was treasurer of the ladies' committee, continued to serve until 1837, when he emigrated to Canada amid expressions of appreciation for his work. [28]

David Buchan's affiliation with the GES was shorter than Johnston's. A "writer to the signet," which entitled him to practise law, the young Buchan evidently was a recent adherent to antislavery. In 1833, W. Kimble, a Baptist missionary to the West Indies, toured Scotland seeking support for the immediate end of slavery in the islands. Buchan was deeply impressed by Kimble's message, and he quickly became involved in the plans to organize the GES. But his friendship with the Baptist cleric proved costly. West Indian planters and their Glasgow mercantile associates held Baptist missionaries in great disfavour, for they were suspected of having aroused slaves to the point of violent resistance. Buchan's familiarity with Kimble – they were seen walking publicly arm in arm – offended some of the young lawyer's relatives who had West Indian ties, most likely the influential James Ewing, and this brought a sharp decline in Buchan's legal practice. The struggling Scot then decided to start anew in Canada, and he emigrated in 1834.[29]

While Stuart recrossed the Atlantic in 1834 to participate in the American abolition crusade, and while Brown, Johnston, and Buchan worked through the Scottish provincial societies before emigrating in the mid-1830s, Burns continued the battle in Paisley. The November 1830 meeting that produced the town's parliamentary petition also spawned an antislavery committee, which Burns helped to lead throughout the decade. Being located in a smaller centre, the Paisley committee never achieved the status of the GES, but it kept slavery before the public with meetings and speakers, and occasionally it contributed funds to the Glasgow society. In 1836, for example, it sponsored several George Thompson lectures in Paisley. Although Burns was away, the provost thanked him for the use of his church, and the Glasgow *Evening Post* numbered Burns and his Paisley ministerial colleague Patrick Brewster "amongst the most zealous supporters we have, of the cause of the oppressed Negro." Burns apologized for missing two antislavery meetings in 1838, an act that would only be necessary for someone accustomed to participating. Later that year, a large meeting in his church marked the end of the apprenticeship system. As principal speaker, Burns gave a detailed historical account of the British antislavery struggle but reminded his audience that the continuation of American slavery meant that there was still much work to do. In 1840 the Paisley committee sponsored a series of lectures by W.L. Garrison, Charles Lenox Remond, and Nathaniel Rogers, all of whom were American delegates to the 1840 London World Anti-Slavery Conference. When Remond challenged the meeting to sustain American abolitionists by boycotting American cotton, Burns conspicuously urged the Paisley residents to comply, and he had them file past the pulpit to extend the brotherly right hand of fellowship to their black American guest.[30]

Although Burns kept his shoulder to the wheel in Paisley, his abolitionism became known farther afield. At the 1839 general assembly of the Presbyterian Church of Scotland, he begged his fellow Presbyterians to strengthen their stand on slavery with a resolution asking Parliament to end the continuing international slave trade and to use its influence to abolish slavery in other countries. He was also active in the GES by this time, for he wrote to the annual meeting in 1839, explaining that he was absent because of illness. Thus, his antislavery reputation had reached Glasgow. The GES was eager for his support, for in 1842 it requested him to take part in the annual meeting, and the following year he introduced one of the resolutions.[31]

Burns never became a leader in the GES, for in 1845 he took up new church duties in Toronto. However, before leaving, he crossed paths with Michael Willis, another Presbyterian clergyman, whose career more than any other symbolized the bridge that spanned British and Canadian antislavery. In 1817 this precocious eighteen-year-old graduated Master of Arts from Glasgow University, with "very high standing" in Latin and Greek as well as in literature and philosophy. His professors urged him to follow an academic career, but he chose the ministry. After theological study, he was ordained minister of the Renfield Street church in Glasgow in 1821, a post he held for twenty-six years. This congregation, which belonged to the Original Associate Synod (Old Light Burgher) branch of Scottish Presbyterianism, had been organized two years earlier to serve parishioners in the new western industrial suburbs of the city.[32]

The young Willis soon gained a reputation as a leader, with interests ranging from the social ills of the surrounding area to the concerns of the entire denomination. Without neglecting his congregation's spiritual needs, he awakened its conscience to local social needs: an almoner to work among the unemployed poor; a cow and dairy equipment so that a destitute widow could provide for her young family. With his encouragement, the church women organized a school and library, where girls from the nearby cotton factories learned to read and write and to improve their domestic skills. Willis's demanding pastoral duties did not prevent him from also cultivating his academic interests, for from 1835 to 1839 he was professor of theology in the Associate Synod Divinity Hall, supervising ministerial candidates from his Renfield Street teaching room.[33]

One cannot be sure what precisely awakened Willis's interest in slavery. A reformed theologian trained in philosophy with disciplined study habits, he may have developed antislavery convictions independently through studying the scriptures in conjunction with writers on natural law. Both were central to his later antislavery pieces. But the rising British antislavery campaign must have been a major influence, for the topic was fully aired in Glasgow, where Caribbean commercial connections were strong. At the university, for example, according to the future abolitionist William King, students and professors shared a "deep interest" in the issue. They held a great twelve-night debate on the nature of slavery in Jewish, Greek, and Roman society, in which the Greek work for slavery – "doulos" – was "thoroughly discussed in all its meanings, in both old and new testament." With the immediatist campaign gathering momentum, events such as this one at his neighbouring alma mater in 1831 would have been irresistible to the bookish young parson with a tender social conscience. For, as one of his parishioners complained, Willis saw "negroes on every page of his Bible."[34]

Willis attended the founding meeting of the GES and became a member of the committee of management, a connection he retained until 1851. How actively he participated in committee affairs during these early years is not known, for clerical members of the society were automatically appointed to the committee, but it is clear that from the 1843 annual meeting, when both Burns and Willis offered resolutions, he occupied a more important position in the group's councils.[35]

This greater role in the GES coincided with changes in Willis's denominational affiliation, for friction soon arose between the society and the new church he helped to form. In 1839 the Original Associate Synod rejoined the Established Church of Scotland, from which it had separated in 1733. Willis received an honorary doctorate from the University of Glasgow largely for his role in promoting this reconciliation, but the reunion was short-lived. In 1843 his congregation, like Burns's Paisley parish, joined a large exodus from the Church of Scotland in the "Great Disruption" to form the Free Church of Scotland. Needing funds and moral support, the Free Church sent a commission to North American Presbyterians in 1844. The delegation, which included Robert Burns, was warmly received by the Americans, and it returned with a substantial sum of money that had partially been contributed by slaveholding church members in South Carolina. An acrimonious dispute ensued between the Free Church and the GES, for the latter had long been opposed to churches having fraternal ties with slaveholding Christians. This fellowshipping controversy, as it was called, raged for the next four years and gradually drew Willis into its vortex, for although he was a Free Church minister, he sided with the GES. Increasingly, he became identified with the society's antifellowshipping forces and with a small but vocal group of Free Church dissidents, who in 1846 formed their own antislavery body. Burns was briefly involved also, but his emigration to Canada removed him from the most bitter phase of the dispute.[36]

The fellowshipping controversy surfaced at a GES meeting in March 1844, shortly before the Free Church general assembly's annual session in June. The GES implored Free Churchmen to act as "Christians and Scotchmen" and to return the money with a "faithful and plain dealing testimony" against Christians holding slaves. At Willis's instigation, the Glasgow presbytery repeated this forthright appeal in an overture to the assembly, but the result was disappointing. The moderator, the Rev. Henry Grey, acknowledged that slaveholding was a foul blot on the social and religious institutions of Southern Christians, as well as a violation of man's natural rights and the spirit of Christianity. Yet, in his opinion, Free Church intervention was unwarranted. The assembly evasively referred the matter to a committee that was authorized to report to the denominational commission.[37] The dismayed GES increased the pressure at a meeting in the Renfield Street church in early July. Robert Burns, whose position on fellowshipping was questioned in GES circles because he had been one of the deputies to America, was invited to explain the church's course, and the plan was to manoeuvre him into criticizing the church in response to Willis's interrogation. But Burns had had second thoughts about the wisdom of his part in the commission, and to everyone's surprise he voluntarily warned the church against fellowshipping with slaveholders. The meeting achieved the GES's purpose. Moreover, even without Willis's intervention, it identified him more closely with the antifellowshipping campaign, for the meeting took place in his church. It also erased all doubt about Burns's antislavery principles.[38]

Although the GES adopted a mildly worded antifellowshipping resolution at its annual meeting in August – a move that was no doubt intended to extend the olive branch to the Free Church – its hopes were quickly dashed. In September the slavery committee's report, which the church commission adopted, advocated retaining the gift and continuing the fraternal tie with Southern churches. Moreover, the Rev. Dr Thomas Chalmers, the church's patron saint, approved this course in a theatrical public letter to Thomas Smythe, the South Carolinan minister whose church had raised a large portion of the infamous money.[39]

Now the GES unleashed a vigorous antifellowshipping campaign against the church's flabby morality, with Willis in the forefront. Yet despite numerous public meetings resonant with incriminating speeches and condemnatory resolutions, which were buttressed by circulars to local presbyteries and by frequent newspaper articles, the GES failed to persuade the Free Church to alter its course. The 1845 general assembly stood firm, and the 1846 session was equally unbending. In fact, at the latter the Rev. Robert Candlish, chairman of the slavery committee, staunchly defended the church's action. When James Macbeth, a minister who shared Willis's views, rose to denounce fellowshipping and implored the church to censure its American cousins, he stood alone. The assembly calmly dismissed the matter with a soothing letter that meekly sympathized with Southern Presbyterians for their awkward position in a slaveholding society.[40]

Although Willis had, from the beginning, been deeply involved in the GES antifellowshipping campaign, he missed the general assembly's slavery debate for he was in Canada in the spring of 1846. The fledgling Canadian Free Church urgently needed clergymen and had appealed to the Scottish church to send deputies periodically to alleviate the situation, a call that Burns had answered the previous year. Similarly, Willis accepted when the Colonial Committee invited him to undertake a brief teaching assignment at the newly opened Free Kirk theological college in Toronto. His enviable reputation for classical scholarship, combined with the recent honorary Glasgow degree and teaching experience at the Associate Synod Divinity Hall, constituted good credentials for this post. Arriving in Toronto in December 1845, he taught during the following winter-spring term and travelled widely throughout the province, preaching wherever he went.[41]

Although Willis was far away from the inflamed Scottish fellowshipping controversy, his abolitionist enthusiasm did not wane, for slavery was a matter of growing concern in Canada West's Free Church circles. Under the guidance of Robert Burns, who was now a minister at Knox Church in Toronto and until recently had been a professor at the theological college, the Canadian church had already remonstrated with the general assembly of the Presbyterian Church in the United States for its laxity on slavery. Moreover, the Toronto *Banner*, published by the recently emigrated Peter Brown, kept Canadian readers well informed about the antislavery struggle.[42]

Before Willis left Toronto, Charles Stuart, still an ardent abolitionist, held two large antislavery rallies which John Roaf, who since 1837 had been minister of Zion Congregational Church, probably helped to arrange. At the second of these, Willis gave an "animated and powerful" speech. These meetings acquainted Torontonians with Willis's abolitionism and resulted in a short-lived antislavery organization in the city. Evidently, it survived only long enough to send Roaf to the annual meeting of the American Anti-Slavery Society in New York in May. But the little-known society, impressed by Willis's abolitionism, also requested him to attend, since he would be in New York on his return trip to Scotland. Being detained in Washington, where reportedly he met the U.S. president but declined to preach to Congress, Willis arrived in New York too late for the meeting, and the left for Europe in mid-May.[43]

Willis reached Scotland in early June, just in time to learn that Macbeth's appeal to the general assembly had fallen on deaf ears, and he aggressively seized the cudgels. Seemingly, his brief contact with North American antislavery had whetted his abolitionism. Having arranged matters with the committee, Willis publicly aligned himself with Macbeth at an open meeting of the GES at which the two men presented a joint letter that was highly critical of the Free Church. Their statement said that while they preferred to attack slavery from within the church, they would gladly cooperate with the society to combat the views of "friends and brethren to whom we owe love and respect; but from whose judgement on the question of FELLOWSHIP WITH SLAVEHOLDERS WE ENTIRELY DISAGREE." They rejected the assembly's contention that maintaining the tie with the Southern church, while reproving its slaveholding, would be more efficacious than severing the connection. The time had come, they declared, for all Christians to proclaim boldly that they would not recognize "as Churches walking orderly those who are faithlessly compromising truth on this momentous subject."[44]

Soon after this dramatic gesture, Willis took the final step that placed him on a collision course with the Free Church. With the blessing of the GES, he and Macbeth formed the Free Church Anti-Slavery Society (FCAS) in September 1846. This Edinburgh-based organization sought to convince Free Churchmen to end the Southern tie and promote immediate emancipation. This was required of every Free Church member who believed that slavery was sinful, stated the by-laws. The appearance of the FCAS intensified the fellowshipping controversy; for, as president of the new body, Willis was now the leader of an embarrassing and potentially disruptive Free Church antifellowshipping faction. Moreover, the society gave Willis a podium for his antislavery views – an opportunity he quickly exploited.[45]

During the winter of 1846–47 the FCAS sponsored seven meetings in Edinburgh. Willis opened the series on 10 December, when he made his major statement on slavery to an "overflowing and highly respectable audience." Citing passages on natural law from Pufendorf, Grotius, and Montesquieu, he declared that slavery was unacceptable because it violated man's natural rights. It was unnatural for anyone to exert the absolute authority over another that slavery imposed, and no right existed whereby this burden could be enforced. Consequently, the slave need not obey it.[46]

If natural law was one pillar supporting his antislavery thought, the other was the scriptures, for Willis was one of those figures in whom, as Duncan Rice has noted, the eighteenth-century Scottish enlightenment critique of slavery and the early-nineteenth-century surge of Scottish evangelicalism merged to produce antislavery activism. He strongly disagreed with those who found biblical sanction for slavery in the apostolic injunction that servants must obey their masters. Doubtless, many servants in the New Testament era were slaves. However, argued Willis, one could just as well claim that the New Testament fathers had sanctioned polygamy when they counselled wives to obey their husbands, for it too was widespread at the time. In fact, asserted Willis, the New Testament taught servants to obey their masters only insofar as that obedience did not violate Christ's law of love. This barred Christians from exercising power that was inconsistent with the principles of brotherhood and equity. Moreover, Willis declared, reverting to natural law propositions, the master-servant relationship was subject to the principle of contract. This bound the servant to fulfil his contract as long as its terms were kept by the master. Between master and slave, however, no contract existed, since the latter was the victim of coercion. Hence, nothing prohibited him from "vindicating his natural liberty, if he only seek it with due preference of peaceful to violent methods."[47]

Willis also drew on his classical learning when expounding the linguistic arguments – which he had probably heard rehearsed at the 1831 Glasgow University debates – against the idea that scripture sanctioned slavery. The proponents of this view frequently claimed that the New Testament Greek term "doulos" really meant slave, even though the translators had rendered it as "servant." Willis agreed with the translators, explaining that "doulos" was a general term denoting one who provided service, whether bond or free. From the biblical context, he inferred that "free servant" was the appropriate meaning, since scripture also used "doulos" to describe prophets, angels, saints, believers, and Christ himself. It was absurd, Willis declared, to think that any of these could accurately be designated "slaves" of God; for example, in New Testament terminology, believers became the sons of God, a status far removed from that of a slave.[48]

Having established that slavery violated natural law and biblical principles, Willis explained why he opposed fellowshipping with slaveholding congregations. It was the duty of churches, he said, to witness to God's truth in the world. The churches accomplished this by screening members, judging conditions in society, and educating the public by witnessing against error. Consistency required the use of rigorous standards in recognizing the legitimacy of other churches, for a mere claim to churchhood did not guarantee scripturally prescribed conduct. In the case of questionable conduct, a church should avoid communion and should remonstrate with the erring church. These principles should guide a church in its establishment of fraternal ties.[49]

To Willis it was perfectly clear that Southern churches were not "walking orderly" on the slavery question. They admitted to membership those who traded in the "bodies of men bred for the market, and sold at auction human beings of one blood with themselves." Some churches even promoted slaveowners to spiritual offices. Yet despite such iniquitous behaviour, the Free Church still extended to them the right hand of fellowship. Moreover, claimed Willis, by accepting the Southern gift, the Free Church had damaged the cause of emancipation, for in the course of defending its actions, it had revived arguments that had been used to defend slavery during the struggle over West Indian emancipation – "arguments ... we had believed to have perished in this country with slavery." This strengthened the oppressor's hand indirectly.[50]

Finally, Willis discredited the subtle argument, heard at the 1846 general assembly, that there was a difference between "slaveholding" and "slavehaving." This made a distinction between masters holding slaves voluntarily and those holding them because the law prevented release or because manumission might place the slaves in the hands of a cruel owner. Some contended that many Southern churchmen were "slavehavers" and therefore were not culpable. Willis scoffed at such reasoning and urged the church to decide clearly whether owning slaves was sinful. "If it be a sin ... no man is, in any circumstances, necessitated to commit it." Churches abroad, he maintained, should be dealt with as if "slavehaving" was the exception:

If the alternative be, that our church at home must either be prepared to recognize the churches of the Slave States at large as orderly societies, or hold itself excluded from fellowship with the ... slaveholders; it cannot be told the Americans too soon or too unequivocally, which horns of the dilemma we prefer.[51]

This lecture, published in 1847 as *Slavery Indefensible*, was only one of at least nine pamphlets that the FCAS issued in its remarkably vigorous publishing program. Two of the others were attributed to the society committee, but both reflected the carefully measured argumentation of Willis's academic style. In *An Address to the Office-Bearers of the Free Church of Scotland*, Willis launched a sharp personal attack on Robert Candlish and James Cunningham, the men who had guided the church's policy, and he refuted the criticisms that they had levelled at Macbeth in the 1846 assembly. For example, Willis ridiculed Candlish's assertion that a person might be placed in circumstances in which he was a slaveholder against his will. The truth, thundered Willis, was that the slaveholder refused to liberate his slaves because he was "so completely under the domination of selfishness, that he [could] not help keeping his fellow-man in bondage, even though the light of nature and the law of God, equally [called] him to liberate them."[52] Cunningham fared no better under Willis's barbed shafts.[53]

This stinging rebuke to the Free Church leaders, which Willis continued in the third pamphlet, *Strictures on the Proceedings of the Last General Assembly*, incited a reaction against the FCAS and its president. In October 1846, Willis for the third time asked the Glasgow presbytery to pressure the assembly against fellowshipping. Previously, the presbytery had supported him unanimously. This time, Willis's motion secured only five votes from the twenty-five presbyters present, and there were ominous complaints. Free Churchmen knew the wickedness of slavery, protested one speaker, and resented being lectured on the point, for it made them appear "hard-hearted and inhuman" to outsiders; Willis should use his energy to help slaves rather than squandering it on "miserable debating." The *Witness* and the *Free Church Magazine* also lashed out at Willis and his supporters, but the bluntest attack came from the floor of the 1847 general assembly. There was no doubt, declared James Cunningham, that the FCAS was an "ingenious device of Satan" to perpetuate the antifellowshipping agitation – an assessment that the assembly greeted approvingly with "shouts of laughter and cheers."[54]

By mid-1847, Willis, who had fought slavery for two decades from his pulpit and through the GES, as well as in church courts and as leader of the FCAS, was locked in a serious confrontation with the Free Church. Although both he and the Free Church agreed that

slavery violated man's natural rights and contradicted biblical teachings, the two adversaries could find no common ground on how to
implement these abstractions in church policy.[55] Willis insisted that
to fellowship with Southern Christians was to abet slaveholders,
injure slaves, and partake in sin. Consequently, the fraternal tie must
be severed. For their part, the Free Church leaders believed that
friendly reproof was the best path, and they saw the FCAS as a tool
of the devil. A rupture seemed inevitable.

A way around this impasse, which saved face for both sides,
fortuitously appeared in Canada West in 1847. Needing a theology
professor for Knox College, the Canadian synod's commissioner,
the Rev. George Bayne, appealed to the Colonial Committee for help.
Seeing a way to defuse the fellowshipping controversy and aid the
Canadian church, the committee requested Willis to take the appointment. Bayne must have welcomed this turn of events, for Willis
had been well received by church leaders in Canada. During his
1845–46 deputation, "various parties" had urged him to remain, but
the position he had been offered had involved teaching at Knox
College and serving a pastoral charge at some distance, and Willis
had declined the offer as being impractical.[56]

By the fall of 1847, he saw things differently. Having served the
same congregation for a quarter of a century and now being in his
mid-forties, a change must have been a welcome prospect. However,
a different consideration probably determined Willis's decision. He
longed for the academic world, with its opportunities for "studious
research and mental application" unhampered by the distractions
of the pastorate. New College, Edinburgh, was the logical place for
Willis, for a chair in theology was vacant, but the fellowshipping
controversy ruled out this possibility. After his attack on several
church leaders, especially New College principal James Cunningham, the two could not have worked amicably in the same
institution. Moreover, New College students were sympathetic to
the FCAS and had voiced their criticism of the Free Church in a
running public correspondence with students at Princeton Seminary. In these conditions, placing Willis at New College was un-
thinkable, and the door to an academic life in the church in Scotland
was closed.[57]

The Canadian offer, on the other hand, was enticing. Without
pastoral duties, Willis could teach and study within the purview of
the church and could enjoy the challenge of building the new theological college. Furthermore, Canadian Free Churchmen were well
disposed towards him and approved of his views on slavery. They
had followed his North American antislavery activities in 1845–46,

and since his return to Scotland the *Banner* had praised both the antifellowshipping campaign and the formation of the FCAS. This meant that he could pursue his antislavery convictions in the company of like-minded Free Churchmen. As he obliquely reminded the Glasgow presbytery in a carefully worded farewell, in Canada, God would enable him to render "as effective and even more widely extended service" to evangelical religion, sound Presbyterianism, and "spiritual and civil freedom, than in my present charge." He took just two weeks to accept the offer that released both him and the Free Church from an intolerable situation. Christmas found him comfortably ensconced in Toronto.[58]

SEVERAL CANADIAN ABOLITIONISTS served their apprenticeship in the lengthy British antislavery struggle that stretched from the amelioration policy to the antifellowshipping controversy. Prior to emancipation, John Roaf and Robert Burns had served at the local level, while Charles Stuart's contributions, through his tireless speaking, aggressive pamphleteering, and inspiration in establishing the critically important Agency Committee, were of national importance. In 1833 Brown, Johnston, and Buchan had helped found two influential Scottish antislavery societies dedicated to ending slavery around the world. After a lengthy term with the Paisley committee, the steadfast Burns had identified with the GES and briefly cooperated in Willis's spirited effort to force the Free Church to sever the Southern tie.

There are indications that other Canadian antislavery advocates had British antislavery ties. For example, Adam Lillie, the influential Toronto Congregationalist, was a convert of Ralph Wardlaw, and doubtless caught the abolition virus from his mentor. William McClure, the Methodist New Connexion clergyman who reached Canada in 1848, had shown interest in antislavery in his native Ireland, where he had met William Lloyd Garrison. But unfortunately the evidence in these cases is sparse and provides little more than a basis for speculation.[59]

With the obvious exception of Stuart, among these figures only Willis, and to a lesser extent Burns and Johnston, could legitimately claim to have exercised any leadership in British antislavery. Burns clearly was an important antislavery figure in the community of Paisley, but Johnston's full role in the influential city of Edinburgh is hidden by the lack of EES files. Willis's valuable work in the GES taught him the importance of organization in achieving social reform, and his enlarged responsibilities in the GES after 1843 gave him experience in managing the affairs of a dynamic public body. While his formation of the FCAS broadened his experience, it was more important in another respect. A weighty step, in which he challenged the church to the point of jeopardizing his career, it was undertaken only after careful consideration. This yielded the anti-slavery ideology, rooted in biblical doctrine and the philosophy of natural rights, that was so meticulously enunciated in his writing. This body of ideas, which was fully matured by the time he reached Canada, provided an intellectually defensible basis for his abolition-ist activity in British North America.

All these figures, regardless of their varying degrees of promi-nence, were veterans of the British antislavery campaign, and in their new homeland in the 1840s they drew on this experience to rekindle the abolitionist flame which, as we shall see, had all but flickered out at the end of the previous decade in the hands of the Upper Canada Anti-Slavery Society.

# 3 Helping the Lord against the Mighty

While Willis and Burns waged abolitionist warfare in Britain, Upper Canadians seemed oblivious to the neighbouring slaves' cry for help in the early 1830s. But under the persistent prodding of Methodist editor Ephraim Evans, and in response to the rising number of fugitive slaves in Upper Canada, by mid-decade abolitionist sentiment began to rise. In 1837, a group of Torontonians optimistically formed an association to spearhead the movement. However, it failed to capitalize on the opportunity presented by the threatened extradition of two fugitive slaves to the United States. The organization collapsed prematurely, without achieving anything significant, in the suspicion-charged political atmosphere that followed the 1837 Upper Canadian rebellion. This ended the first phase of Canadian antislavery, leaving the movement disorganized and leaderless.

THE WINNING OF BRITISH EMANCIPATION in 1833 inaugurated a dynamic era in the history of the antislavery movement. It saw the organization of the Edinburgh and Glasgow emancipation societies, which were devoted to ending slavery in the American South. Meanwhile, in the United States, the American abolitionist William Lloyd Garrison and his supporters had formed the New England Anti-Slavery Society and, in late 1833, the American Anti-Slavery Society. The people who led these organizations no longer viewed slavery merely as an undesirable social institution destined for eventual termination, as previous antislavery advocates had defined it. Instead, the new generation of opponents to slavery declared it to be a sin with which there could be no further compromise. For them, immediate abolition was the only acceptable solution.[1]

Britons and Americans watched these developments closely, but British North Americans were decidedly complacent about them. Residents of Toronto, Niagara, Hamilton, St Catharines, and Kingston were informed about the triumph of British antislavery, since newspapers in these towns published summaries of the emancipation bill's progress through Parliament, although only five papers bothered to comment.[2] The Niagara *Gleaner*, for example, congratulated the "noble, humane" British for spending £20 million to secure the "glorious boon" of liberty for 800,000 slaves.[3] But such enthusiasm was an exception to the general lack of interest and even the outright hostility exhibited by many Upper Canadians. Callously disregarding what freedom meant to the slaves, the Niagara *Reporter* lamented that emancipation would induce dissatisfied planters to leave the West Indies, and the Toronto *Patriot* condemned the step as a failure. "Everybody knows," the editor caustically declared, that the "natives of Africa and their descendants are a lazy race. Nothing but want, which is every man's master, will make them work; and when the cravings of nature are satisfied, like other animals, they go to sleep."[4]

In some measure, the appearance of British antislavery groups in the 1830s was a tacit admission that, having permitted slavery to take root in colonial America, the mother country shared responsibility for its existence and therefore was obligated to see the battle through in the United States now that slavery had ended in the empire. It would have been natural for Upper Canadians to have shared this sentiment and, given their proximity to the United States, to have applauded every step their neighbours took to end the "peculiar institution." But judging from journalistic comment, this was not the case. The Canadian press was strangely silent on the appearance of the American Anti-Slavery Society (AAS) as well as the British organizations, and it certainly did not praise them. Instead, the newspapers saw the continuation of slavery in the United States as cause for smug self-congratulation. The Niagara *Gleaner*, for example, self-righteously declared that while others

prattle about liberty and equality, the kingly government of Britain acts upon the principle, and sets an example to the whole world ... It is disgusting to hear our neighbours of the United States boast of their liberty and equality, while thousands of human beings are chained together and driven from place to place and sold like beasts ... to the everlasting disgrace of the people of that Republic. We glory in being a subject of the greatest and most benevolent nation ever in existence, either of the present or subsequent ages of the world.[5]

There was more evidence of Upper Canadian coolness towards antislavery in September 1835, when Captain Charles Stuart, who had contributed so significantly to British emancipation, visited Toronto. With the end of British slavery, Stuart had crossed the Atlantic to push the cause in the United States. In 1835 he became an agent for the AAS, and he travelled widely throughout the northwest holding antislavery meetings and organizing local committees.[6] Stuart likely went to Toronto to see his sister, but he took the opportunity to hold several antislavery meetings in city hall. In view of his burgeoning antislavery reputation, the little provincial capital could have been expected to welcome him with considerable fanfare, but Stuart and his antislavery meetings went largely unannounced. It is conceivable that the busy agent arranged his itinerary so hastily that there was no time for advance publicity. The only newspaper to mention his presence was the *Patriot*, voice of the Tory establishment. In a harsh review by "Philo Libertas," it declared that if this "babbler" was serious, he should manfully concentrate his efforts on the slaveholders instead of retreating to a place where slavery did not exist. It was improper for Canadians to combine against slavery or to desecrate their pulpits with the subject, the paper said, and the notion that British North Americans should entice slaves to leave their masters was "vicious" and "immoral" and was rooted in the barest "fanaticism." The *Patriot* hoped that such a "bloody-minded preacher" would not be welcomed in the province, for slavery was a puzzle for Americans to solve without Canadian meddling.[7]

Despite the *Patriot's* opposition, Stuart's meetings were well attended, and soon there were signs that not all the seed had fallen on stony ground. A key influence in fostering the growth of abolitionist sentiment was the Toronto *Christian Guardian*, the provincial Wesleyan Methodist mouthpiece and the most widely read newspaper of the decade. It had kept its readers informed about recent antislavery events, and when the English-born cleric Ephraim Evans became editor in 1835, the journal moved towards an avowedly abolitionist position, for, in Evans's view, slavery was a topic that could not be discussed "without strong excitement of feeling."[8]

Evidently, it was the friction that slavery was causing among American Methodists in the 1830s that aroused the *Guardian's* concern. Some Northern Methodists, particularly those in New England and at some locations in New York, were sympathetic to the abolitionists. The Methodist church as a whole, however, feared the threat of division that the slavery issue represented, for there were many slaveholding members in its Southern conferences. It therefore sought to avoid discussing the question. This evasiveness had induced the AAS to criticize American Methodists pointedly in 1834 for failing to denounce slavery as a sinful practice, and British Methodists echoed the charge in an address to their American fellow churchmen the following year. These actions no doubt encouraged the 1835 New England Methodist Episcopal annual conference, an antislavery stronghold, to denounce slavery and demand immediate emancipation. The *Guardian*, now in Evans's hands, welcomed this step, and it edged closer to adopting immediate abolition in a ringing attack on South Carolina Governor George McDuffie, who had made an inflammatory speech advocating the death penalty for all antislavery agents.[9] Meanwhile, the quadrennial Methodist Episcopal general conference met in Cincinnati in the spring of 1836 and apologetically replied to the British Methodists, saying that if they had fully understood the complexities of the slavery question in the United States, they would have been more sympathetic to their American brethren. The conference also sternly censured two of its members for participating in a recent Cincinnati antislavery meeting, and it denounced "modern abolition" (immediatism), disclaiming any wish to interfere in the master-slave relationship. These measures left the abolitionist Methodist minority dissatisfied, and when the New England annual conference met on the heels of the general conference, it defiantly retaliated, calling slavery a sin and advocating immediate emancipation.[10]

Evans's presence at the New England meeting seemingly whetted his antislavery appetite, for the 17 August edition of the *Guardian* praised the New England Methodists, giving extensive coverage to the slavery committee's report and the resolutions that were adopted. In the same breath, Evans lashed out at the New York annual conference for requiring that, before new ministers could be ordained, they must promise to refrain from advocating abolition. The Toronto editor continued his antislavery crusade in the fall of 1836 by praising British Wesleyans for renewing their plea that American Methodists declare forthrightly the sinfulness of slavery. He also sharply criticized the prominent American Presbyterian minister, R.J. Breckenridge, who had attacked George Thompson and the abolitionists while defending his own slaveholding countrymen during a widely publicized Glasgow debate. "We tell Mr Breckenridge and all who act with him," Evans declared, "that it is not by exposures such as theirs that slavery will ever be locked out of countenance in any country – and that they will have to account to the Great Master for all the contempt they have sought to pour upon that honoured band of men in their land, who have suffered worse treatment at the hand of the church and the world – and for what – why for nothing more than they have demanded the instant abolition of slavery."[11]

The *Guardian* reserved its strongest antislavery declaration for the first editorial of 1837, when it published a letter by Timothy Murilb, an American Methodist minister, which attacked slavery on scriptural grounds. Always zealous to preserve Methodism's good name, Evans was gratified that a respected Methodist had finally spoken out about the

crying sin of his nation; – a sin excelling in magnitude ... any other which has ever enlisted in its support the sanction of law – a sin, against which, as such, the founders of American Methodism lifted up their voices loud and long, and which, as the records of the church will show, they zealously laboured to exterminate ... O that this foul blot could be erased from the records of history! But it cannot. One course is, however, open to our American brethren, if they would sustain the character of Wesleyan Methodism within their borders. Let them immediately fly to the rescue, by proclaiming to the world their detestation of the system of oppression. Let them denounce it, not on political grounds, but as a *moral evil*.[12]

The growing number of fugitive slaves who found their way to safety in Upper Canada also awakened British North American interest in antislavery in the mid-1830s. Some had come to the southwestern portion of the province after the War of 1812, and as prejudice mounted in the American North in the following decades, the flow increased. As the fugitives became more numerous, their presence drew attention to the slavery question in various ways.[13] The destitution of some of the newcomers elicited help from the community. On the other hand, as earlier refugees established themselves, they built institutions that articulated the black community's interests, and this fostered hostility and discrimination on the part of some whites; but it led others to fight slavery abroad and to reduce prejudice at home.[14] Moreover, the presence of fugitive slaves in Canada assumed a symbolic importance for the entire antislavery movement. Some antislavery activists maintained that if blacks prospered in Canada, it would show that they were ready for freedom, while others claimed that if blacks failed, it would prove the proslavery contention that they could not compete with whites and that liberation would be a mistake. [15] How fully aware Upper Canadians were that their province was an antislavery proving ground is unclear, but the combined effect of these influences was to make it more difficult for them to ignore antislavery, as they had done earlier in the decade.

Three men were particularly important in awakening antislavery sentiment through their efforts to assist the fugitives. One was Thomas Rolph, an English physician who became well known in the black community. Rolph had lived in Essex, where he had imbibed antislavery in part from Agency Committee lecturers. He emigrated to Canada in 1833 and opened a medical practice at Ancaster, near Hamilton, where the black population was growing, and he soon became a notable public figure. In later years, this self-declared "ardent friend" of blacks claimed to have been elected their agent in Upper Canada in 1834, although there is no independent confirmation of this and it seems likely that the actual year was 1837. However, there is no doubt that somehow he won the black community's confidence and was a frequent speaker at their gatherings – such as that at Hamilton Anglican church in August 1837, when they met to celebrate the anniversary of West Indian emancipation. [16]

In 1836, Rolph published a book about his West Indian experiences (on his way to Canada, he had spent four months on the Barbados sugar plantation of a friend). His glowing picture of Canada as an ideal place for British settlers gained wide recognition for the volume, but it was the book's harsh description of American slavery, in comparison to the mildness of the slavery he had observed in Barbados, that boosted the antislavery movement in Upper Canada. In Rolph's judgment, the British slaves were well cared for and had enjoyed a full and secure social life even before Parliament had wisely adopted compensated emancipation. The benevolence of British slavery, in his view, was symbolized by one island governor's recommendation of public funding for black education. Rolph contrasted this with the situation in the United States where, he said, "slavery is to be perpetual – instruction and amelioration a crime. Nay, they almost justify the strippings, scourgings, tarrings, featherings, shootings, hangings, and assassinations that bands of murderous tyrants, under the name of Lynch law, have exercised against those who would attempt the introduction of better and milder institutions." [17]

Hiram Wilson was another figure who contributed to the rise of the Upper Canadian antislavery movement in the mid-1830s. Wilson was one of the Lane Rebels – a group of students and faculty from Lane Seminary in Cincinnati who were dismissed for abolitionist activities and who migrated to Oberlin Institute in Ohio, where antislavery sentiment was welcomed. In October 1836 the AAS commissioned him to examine the condition of fugitive slaves in Upper Canada. He located himself in Toronto and systematically collected information on the six hundred blacks who allegedly were living in the vicinity, by circulating a questionnaire to prominent and supposedly knowledgeable figures. The questionnaire probed such areas of black behaviour as work habits, criminality, sobriety, and the need for public charity. Wilson's findings – that the social behaviour of blacks compared favourably with that of the general white population – were published in several abolitionist periodicals. This devoted agent also laboriously crisscrossed the province on foot, counselling blacks and promoting antislavery. The AAS's annual report stated that his efforts produced a number of schools for the fugitives and "several flourishing [black] societies" that could be counted on for co-operation.[18]

Robert Graham Dunlop was the third member of this antislavery triumvirate. He had come from Britain to Canada in 1833 at the invitation of his more famous brother, William "Tiger" Dunlop, a physician. The latter was involved in the Canada Land Company, a real estate group concentrated in the region that became Huron County, and he settled at Goderich on the shores of Lake Huron, where his residence was known as Gairbraid. Robert Dunlop devoted much time to improving Goderich, becoming a justice of the peace, helping to organize the Anglican parish, and opening a school in a room at Gairbraid; and when Huron County was organized in 1835, he was elected to the assembly. His duties frequently found him in the provincial capital, where he took an interest in the fugitive slaves, and he was one of those whom Hiram Wilson consulted. Dunlop stated that after "much observation and some experience," he was certain that there was not a "more loyal, honest, industrious, temperate and independent class of citizens than the coloured people of Upper Canada," and he encouraged Wilson to continue his benevolent work among them. Dunlop was also known for his "ardent desire to elevate the character of our coloured population": during the winter of 1835–36 he gave blacks a series of lectures on the "importance and advantage of education" as stepping stones to success in their new homeland.[19]

By late 1836, the philanthropic work of Rolph, Wilson, and Dunlop, together with Evans's campaign in the *Guardian*, had awakened considerable antislavery sentiment in the province. It was with great anticipation that the *Guardian* announced that a meeting would be held on 4 January 1837 to organize an antislavery society in Toronto.

Identifying the moving force behind the organization of the Upper Canada Anti-Slavery Society (UCAS) is a difficult task, for there are several candidates. James Johnston, a member of the executive committee, who before emigrating to Canada in the mid-1830s had been treasurer of the GES, is one possibility. Hiram Wilson is another, for his arrival in Canada virtually coincided with the appearance of the new society. Ephraim Evans has been credited with that role, and surely Dunlop, who chaired the founding meeting and became president of the society, is a fourth candidate. In retrospect, Wilson seems the least likely, for it is doubtful that he actually participated in the first meeting. Moreover, given the antirepublicanism of many Canadians, it would have invited opposition to have this young and recently arrived American as the spearhead of the society. Johnston, like Wilson, was an outsider, but he was also an antislavery veteran with good British credentials – a coveted addition to any new society in the young province. Surprisingly, however, neither Johnston nor Dunlop participated in the society's second meeting, so it seems unlikely that either had guided the group's formation, unless some unseen consideration entered the picture.

On balance, then, it seems probable that Evans was the principal force in the birth of the UCAS. His antislavery editorials had reached a crescendo by early 1837, and unlike the Goderich-based Dunlop or the peripatetic Wilson, Evans resided in Toronto, the best location from which to make arrangements for the society. Evans's influence in Wesleyan Methodist circles merits consideration as well, for the founding meeting was held at Newgate Wesleyan Methodist Church, and Wesleyans predominated among the participants and among those who were elected officers and committee members. Undoubtedly, Toronto Wesleyan Methodists were the main force in the founding of the UCAS and Evans was chief among them.[20]

There were no international abolitionist heavyweights present to dramatize the organization of the UCAS, and, except for the full-scale participation of blacks, it was an unexceptional meeting. In his opening remarks as chairman, Dunlop complimented the city's black community for its responsible conduct and its eagerness for education, and he commented optimistically on the influence that such a "decided" expression of public opinion as the meeting represented could have on a great question of public morality such as slavery. The evening's resolutions ranged from praising the "lofty justice" of British emancipation and identifying slavery as a sinful practice requiring immediate abandonment, to welcoming the "correct views" and efforts to extinguish slavery that were at last appearing among some Americans. Recalling William Wilberforce's long battle to secure British emancipation, the fledgling society pledged itself to "prosecute unceasing efforts" to end slavery so that the wicked institution would be only a memory to the next generation. The *Guardian* reported that the meeting was well attended with 106 claiming membership.[21]

Reaction to the formation of the UCAS was mixed. Predictably, the *Guardian* welcomed it enthusiastically, while the *Upper Canada Herald* merely summarized the events of the founding meeting. Neither the reformist Toronto *Constitution* nor the rival *Patriot* took any notice. The distant Quebec *Gazette*, echoing earlier sentiments of the *Patriot*, harshly criticized the society; the paper deplored its formation, arguing that slavery was a matter for Americans to deal with free from foreign interference: "It seems to us, uncalled for; slavery does not exist there, nor in any part of the British dominions. Where then is the use of such a society? Is it intended to operate in the United States? We can conceive of no greater offense toward any people ... It is neither consistent with prudence nor good neighborhood." The *Guardian* defensively replied that Christianity's mandate was not limited by national boundaries; it was just as legitimate to seek to abolish slavery wherever it existed as it was to advocate eliminating infanticide and sutteeism in India. With British and American Christians jointly arrayed against the forces of evil, the *Guardian* rejoiced that "Canada will also put forth her aid, and come up 'to help the Lord against the mighty.'"[22]

The UCAS doubtless assumed that its primary task was to educate public opinion about the evils of slavery. If Upper Canadians could be brought to support abolition, the society would have done its part towards bringing world opinion to bear on hard-hearted Southern slaveholders. In the fall of 1837, however, the immediate issue that confronted the Canadian antislavery movement was protecting the escaped slaves who were living in Upper Canada. Judging by an earlier case, governments in British North America were inclined to extend a large measure of protection to them. In 1829 the American government had formally requested the administrator of Lower Canada, Sir James Kempt, to return a slave who had made his way to Montreal. After consulting his council, Kempt refused to comply, claiming that a fugitive slave could only be returned if the alleged offence made him subject to arrest in the province. Since slavery did not exist in British North America, an escaped slave was not guilty of violating any law merely by fleeing from servitude. However, in late 1837 there were two fugitive-slave cases in which the Upper Canadian government seemed prepared to meet American wishes. These incidents were tailor-made to provide an opportunity for the UCAS to make its mark.[23]

Solomon Moseby had escaped from his owner in Kentucky and had made his way to Upper Canada, where he settled in the Niagara region in the spring of 1837. While escaping, he had taken a horse from his master's plantation, and when the owner traced him to Upper Canada, the authorities jailed him for horse theft and Kentucky requested his extradition. When the executive council of Upper Canada concluded that there was sufficient evidence to show that Moseby was guilty, the government decided to return him, despite a petition on his behalf from the citizens of Niagara. To prevent their brother from being returned to likely punishment and certain re-enslavement, a crowd of blacks assembled at the Niagara jail. When Moseby was brought out, the blacks briefly overpowered the attending militiamen, and in the ensuing confusion the prisoner escaped and the soldiers fired on the crowd, killing two men. The incident was widely reported in the press and caused much excitement.[24]

The second case, which involved another fugitive from Kentucky, surfaced before the Moseby affair had been resolved. The circumstances were nearly identical, except that the defendant, Jesse Happy, had left his horse on the American side of the border and had written to his owner explaining where the animal could be found. When Attorney General C.A. Hagerman and Chief Justice John Beverley Robinson advised that there was sufficient evidence to return Happy, the government behaved cautiously. Criticism over the decision to return Moseby and the accompanying violence had not yet subsided, and now residents of Hamilton, where Happy was jailed, were petitioning. This time the government referred the case to the Colonial Office for advice. Eventually, Happy was released, for the law officers of the crown decided that informing the owner where the horse was located absolved Happy of felonious intent in taking the animal.[25]

The remarkable fact about these incidents was the inaction of the UCAS. While residents of Niagara and Hamilton petitioned against extradition, the society remained silent. In similar circumstances twenty-three years later, the Anti-Slavery Society of Canada swiftly challenged the Canadian government with a large protest meeting in Toronto after the government had threatened to extradite the fugitive John Anderson.[26] But not until 8 November, nearly two full months after the Moseby fiasco, did the apathetic Upper Canadian abolitionists arrange a meeting, and there is no evidence that in the meantime the society did anything whatsoever on behalf of the two men. If the meeting was intended to rebuke the government, at best it dealt but a glancing blow with a resolution expressing "unfeigned disapprobation and abhorrence of the mercenary motives which would induce any foreigner to set foot upon our favoured shores for the purpose of entrapping, and again subjecting to the horrors of slavery, those who have sought the pure air of freedom in a British province."[27]

The meeting itself holds some clues that shed light on why the society remained inactive during the Moseby and Happy incidents. Dunlop, the president, did not participate, and it is possible that his withdrawal from public life, which became complete by 1839 and eventuated in his early death in 1841, had already begun. This would have weakened the society's leadership at a critical juncture. Changes had also occurred in the makeup of the organization since its formation ten months earlier, when Methodists predominated. Not only were founders such as Dunlop, Johnston, and the influential John Ryerson, the minister of Newgate Wesleyan Methodist church in Toronto, absent from the November meeting, but several new figures had appeared. Most evident were two Presbyterian clergymen, William Rintoul and David Ferguson. Other new members were John Roaf, who had just arrived in Toronto to take charge of the newly formed Congregational church, and Hiram Wilson. Unfortunately, the new members seem to have offered no effectual leadership to guide the young UCAS after Dunlop's apparent withdrawal.[28]

But more than faltering leadership brought the collapse of the UCAS in the wake of the Moseby and Happy incidents. The crackling political climate in Upper Canada was about to erupt in the Rebellion of 1837, and this event cast a dark shadow over the antislavery struggle. In the 1830s, Upper Canada was governed by an oligarchical political system that had become too restrictive for the growing province. Political authority resided in the governor, who was aided by appointed executive and legislative councils. An elected assembly levied taxes and passed laws, but some areas of responsibility were reserved and legislation could be revised by the legislative council. The appointed officials, many of whom held office for life, came primarily from a small group usually known as the Family Compact, because its members were bound together by business and family ties, by Loyalist roots, and by Anglicanism. A reform movement had appeared demanding changes in this state of affairs – a condition that seemed even more oppressive to those beyond the "charmed circle" when compared to the prosperity and political liberty glistening just south of the border in Jacksonian America. Under the leadership of William Lyon Mackenzie, the reformers demanded a more open land policy, public education, reform of the banking system (which was symbolized by the Bank of Upper Canada), an end to corruption in public works, and political institutions that were responsible to the people.[29]

A particular bone of contention was the clergy reserves. Under the Constitutional Act of 1791, which had created the provinces of Upper and Lower Canada, one-seventh of the unoccupied land in Upper Canada was set aside to support a Protestant clergy. With the passage of time and the support of the oligarchy, the Anglican church had made good its claim to be the sole beneficiary of the grant. Anglicans assumed a semi-established status, even though they were outnumbered by the Wesleyan Methodists, the largest Christian communion in the province. Under the leadership of Egerton Ryerson, its most prominent minister in the early 1830s, the Wesleyans began a campaign against this religious privilege and joined forces with Mackenzie's political reformers in an effort to have the proceeds of the clergy reserves applied to public education. However, while Ryerson and the Methodists opposed the religious privilege which the clergy reserves represented, they were firmly attached to the British connection as a means of countering republican influences from the United States – and Mackenzie increasingly seemed to be moving towards republicanism. Accordingly, Ryerson broke with Mackenzie and the Reform party in 1833 and delivered the Methodists to the Constitutionalists, as the oligarchists were called. From that time forward, the Wesleyan Methodists generally advocated a progressive constitutionalist position which, while opposing the principle of responsible government (a legislative council chosen from the majority party in the assembly, to which it would be responsible), continued to call for an end to the abuses of the oligarchy and for the income from the clergy reserves to be applied to education. In the election of 1836, Methodist votes secured the assembly for the Constitutionalists.[30] This, combined with the political ineptitude of the new governor, Sir Francis Bond Head, led Mackenzie and his followers to despair of securing reform through political means and thus to resort to an ill-conceived coup in Toronto in December 1837. Easily routed, the unsuccessful revolutionaries fled across the border to New York State, where they fruitlessly pursued their goals the following year.

It was in the suspicion-charged atmosphere of the post-rebellion months of late 1837 and early 1838, when Upper Canadian Tories were "hunting hard for treason and crying 'rebel' after even moderate reformers," that the UCAS foundered. While the courts were rounding up and trying those suspected of disloyalty during the rising, even the Wesleyan Methodists were feverishly trying to show that their hands were clean. The Rev. William M. Harvard, president of the Methodist conference, directed local ministers to examine their class lists for the names of people of doubtful loyalty and to tell any person "ill-affected towards the Crown" who applied for membership in the future that he had come to the "wrong door." With such paranoia engulfing the province – and evident even in Methodist circles – Wesleyans who had pressed for reform too vigorously may well have been uneasy and have sought to avoid any further action that would attract the attention of the vengeful establishment. The position of the oligarchy on the antislavery question which, as we have seen, was enunciated by the semi-official *Patriot*, was that slavery was an American question that should be left to Americans to settle. Moreover, some voices among the favoured few already were pointing the finger of blame for the rebellion at Methodists and Presbyterians – the very people who were most closely associated with the UCAS. Alexander Macdonell, the Roman Catholic bishop of Upper Canada who clung tightly to the skirts of the oligarchy, strongly opposed all republican and American influences because of the attraction they might hold for his beloved Scottish immigrants. Identifying Methodists with these corrosive forces, Macdonell held that "Protestants, Presbyterians and Methodists" had been the "leaders and chief contrivers" in the uprising. In such a climate, Methodists and Presbyterians might well be expected to soft-pedal the antislavery theme, especially if the former were to have any hope of achieving the secularization of the clergy reserves or funding for the struggling Methodist Upper Canada Academy at Cobourg, which the mother country had promised but the provincial authorities had withheld.[31]

Upper Canadian antislavery suffered another serious blow in the spring of 1838 when the annual conference removed Evans from the helm of the *Guardian*. The paper had been the one prominent abolitionist journal since 1835, and its voice had become more strident in 1836 as American Methodists faltered on the slavery question. However, the *Guardian* was criticized for discussing political issues, and the 1837 annual conference reprimanded Evans by removing his name as editor from the title page and by appointing a committee to supervise his work. The complaints were renewed the following year when the *Guardian* attacked the American government for sympathizing with the patriots in the rebellion. Evans was reassigned to an administrative post in the London District, far from the Toronto seat of the UCAS. This prevented him from assuming leadership of the society as the logical replacement for Dunlop. It also silenced his antislavery pen, depriving Upper Canadian antislavery of its chief editorial voice just when this was critically important to the welfare of the organization.

Whether Evans's harsh words about the American Methodists' stand on slavery contributed to his removal is unclear. But it seems plausible, for at the time many Canadian Methodists were anxious to avoid offending American Wesleyans in order to maintain a good "connexional" tie with them. Among these people was Egerton Ryerson, the *Guardian*'s new editor. By 1839 he was weary of the continual political struggle on behalf of Methodist interests that he had waged throughout the decade. The following year he even considered taking the pulpit at a large New York City Methodist church in order to escape from the Upper Canadian turmoil. Given the controversy that the slavery question had aroused in American Methodist circles, anyone considering such an appointment would have been unwise to exacerbate the matter. In any case, in Ryerson's hands after mid-1838 the *Guardian* abruptly dropped the antislavery theme, and ironically the new editor soon became a target for antislavery journals. [32]

It was unfortunate for Canadian antislavery that Thomas Rolph was not a member of the UCAS. He continued to assist fugitives until his return to England in 1843. An experienced speaker and gifted publicist, Rolph should have been a prime recruit for the society. However, in 1836 Evans had reviewed Rolph's book on his West Indian excursion somewhat negatively, charging that the physician's view of slavery in the islands was unrealistically mild. This likely created friction between the two men, and anyone who was a member of the society would have had to be able to work with Evans. Sectarian religious considerations may also have steered Rolph away from the UCAS, for he was a recent convert to Roman Catholicism, and in the religious climate of the day, in which sectarian views were strongly held, he would undoubtedly have been uncomfortable in a body that was dominated by evangelical Methodists and Presbyterians. Although there is no evidence that the Tory, Rolph, shared his friend Bishop Macdonell's interpretation of the role of Methodists and Presbyterians in the rebellion, Macdonell's attitude may well have inhibited Rolph when it came to working with Methodists and Presbyterians, even in so urgent a matter as antislavery. Sectarianism may also explain why Rolph, a tireless provincewide traveller, failed to sign the Hamilton petition on behalf of Jesse Happy, even though the town was virtually next door to Ancaster.[33]


THE UCAS WAS NOT SYNONYMOUS WITH the Upper Canadian antislavery movement in the 1830s, as the independent activities of Thomas Rolph and Hiram Wilson show. Moreover, there were nearly three hundred signatures of citizens on the Hamilton and Niagara petitions who were likely candidates to form either independent or branch groups, as was happening widely in British and American circles. Yet there is no evidence that the UCAS attempted to coordinate its efforts with abolitionists in the Hamilton-Niagara region. Nor did the Toronto abolitionists establish ties with the black antislavery groups that Hiram Wilson organized or with the major societies in Britain and the United States. The UCAS provided a potential nucleus around which Canadian antislavery might have coalesced; but because it suffered from a crippled leadership, was intimidated by the rebellion-induced paranoia of the oligarchy, lacked a media voice after mid-1838, and was perhaps stifled by sectarian religious divisions, this failed to occur. Instead, the UCAS collapsed in late 1837, and with it ended the first phase of Canadian antislavery. Rejuvenation of the movement did not occur until a decade later.

# 4 A Feeble Voice from the Backwoods of Canada

The 1840s marked a quiescent interlude in Canadian antislavery between the decline of the UCAS and the resurgence of a more militant abolitionist movement, following passage of the 1850 Fugitive Slave Law. Abolition in the province found expression in the activities of isolated individuals such as Thomas Rolph and Hiram Wilson, who directed their energies towards the immediate task at hand – helping fugitive slaves who, with few resources, faced the challenge of adjusting to life in an adopted homeland. Promising efforts to arouse public opinion resumed when Peter Brown's Toronto *Banner* seized the antislavery mantle that had once been worn by the *Christian Guardian*. However, John Roaf's efforts to form a new antislavery society foundered, leaving Canadian antislavery leaderless and disorganized. Not until the end of the decade did British North Americans effectively respond to the needy fugitives who were arriving in increasing numbers.

THE IMMEDIATE ISSUE FACING the few Upper Canadians who concerned themselves with slavery in the late 1830s was the safety of the growing number of fugitives in the province. An 1840 canvass of the various communities where they lived in 1840 counted approximately 12,500, and, as the Moseby and Happy incidents showed, they were in some danger of extradition to the United States on criminal charges. As a consequence, Upper Canadian blacks sought help from their friend and "staunch abolitionist," Thomas

Rolph. At a December 1837 Toronto meeting, with the events of the previous months still a vivid memory, they appointed Rolph their agent and asked him to present their case to the imperial government. Since public attention was still riveted on events surrounding the Mackenzie rebellion, Rolph wisely delayed any action until the following summer when Lord Durham, who had been appointed to investigate the uprising, was on the scene. Then, with Durham in the city, Rolph, at a meeting of Toronto blacks, called for a revision of the law so that slaves charged with committing a crime before entering British North America would be tried by a provincial jury rather than being extradited. The memorial also asked authorities to provide competent teachers and access to public schools for the fugitives' children. In a rousing speech, which praised blacks for their model behaviour and their loyal support of Britain in the recent rebellions, Rolph contrasted the enlightened British policy of compensated emancipation with America's dogged adherence to slavery. The meeting heartily endorsed the memorial, which was entrusted to Durham for presentation to the Colonial Office. Durham acknowledged the justice of its requests and promised to use the "whole weight of his influence" to win the British government's support. [1]

Durham's forthright endorsement must have heartened Rolph and his clients; however, when nearly a year passed with no response, Rolph asked the lieutenant-governor, Sir George Arthur, about the status of the memorial. Arthur had no information but promised to take up the matter with the Colonial Office. But he cautioned Rolph not to be surprised if the British government did not concede the memorial's main wish, regardless of the praiseworthiness of protecting the fugitives, for he said that the mother country would hesitate to claim the right of trial in Canada for people charged elsewhere. The lieutenant-governor also implied that the petition impinged on some unspecified negotiations that were underway between Britain and the United States. [2]

In the meantime, Rolph went to England in the summer of 1839 to promote British emigration to Canada and to assist Bishop Macdonell with church matters. He appealed directly to the Colonial Office for information about the memorial, requesting to see Colonial Secretary Lord John Russell. The Colonial Office diffidently answered that it had already sent Arthur a reply to the petition, and Russell refused to see Rolph. When Rolph persisted, the "substance" of the dispatch, though not the document itself, was communicated to him. [3]

It revealed that the law officers of the crown had concluded that the security of the fugitives was not in jeopardy. Upper Canadian law did not distinguish between whites and blacks, and therefore it would be illegal, they claimed, to surrender fugitive slaves in circumstances in which white men would not also be given up. Changing the law, therefore, was not necessary, and the government concurred in this. Since education was a local issue, they recommended that the school question be taken up with provincial authorities.[4]

Rolph "deeply deplored" this decision. In light of the petitioners' "eminent services" during Mackenzie's rebellion, Rolph told Russell, they deserved better treatment. Britain's position ignored the key fact that it was not the American government that requested extradition in these cases, as Russell's dispatch assumed, but state governors acting for slaveowners. It was crucial to understand this, for in most Southern states only rape, arson, and murder were recognizable slave offences; in other cases, the authorities returned slaves to their owners for punishment. If the law remained unchanged, Rolph warned, any slave in Upper Canada could be subject to a felony charge and possible extradition merely for carrying away the clothes he wore, since these belonged to his owner.[5]

When word of the British government's decision reached blacks in Canada, they urged Rolph to renew the appeal, for they saw a contradiction in the government's policy in the Moseby and Happy cases. The two incidents were virtually identical, they argued, but in the former the decision was to extradite, while Happy was freed. The government should place such decisions beyond the influence of such "expediency and caprice," they argued, and should thereby ensure their security in the province.[6]

Russell did not reply when Rolph communicated these sentiments in early November, but the persistent agent shortly renewed the attack, for in the meantime he had received disturbing information from Edward de St Remy, who was acting as secretary for the Upper Canadian petitioners in Rolph's absence. De St Remy, undoubtedly through correspondence with Arthur, had learned the full contents of Russell's dispatch (which had been described only partially to Rolph). The reason for the long delay in responding to the memorial was that the Colonial Office had never received it; Durham had either misplaced it or been negligent. Rolph penned Russell a scathing letter. Since former bondsmen might be re-enslaved and since more lives might be lost, the memorial was a matter of "momentous importance" to the patriotic blacks of Upper Canada, and Durham's behaviour amounted to "criminal negligence," claimed the incensed advocate. Again, he rehearsed the arguments about fugitives charged with pre-escape felonies being tried by provincial

juries; but Russell was unmoved. Deeply concerned about the security of the fugitives, Rolph continued to appeal until the following
spring. He even hinted that he might take the issue to Parliament
through Lord Brougham, the British antislavery veteran, but the
veiled threat did not impress the Colonial Office and it looked as if
this lengthy struggle was about to end in failure.[7]

The vulnerable fugitives, however, were unwilling to accept de-
feat, and they appealed over Britain's head, probably at Rolph's
suggestion, directly to the forum of world opinion. A convenient
opportunity was at hand, for the British and Foreign Anti-Slavery
Society (BFAS) had called an international convention to meet in
London during the summer of 1840. Leading abolition societies from
the United States, Europe, and Britain were to be represented, and
blacks in Upper Canada asked Rolph to represent them. He was to
inform the convention of their desire that fugitive slaves who were
accused of pre-escape felonies should be tried by Upper Canadian
juries; and also that they wanted a Canadian naturalization law that
would make fugitive slaves British subjects as soon as they crossed
the border. This would protect them, they believed, and would
guarantee access to churches and schools, which discrimination now
prevented in some areas.[8]

A gifted orator, Rolph represented the Upper Canadian blacks
very effectively at the London convention. Knowing the romantic
tastes of his nineteenth-century audience, he cited dramatic examples of fugitives' harrowing escapes to the province and detailed the
conditions under which they lived in their new homeland. He glowingly claimed that those "who have settled upon lands, which they
have purchased by their industrious accumulation, have succeeded
and are prospering." After reciting the Canadian resolutions, Rolph
suggested two possible courses of action. Parliament might pass a
law such as the petitioners wanted, requiring that fugitives charged
with pre-flight felonies be tried by provincial juries. However, he
preferred another course, namely, that of having the Colonial Office
instruct Canadian officials to treat all blacks as political refugees who
could not be extradited. This would avoid the risk of offending the
Americans, who would be almost certain to take umbrage if the law
was passed. Moreover, it would protect free blacks under indictment
in the United States who had crossed the border. These people also
deserved the even-handed protection of British justice, he observed,
for while they might be guilty of a crime, as blacks they would suffer
harsher penalties under American law than whites would. The convention referred the subject to a committee, on which Rolph served.
Evidently it supported his arguments, for it recommended asking

the colonial secretary whether Canadian officials had received instructions that prevented black refugees from being surrendered. The committee also advised the conference to recommend that the Colonial Office require blacks to be admitted to Upper Canadian schools. After endorsing these recommendations, the meeting committed them to the executive committee of the BFAS for implementation; but although the committee sent petitions to the British government in 1840 and 1841, nothing came of them.[9]

Thus, Rolph's efforts to protect the fugitives from extradition by appealing to the world's highest antislavery court were no more effective than his long personal campaign at the Colonial Office. Ironically, the only benefit to come from his labours turned on a question of chance, for while he was beseeching the Colonial Office, the British government was considering the terms of a possible extradition treaty with the United States. A previous agreement had expired in 1807, and since then extradition had been handled on an ad hoc basic. The escape of several notorious criminals to the United States in 1839, and the recent border troubles in the wake of the 1837 rebellions, convinced the government that a new agreement was desirable. Henry S. Fox, the British minister in Washington, advised that great care be taken to accommodate the prospective treaty to the needs of the fugitive slave question, for this was the aspect of the matter which the government of Upper Canada would have to act on most frequently. Upper Canada's chief justice, John Beverley Robinson, recommended that the agreement encompass a broad list of crimes, including robbery and horse stealing. Heeding Fox's advice, the government began to draft a treaty that would circumvent extraditing fugitive slaves. While the draft was circulating in the government, Rolph's letters arrived, pointing out how a slave might be returned because he was charged with a felony for having stolen the clothes he wore. Palmerston, the British foreign secretary, evidently found these arguments convincing for he dropped horse stealing and robbery from the draft. Thus, Rolph unknowingly helped shape the extradition clauses that eventually found their way into the Webster-Ashburton Treaty of 1842, and so in the long run he helped to safeguard his clients.[10]

Clearly, however, Rolph's single-handed campaign to have the British government erect ironclad barriers against the return of fugitive slaves failed to achieve its goal. Surprisingly, this was not the impression he gave his black clients when he returned to Upper Canada. At a packed meeting in the Toronto Baptist chapel in September 1840, he reported on his dealings with the Colonial Office and the measures taken by the London convention, emphasizing the "success which at length followed his efforts." The meeting grate-fully thanked him with a warm resolution accompanied by "hearty and prolonged acclamations," and it urged blacks throughout the province to publicize "the happy results of the mission of our worthy agent, Dr Rolph." Even Peter Gallego, the university-educated black who had helped write the petition given to Durham, attributed great results to Rolph's efforts, for the following year he told the physician that Upper Canadian fugitives "owe it to your instrumentality, that in this country the imperial government extends to us the protection of political refugees." Blacks clearly believed that Rolph had accom-plished what they had asked him to, an unwarranted claim for which Rolph himself was largely responsible.[11]

Rolph's deception casts a shadow over what otherwise was un-doubtedly a high-minded effort to protect the fugitive slaves. As an isolated incident, it might have had little significance, but the An-caster physician also concocted a curious scheme to colonize Ca-nadian blacks in Trinidad. At first glance, this appears to have had credibility, but in light of his furtiveness about the results in Britain, it raises doubts concerning his candour in both instances.

As the number of blacks in Upper Canada increased, antiblack prejudice rose accordingly. Blacks were denied access to schools in some regions and were sometimes barred from lodging and trans-portation facilities. In 1840 a group of magistrates in the Western District even petitioned the legislature to check the "rapid impor-tation of this unfortunate race, such as have of late inundated this devoted section of the province, to the great detriment of the claims of the poor immigrant from the mother country." Rolph deplored these attitudes but saw them as inevitable obstacles to blacks in the province. The solution he proposed was to relocate provincial blacks in the West Indian island of Trinidad, where there were many op-portunities. After British emancipation, some island freedmen had declined to become wage labourers for their former owners, prefer-ring to work for themselves as small landowners. This created a shortage of agricultural workers, and in 1838 the island's legislative council subsidized the importation of farm workers.[12]

It is not known when Rolph first thought of colonizing Upper Canadian blacks in Trinidad, though he may have developed the idea while in London, for immediately after returning to Canada in August 1840 he wrote Sir Henry MacLeod, the lieutenant-governor of the island, and it is apparent from his letter that the two had already discussed the scheme. Rolph claimed that his consultation with the blacks revealed that there were from two to five hundred who were ready to go to Trinidad if he accompanied them as their surgeon. These industrious, loyal people, Rolph assured MacLeod, would be a "most valuable acquisition" for the island, but August was rather late in the season to organize an expedition via Quebec. Rolph asked the governor what "encouragement" the Trinidad council would offer if he accompanied the black settlers. Eager to accommodate the labour-pressed planters, MacLeod replied that an industrious worker could earn a dollar a day with medical attendance, free housing, and provision lands. But Trinidad would only pay to transport agricultural workers, he reminded Rolph, and he requested full information on the class of people who might come and sufficient notice of their time of arrival to make preparations. Rolph would be appointed British North American emigration agent for Trinidad the following year at a stipend of £150.[13]

The prospective size of the migration led MacLeod to consult the Colonial Office, and this caused the British government to look into the plan. Russell referred it to the colonial land and emigration commissioners and also to the governor general of British North America, Lord Sydenham, for his assessment. The commissioners found no obstacles, provided that emigrants were fully apprised of working conditions in Trinidad, for the scheme met the objectives laid down by the 1838 Trinidad law to attract labour. Yet they were far from enthusiastic about the plan, for in view of the labour shortage in Canada, they doubted that blacks would be any better off in Trinidad. Sydenham was openly critical; he assumed that since there was no evidence that Lieutenant-Governor Sir George Arthur had discussed the plan with Rolph, the idea must have originated with the doctor himself. Nor could Sydenham verify Rolph's claim that numerous blacks were ready to leave for Trinidad; in fact, he questioned whether Rolph had actually consulted the black community. Sydenham declared that he had no intention of encouraging the fugitives to emigrate, for in his opinion they were a "well conducted and orderly set of people" whose prospects were at least as good in Canada as they would be in Trinidad. Russell, too, denigrated the Trinidad scheme, for he advised Sydenham to work at improving the conditions of blacks in Canada by winning from the legislature the maximum protection that it was willing to provide for them.[14]

Despite this official hostility, Rolph and MacLeod pursued the objective of colonizing Upper Canadian blacks in Trinidad, and after several London meetings in early 1843 the governor appointed Rolph as the island's British North American immigration agent. Rolph returned to Canada and was soon promoting emigration with a series of fall meetings in Colchester, Sandwich, and Amherstburg, which he reported were well attended. He reminded his audiences that

prejudice had crossed the border surreptitiously with American settlers, effectively barring "every individual of your colour from holding any situations in the church, at the Bar, in the magistracy, in
the Senate," a handicap which their small numbers would never
overcome. On the other hand, he said, in Trinidad there was ready
employment in a fertile land with a pleasant climate, where schools
were ready to receive their children and where no social barriers
would restrict their advancement. Blacks had "thronged" the meetings, he claimed, and "vast numbers" were "most desirous of pro-
ceeding to Trinidad." But the colonization scheme foundered when
neither the island legislature nor the mother country would appropriate sufficient money to implement it.[15]

After the collapse of the Trinidad colonization plan, Rolph returned to England and disappeared from Canadian antislavery. How
he had initially gained the confidence of Upper Canadian blacks
remains a mystery; conceivably, it depended on his conservative
politics. They were unswervingly constitutionalist, and he was the
only Tory political activist to defend Upper Canada's blacks. At a
time when they had few spokesmen of any description, he ener-
getically sought to have the British government give firm guarantees
against extraditing them from the province. Although he failed in
this, by taking their case to the London convention he brought them
to the attention of British and American antislavery leaders, who
previously had given them little thought. The Trinidad colonization
scheme, on the other hand, was of questionable benefit to Canadian
abolition. Sydenham's scepticism about whether Rolph had consulted Upper Canadian blacks on the topic in the late summer of
1840 is well founded. Rolph was in London until at least June when
the antislavery convention adjourned, and it is doubtful that he
would have had enough time to return to Canada and consult the
black community before writing to Governor MacLeod on 31 August.
Newspaper accounts of the Toronto meeting on 13 September, when
Rolph reported on the London mission, do not mention the colonization scheme – a surprising omission if Rolph was then actually
questioning blacks about emigration, for the large gathering would
have been too good an opportunity to miss. Nor are there any other
grounds for saying that he raised the Trinidad scheme with Canadian
fugitive slaves at the time. Evidence of large crowds attending the
October 1843 meetings in the southwestern part of the province is
lacking, except for Rolph's own claims. One is left with the nagging
suspicion that Rolph (who, interestingly enough, was disciplined in
1840 by the Upper Canada College of Physicians and Surgeons for
claiming to be a surgeon without having the proper credentials) was

mainly concerned about being appointed emigration agent for Trinidad and did not mind bending the truth, just as he had done when reporting the success of the London mission, if it would advance his case.

The other figure who stepped into the vacuum left by the collapse of the UCAS was Hiram Wilson, one of seventy workers whom the AAS commissioned in the 1830s.[16] For the next fifteen years, the humble Wilson worked tirelessly among the province's blacks, offering counsel and distributing aid, and his stream of letters to antislavery journals kept British and American abolitionists informed about events in Canada. Wilson's initial four-month assignment in late 1836 was to examine living conditions among the refugees, and by late winter he had visited numerous black communities on foot, holding meetings, gathering information, and giving encouragement. He reported his activities to the Boston-based *Emancipator*, and the AAS published his findings on the conditions of blacks in Canada in its *Fourth Annual Report*. Although his appointment was extended to ten months, by late 1837 he was entirely dependent on his own resources.[17]

Wilson's chief concern throughout the 1840s was the educational needs of blacks in the province; the fact that he lacked a regular source of income makes his educational efforts especially remarkable. Even before completing his 1836 tour in the southwest, he had organized schools at Colchester and Amherstburg, and had secured teachers on condition that the communities provided board and ten dollars a month for their support. He lamented the lack of schools elsewhere – for example, at Wilberforce, a black community of nineteen families near London, and at Ora, where he estimated there were about thirty school-age children. Nevertheless, by early 1838 Wilson was claiming that "our schools at Brantford, Niagara, and St Catharines are flourishing," and within a year an evening school had opened in Toronto. By 1841 the resourceful recruiter had twelve teachers working at different locations throughout the province.[18]

Funding to support this burgeoning educational program – the Canada Mission, as it was known – was a constant worry, and the hard-pressed Wilson tapped whatever source was available. When the province's disturbed political climate following Mackenzie's uprising dictated that Wilson withdraw until the air cleared, he seized the opportunity to visit Rochester, where an antislavery convention was in session; he reported on his efforts among the fugitive slaves and stayed in the area for several weeks, organizing abolition societies and raising funds. The annual meeting of the AAS in the spring of 1840 in New York afforded him the chance to publicize his work in a national forum, and the meeting bestowed its blessing with a supportive resolution and a collection for the schools. Wilson returned the following year, arriving early enough for a pre-convention fund-raising swing through several northeastern communities, since money had arrived from local groups there, such as the Milford, New Hampshire, Ladies' Anti-Slavery Society. Additional support came from abroad, enabling Wilson to pay off the debts of the mission in 1840.[19]

Operating the schools required more than money. Teachers were in chronically short supply in Upper Canada, where training facilities were limited and working conditions were harsh. Rising antiblack prejudice further complicated the staffing of black schools. The resourceful Wilson resorted to using students from the Oberlin Institute in Ohio and the Oneida Institute in New York, for these training schools were filled with idealistic youths who were eager for humanitarian service. Oberlin, the source of most of the teachers, had been formed in the early 1830s when some students and faculty from Lane Seminary were disciplined for antislavery activity in Cincinnati. Refusing to abandon their cause, as the Lane board demanded, they withdrew and, aided by two like-minded New York philanthropists, Arthur and Lewis Tappan, they organized Oberlin Institute near Cleveland. There they were educated and were inspired with antislavery ideals by Theodore Dwight Weld. Oberlin students, wrote Wilson, often used their summer vacations to gain practical experience in philanthropic work. Some ventured as far as the West Indies, preaching, teaching, organizing schools, and collecting antislavery libraries. Others went to Canada, "lifting the intellect of the poor fugitive into a fitness for the state of freedom they have attained," Wilson declared. Occasionally they suffered great hardship for the cause, taking "deck passages upon the lakes, exposing themselves to chilling blasts and midnight damp; and in walking upon the land, they have weary limbs, blistered feet, and in some cases hardly a penny in their pockets." After their vacation was over, those who were unable to find replacements or who conscientiously felt that they could not leave their posts served through the winter with little hope of remuneration and often returned "pennyless and in debt" to Oberlin and Oneida to resume studying. Despite these trying conditions, by 1841 Wilson had recruited forty-three teachers for his schools, keeping costs to a minimum.[20]

The year 1841 was especially difficult for Wilson, for the voice of criticism sounded. At a convention in Le Roy, New York, management of the Canada Mission was placed in the hands of an executive committee of three Rochester men. Seemingly, this reorganization was a wise step, for a formalized directorate with roots in American antislavery – Rochester being an important abolitionist centre – would bring greater status and wider contacts and would ease the burden of fund raising. A broadened leadership would also enable Wilson to share his heavy responsibility. Nevertheless, Peter Gallego wrote a hostile letter to the *National Anti-Slavery Standard*, calling the Canada Mission a "specious humbug" that had been foisted on an unsuspecting public. He complained that the mission was drawing funds away from the abolition cause in the United States. Furthermore, Gallego believed that Wilson's incessant pleas for support cast the fugitives in a bad light; without schools and churches, they appeared to be destitute and unable to take care of themselves, when in reality, he declared, blacks in Canada lived in circumstances that compared favourably with those anywhere else on the continent. He maintained that many blacks prospered soon after arriving in Canada and that, regardless of Wilson's assertion, most of the schools were open to them. In cases where prejudice denied them access, Gallego insisted that the courts were the proper remedy.

These charges briefly raised doubts among Wilson's supporters. The *Coloured American*, for example, admitted Wilson's good intentions but shared Gallego's scepticism, while the *American Citizen*, another black journal, believed that Wilson deserved support. However, James Canning Fuller came to Wilson's aid. An English Quaker philanthropist living in Skaneateles, New York, Canning had spent five weeks in late 1840 examining the Canada Mission. In a long letter to the *Standard*, he attributed Gallego's criticism to "jealousy," declaring, "After what I have seen ... no human tongue can portray the good effect of it [the Canada Mission], nor what its ultimate effects may, and I trust will be, on that portion of the family of man, for whose benefit it is, and ought to be vigorously sustained." The *Standard* vacillated for a while, but by spring the *Liberator* had thrown its support behind the Canada Mission, and the other antislavery journals soon fell into line. The dispute left Wilson unscathed, and the 1842 school year opened with four hundred students at eleven schools.[21]

Wilson's antislavery vision extended beyond aiding the destitute and providing elementary education to fugitive slaves in Upper Canada. He believed that if there was an institution to give black students advanced training, there would be a supply of teachers for the Canada Mission's lower schools, as well as a surplus of instructors ready to educate the host of freedmen who would be certain to seek schooling when abolition finally triumphed in the American South. Whether Wilson originated the idea or whether he borrowed it from

Fuller, the notion was in the air by the end of 1840. Fuller had attended the London antislavery conference and had used the opportunity to raise funds for the Canada Mission, and at the close of the year he spent several weeks visiting the schools and consulting Wilson. They decided to use part of the $1700 that Fuller had collected to build such an institution, for shortly after returning to Skaneateles he hinted that something big was afoot. A black meeting at London gave its support, struck a committee to locate a suitable site, and within two months the project was underway. Two hundred acres of land were purchased in Dawn Township on the Sydenham River near Chatham, and the property was conveyed to three black and three white trustees. Wilson planned to move his family from Toronto to the site in January and to open the school in May 1842, but shortage of funds delayed construction. The British-American Institute of Science and Industry, as it was officially called, opened with nine students in December 1842. There were at least four buildings, three dwellings and a school capable of handling sixty, with dormitories for twenty. Students of fifteen years and older were admitted for training as teachers, and they paid tuition and board of one dollar a week by contributing labour at the rate of five cents an hour. Twelve acres had been cleared and fenced.[22]

The manual labour school greatly increased Wilson's responsibilities. A board of tuition and an executive committee managed the institution, the former directing internal affairs and the latter handling external matters. Although the record is vague, Wilson apparently was president and chaired both committees. The combined demands of the Canada Mission and the British-American Institute created heavy financial needs. Wilson contrived to be designated delegate of the "Central Corresponding Committee for the Coloured Population of Canada" to the 1843 London Anti-Slavery Conference, and this enabled him to meet the leading abolitionists of the day. After calling on the convention for continued protection for the Upper Canadian fugitives, he stayed on in Britain to raise funds. His tour yielded $1100 and several hundred Bibles and Testaments, and the connections he established with the upper levels of British antislavery seemed to assure him a continuing source of support. When, shortly after his return from England, fire destroyed a newly built women's residence that had been funded with money from Maine, the buoyant Wilson confidently claimed that providence would make good the loss, and he optimistically announced plans to erect more buildings and acquire more land in the spring. A two-month tour through New England and New York in 1844 netted another $400, and by the middle of the decade Wilson reported that there were sixty-six students, half of whom were adults and about twenty of whom contributed part-time labour.[23]

From this plateau in 1847, when the Toronto *Globe* announced that the British-American Institute was flourishing, the affairs of the school began to decline, as did the Canada Mission, which had already reached its apex. Wilson's serious illness ("nigh unto death," he claimed) in early 1847 signalled that worse was to come. By spring he was in New England on a "health-restoring" tour, urgently needing $300 to meet "vexatious embarrassments," and before he returned word came of his wife's death. These events undoubtedly deflected Wilson's attention from an enterprise that required his constant supervision, but more serious were the management problems that were about to come to light.[24]

Josiah Henson, a fugitive slave and methodist minister who was illiterate until the age of forty-five, had participated in the 1841 London (Canada West) meeting at which western provincial blacks had given their support to opening the manual labour school. Recounting his own experiences, Henson had made a strong plea for the education of black youths, and he became closely associated with the leadership of the British-American Institute, although his precise role, other than being an agent after 1844, is unclear. Wilson should have been alerted by the questions that William P. Newman, a teacher and the secretary of the executive committee, raised about the school's accounting practices shortly after he arrived in 1845. Newman eventually insisted that agents, especially Henson, must give a satisfactory accounting of the funds they had collected, and the executive committee agreed. Wilson and Henson defended their practices, but when the latter could not produce a suitable statement of the funds he had raised, the leadership split over whether to discipline him, and Newman resigned.

Despite the evidence that the well-intentioned but unsophisticated Henson often did not use good judgment and that he lacked skill in business matters, the executive committee encouraged him to undertake an expensive project that was to have disastrous results for the institute. The land on which the institute was situated contained extensive stands of black walnut timber, which Henson believed could be marketed profitably rather than being wastefully burned in land clearing. He convinced several Boston philanthropists to assist him with funds to build a steam-powered sawmill so that the timber could be prepared for market. They raised $1400, but Henson could not complete the project with this sum and he returned to the Boston backers for a loan of $1800.

Before the fate of the sawmill was known, a dispute occurred within the management of the school, the details of which are unknown, and this resulted in Wilson's resignation in late 1847 or early 1848. Matters became so serious that the board of trustees, which ordinarily was not involved in internal operations, investigated the executive committee in the spring of 1848. It was not convicted of wrongdoing, but clearly there had been a mishandling of funds, and the following year the manual labour school was divided into two departments, one being responsible for the mill, lands, and debts, and the other for the school and buildings. These efforts at reorganization failed to arrest the rapid desintegration of the institute, although the settlement that had grown up around the site – Dawn – remained active for more than a decade. By 1850, in Wilson's judgment, the British-American Institute was so run down and so deeply in debt that it was contributing nothing to education and only a miracle could revive it. The sawmill lay idle in disrepair, never having met the cost of construction. [25]

With the burdens of Dawn institute behind him, Wilson turned to teaching at the nearby Canada Mission school. As we have seen, the mission began 1842 on a strong note with eleven schools; but a shortage of teachers caused six closings, and there was a debt of $451 by year's end. The picture improved somewhat the following year, for Wilson reported that their "nine or ten schools" were in a "prosperous state." However, the Canada Mission reached a turning point in 1846 when the Rochester board, under whose authority it had functioned since 1841, relinquished its duties to the American Missionary Association, an umbrella group established to coordinate the numerous mission activities of American evangelicals. This weakened the financial position of the mission, since the association merely channelled designated gifts, while contributors evidently assumed that regular grants were being made to the Canada Mission from the treasury. Within three years, the Canada Mission functioned only at three locations – Amherstburg, Dawn, and Queen's Bush – with ten teachers serving as volunteers, because, as Wilson explained, there was "no regular or reliable support guaranteed us from any source under the heavens"; despite wise planning and strict economy, it was necessary to "sacrifice our own effects," he wrote, "or to put what little worldly substance we have in jeopardy, to keep up credit and enable us to live."

Wilson's report to the *Liberator* in the spring of 1850 referred to only two schools at Dawn, with sixty students, without mentioning the Canada Mission. The battle-weary veteran announced that he would "quit the field soon from dire necessity" after having campaigned for fourteen years but that he would do so with a clear conscience. However, circumstances caused the disheartened abolitionist to change his mind. A trip to New England yielded $300, and this enabled him to pay off the Dawn mission debt, and the passage of the 1850 Fugitive Slave Law in the United States convinced him that large numbers of refugees would soon pour across the border. He therefore decided to remain in Canada but moved to St Catharines in the Niagara peninsula, where he felt there was bound to be a concentration of destitute newcomers. He remained there until his death in 1866, using whatever resources were available to assist arriving refugees and working among blacks who found employment on the Welland Canal.[26]

Wilson contributed to Canadian antislavery during the 1840s because he was deeply moved by the illiterate fugitives' suffering. An abolitionist who demanded the immediate end of slavery at every opportunity, he considered his primary task to be meeting the needs of its victims as they arrived at the missions or at his Toronto home – "Hiram Wilson's free tavern" one editor named it because of the steady flow of refugee traffic that passed through its doors. A manual labour school was not an untried visionary concept, for Oneida and Oberlin were demonstrating its viability, and it seemed well suited to the needs of the impoverished blacks. Wilson was far-sighted in envisioning the role it might play in the post-emancipation era, as graduates of William King's yet-to-be-founded schools at Buxton demonstrated in Reconstruction America. Much remains undiscovered about those who attended the British-American Institute. Did they enter with enough schooling to prepare them for advanced learning, or was the institute in reality a place where either youths or adults received elementary education? Did they stay for the three to five years that Wilson intended? How many eventually became teachers or leaders in their communities? Without answers to these questions – and they will probably never be answered – one cannot assess the full significance of the institute.[27]

No hint of self-interestedness touched Wilson's work, as had been the case with Rolph, but he lacked the leadership qualities necessary to manage the institutions he founded. This was readily apparent in the manual labour school when the substantial sums raised were not used wisely and when the inexperienced Henson was given a free hand in the risky sawmill enterprise. Joshua Leavitt, editor of the American Anti-Slavery Society's *Emancipator*, shrewdly assessed Wilson's limitations in a letter to John Scoble when the British and Foreign Anti-Slavery Society was considering whether to support the British-American Institute. "I think that Wilson has done great good as a most laborious pioneer in looking after the fugitives from American oppression," he wrote, "but I confess I do not feel so much confidence in his ability to manage an institution of learning or any other matter involving a large expenditure of money." Moreover, Wilson lacked charisma; his "sound common sense" speaking style did not inspire the clientele whose support was essential for projects of the magnitude he undertook. The institute and the Canada Mission were fatally vulnerable when the Rochester board and the American Missionary Association failed to provide funding and when British revenue dropped off in the wake of the Irish famine in 1847. But Wilson did make two lasting contributions to Canadian antislavery. Although the schooling that the Canada Mission offered may have reinforced the isolation of some blacks in their new homeland, it provided education to unlettered fugitives who lived where there were no public schools or who, being excluded from white schools, were too poor or too timid to obtain legal redress. Hundreds benefited until 1847–48. Moreover, blacks who participated in managing the Dawn institute and the Canada Mission gained valuable experience in managing autonomous institutions. [28]

Except for Rolph and Wilson, the white antislavery movement was virtually nonexistent in the province after the demise of the Upper Canada Anti-Slavery Society. The key to the movement's success in the late 1840s lay in awakening dormant public interest, and neither Rolph nor Wilson gave this much attention. The figure who played the leading role in this process was Peter Brown who, as will be recalled, had been a charter member of the Edinburgh Emancipation Society. After rising to prominence in Edinburgh politics as collector of assessments, Brown encountered a substantial setback when £2800 in city revenues became entangled with his business accounts. There was no question of personal dishonesty, but to meet obligations to his guarantors when world depression created an unfavourable business climate in Edinburgh, he decided to start afresh, and he emigrated to New York in 1837. Success at the dry goods business he opened enabled him to try his hand at writing for the New York *Albion*, a journal of the British immigrant community. Although Brown was a Liberal who had supported British electoral reform in the 1830s, he disapproved of the universal suffrage practised in the United States and frequently criticized American political institutions. In his view, nothing symbolized the shortcomings of American republicanism more than the existence of slavery in a society that claimed to have political democracy and personal freedom. [29]

An opportunity for Brown to air his views more fully appeared in 1842 with the publication of Charles E. Lester's *The Glory and Shame of England*. The American abolitionist painted a derogatory picture of British institutions and British government while projecting a glowing image of the United States. Brown spiritedly replied in *The Fame and Glory of England Vindicated*, which praised Britain and attacked American slavery, a topic that Lester had soft-peddled. This was a crucial flaw in Lester's analysis, so far as Brown was concerned, for Brown saw American slavery as a fatal weakness. He envisioned countries advancing to liberty, every nation's ultimate goal, through three distinct phases: winning independence; achieving personal freedom and the social and political privileges that mark the citizens of enlightened communities; and extending liberty to less favoured peoples. Both Britain and the United States had passed the first stage, but America, unlike Britain, had failed to achieve the second step because of slavery. America denied personal freedom to millions, and it limited freedom of speech and the right to petition, for the proslavery forces in Congress (the very forum where free speech was most essential) applied the notorious "gag rule" to prevent discussion of slavery. Even clergymen were muzzled, declared Brown, for they dared not use the pulpit to denounce the iniquitous institution. Only by excising this malignancy would American society achieve full liberty.

Brown went on to point out that whenever Lester ventured to raise the forbidden topic, it was always in "guarded and submissive" tones. A case in point was his deferential manner in a public letter from London to John C. Calhoun, slaveowner and Southern spokesman. Although Lester was an avowed abolitionist, he had timidly reminded Calhoun that ending slavery might in the long run benefit slaveholders, and he had carefully skirted the glaring fact that slavery violated God's law. Lester also faulted British merchants for buying slave-grown cotton, and the British government for allowing it to be imported. Brown countered by reciting the antislavery record of British governments, from their termination of the slave trade to West Indian emancipation. But Lester disparaged British emancipation, contending that Parliament, by paying planters £20 million to release their slaves, had burdened English workers with heavier taxes to finance the enlarged public debt. Brown found Lester's objection "utterly base and heartless," arguing that the tiny increase in taxation was nothing compared to the "inestimable blessing conveyed to 800,000 of our fellowmen." Nothing in history compared with the "moral grandeur" of British emancipation, boasted Brown, for the money had been "freely given from a sense of moral justice alone."[30]

Brown's rebuttal gained considerable attention in both Britain and North America, and the book's success no doubt influenced Brown's decision to start his own newspaper, the *British Chronicle*. Directed at the Scottish immigrant community in New York and Canada, it flourished and predictably took up the issue of the "Great Disruption" that was then convulsing Scotland, for Brown was a thorough-going evangelical Presbyterian. He applauded the Free Church decision to separate from the Church of Scotland, a stand that ingratiated him with the Canadian wing of the newly formed church. When Toronto-based Free Churchmen urged him to relocate there and, with their support, to establish a newspaper devoted to the new denomination, he accepted the invitation. The first number of the *Banner*, as the new journal was called, appeared in August 1843. Devoted mainly to the interests of the Free Church, missions, and evangelicalism, the *Banner* also identified with the Reformers in provincial politics and became a strong antislavery mouthpiece – the voice that contributed most to reawakening provincial antislavery sentiment.

Brown raised the issue in the second edition when, in response to a call by the New York *Journal of Commerce* for a national conference to consider ways of remedying the shortcomings of American politics, he offered his own cure. The best solution, he said, would be to enhance the voice of the propertied classes by altering the franchise, but this would be unworkable in egalitarian America. The country, therefore, should concentrate on educating the electorate, although it was doubtful that this could be accomplished in time to avoid the collapse of America's flawed political system which Brown believed to be rapidly approaching. But any change would be futile unless slavery was removed, Brown told his readers, for it was a "cankerworm" that would "destroy the vitality of the most perfect government on earth."[31]

This was the first of an unending stream of antislavery editorials that lasted until the journal ceased publication in 1848, when Brown retired. Often, the *Banner* reported the acts of bravery and violence that punctuated the flight of fugitive slaves. It idolized aged John Quincy Adams's heroic congressional battle to kill the "gag rule" which, during much of the decade, prevented antislavery petitions from reaching the floor of the House. Readers learned of the Kentucky mob that destroyed Cassius M. Clay's antislavery newspaper, and they heard Brown heap scorn on the New York Whigs whose opposition forced O.A. Bowe to resign as editor of the abolitionist Herkimer *Journal*. Sometimes Brown's tactic was to arouse subscribers by informing them of the progress of antislavery, for instance, by printing summaries or reports from antislavery journals such as the British *Anti-Slavery Reporter*. Current political events also served the watchful editor as a useful springboard for attacking slavery: the annexation of Texas would be disastrous, he warned, for by strengthening the voice of slavery in Congress, it would permanently rivet the slaves' fetters; and he regretfully justified calling for an Anglo-American war over the Oregon Territory on the grounds that Britain would win and would then demand an end to slavery as the price of peace.[32]

A zealous Presbyterian, Brown seldom missed the chance to lash Old School American Presbyterians (the more orthodox branch of the church, which had emerged when the denomination divided in 1837) for their laxity on slavery. Initially, the Old School had said little on the topic, relying on the former church's 1818 disciplinary statement. But as the antislavery movement gained momentum, there were demands that the church take a stand, and in 1845 the general assembly passed resolutions accommodating slaveholding members. The assembly declared that scripture did not command New Testament slaveowners to free their bondsmen; it simply commanded them to treat the bondsmen kindly, and it told slaves to be obedient to their masters. Accordingly, slaveholding as practised in the United States could not be a barrier to Christian communion. The assembly further stated that petitions requesting the synod to discipline owners were deplorable, for they threatened to divide both church and nation.

Brown attacked with slashing prose. This compromise by a "highly influential" church filled with "intelligent, wealthy, and respectable Scotsmen" from the "middle ranks" brought the "deepest disgrace" on the Old School, declared the *Banner*. Considering that this church was universally regarded as one of America's "most enlightened" and was viewed as the special guardian of Westminster orthodoxy, it was, wrote Brown, "truly painful" to see Presbyterians "deny openly that slavery is a sin, and most unrighteously try to back themselves out, by drawing their defense from the Word of God." "Shame on Presbyterianism!" he cried. The following year, the assembly rejected fresh appeals, abruptly declaring that its position on slavery was abundantly clear. Again the *Banner* protested, saying that this was a "hard-hearted and unchristian" way to deal with a "great national crime." Repeatedly, too, Brown flayed the Philadelphia *Presbyterian* for defending the church's spineless position while ignoring the oppressed.[33]

Despite all this activity, Brown's main front in the antislavery campaign in the 1840s was the fellowshipping controversy that afflicted his beloved Free Church. This dispute filled the *Banner*'s columns and coincidentally aroused Canadian interest in antislavery. The journal showed little concern in the early stages of the controversy in 1844; but when, just before the 1845 general assembly, Brown's native Edinburgh presbytery debated a petition, asking the church to give a "clear and decided utterance" on slavery and to send an "uncompromising remonstrance" to those American Presbyterian churches that welcomed slaveholding members, Brown followed events closely. The *Banner* published the petition, along with several speeches by Edinburgh ministers on both sides of the question. The presbyters decided to let the assembly deal with the topic as it saw fit, but Brown clearly hoped that it would take a strong antifellowshipping position, and he approvingly printed a letter by Henry Grey, one of the petition's supporters, stating that he would be disappointed and aggrieved if the church took an "infirm and compromising" position on this "important question." Moreover, the concerned editor warned the petition's opponents that their arguments against the overture were being used effectively by the Philadelphia *Presbyterian* as a "palliation" for the lax conduct of the Old School.[34]

The 1845 Scottish general assembly must have greatly disappointed Brown when it refused to change its policy (even though the *Banner* took no notice of the fact, possibly because the Canadian Free Church was then also grappling with the issue). However, the fellowshipping controversy soon reappeared in the columns of the paper when St Peter's Kirk session presented a resolution in the Dundee presbytery in Scotland asking the church to "lift up a decided testimony" against the American churches and "withdraw from fellowship with them until they be brought to an acknowledgment and renunciation of their sin." The cautious presbyters tabled the request, claiming that it should have been framed as a petition rather than a resolution. But the *Banner* ridiculed this legalistic manoeuvre as a tactic worthy of slaveholders, who characteristically avoided facing "unpalatable truths" by preventing them from being discussed, and reminded the Dundee court that as Free Churchmen they were bound to hear appeals from their brethren. The plain truth, asserted Brown, was that it had been a great mistake to send deputies to America in the first place. The money they had received was a trifle; the real problem was that all the deputies except Burns had been duped by their hosts into believing that slavery was not as bad as it seemed, and consequently they had returned to Scotland more critical of the abolitionists than the slaveholders. As a result, abolitionists had become suspect in Scotland, the deputies having been misled by the very people in the United States who would not lift a finger to defend the slaves. Abolitionists were even being attacked in Free Church courts. Nevertheless, the *Banner* predicted that "deep-thinking" Scots would soon see the truth of abolitionism. "Feeble and little regarded will be a voice from the back-woods of Canada," declared Brown, but "if that voice could be heard, it would be in the language of earnest entreaty that the fair fame of the Free Church should withdraw from every connection with Slaveholding Churches, and raise their solemn voices against the deadly sin, or rather collection of sins."[35]

When the general assembly reconvened in 1846, the *Banner*, anxious for the church to mend its ways, kept readers fully informed with lengthy transcripts of the proceedings. It cited the slavery committee's report, as well as a long speech by chairman Candlish defending the church's course and advocating continuation of the fraternal tie with the admittedly offending American Presbyterians, together with Macbeth's lone plea that it be severed. The final decision – to send another mild remonstrance but to maintain the tie – exasperated Brown, and he forcefully attacked the Scottish church in searing language. "We wish there were no alloy" in the assembly's work, stated the *Banner* before going on to say that the Free Church leadership had "erred seriously on this great question," which was second in importance only to the preaching of the Gospel. "Two millions and a half of human beings [had been] pleading at the bar of the General Assembly," declared Brown, and only Macbeth's voice had been raised on their behalf. But though the court had shamefully rejected their pleas, he said, "they have gone up to the Appeal Court of the Judge of all, where the pleader for the oppressed never pleads in vain." Despite this discouraging outcome, Brown continued to believe that the assembly would soon see the real character of the American Presbyterians and would take a "bold and determined" stand on the question.[36]

The one bright spot in the disheartening events of the summer was that when Willis arrived in Glasgow in July, after completing his deputation at Knox College, he immediately sided with Macbeth in the fellowshipping controversy. As we have seen, with the support of the Glasgow Emancipation Society, the two men issued a joint public letter that was highly critical of the general assembly. The *Banner* published it with glowing praise, and thereafter the paper kept close track of Willis's antislavery activities. It was encouraged to learn in September that he would again be raising the issue of slavery with the Free Church through a lecture on "doulos," the Greek word for servant, in which he would instruct his fellow clergymen in some "valuable truths." Moreover, when in November Willis moved that the Glasgow presbytery ask the general assembly to reconsider breaking fellowship with American Presbyterians, Brown copied the speech and accompanied it with a long supportive editorial insisting that Willis had held the upper hand in the ensuing debate even though his motion had lost.[37]

But it was the news that Willis had organized the Free Church Anti-Slavery Society, a body "diametrically opposed" to the position of the general assembly, that Brown welcomed most. It was now certain, exulted the *Banner*, that the right view would prevail and that the Free Church would be "delivered from the false position she has hitherto occupied upon one of the most vital questions which can engage the attention of the Christian world." The paper believed that Willis could now bring the matter before the general assembly for consideration, with a good chance of success, and it published the society's *By Laws and Preamble*, which sharply indicted the Free Church. However, being remote from the climate of opinion in Scotland, Brown seriously overrated the influence of the Free Church Anti-Slavery Society, as events at the 1847 general assembly soon revealed. A debate on slavery and fellowshipping occurred when St Bernard's Church offered a petition that forthrightly denounced slavery as sinful under all conditions and asked the church to inform the tainted American Presbyterians that it could no longer commune with them. This was the occasion, as will be recalled, when Cunningham, accompanied by laughter and shouts of approval, derided Willis's society as a device of the devil designed to afflict the church. The synod decided that it was "inexpedient" to make any judgment about the issues raised in the petition and merely reappointed the slavery committee.[38]

Although the "feeble voice" from the "back-woods of Canada" had gone unheeded in the far-off courts of the Free Church, there were signs that it had been heard in central Canada. In the spring of 1843, only four months before the *Banner* first appeared in Toronto, John Roaf, the Wolverhampton abolitionist who since 1837 had been shepherding the flock at Toronto's Zion Congregational Church, had told John Scoble that antislavery sentiment was so low in the city that he doubted there was enough interest to "keep a society alive" or even "whether any considerable number of people could be induced to take up the matter." Yet by the middle of 1846, Brown's tenacious editorializing was already arousing concern. On 3 April, the *Banner* announced that Captain Charles Stuart, the abolitionist workhorse, who since the end of British emancipation had been championing the cause in North America, would speak in Toronto. At a second meeting Willis, who was still at Knox College, joined Stuart in making a spirited abolitionist speech.

These meetings, in which Roaf, Willis, and Stuart cooperated, with Brown's editorial support (all of them veterans of British antislavery), brought the formation of an antislavery society. Its special purpose was to serve the needs of the growing number of fugitive slaves in the province. The fledgling organization sent Roaf, who seems to have been its president, to the annual meeting of the American and Foreign Anti-Slavery Society in New York, where he reported on the formation of the group and praised the English Evangelical Alliance for excluding slaveholding American Churchmen from its annual meeting. Unfortunately, virtually nothing is known about the society's activities beyond these few details; the *Banner* promised to print committee lists and to inform readers of its work, but no further information appeared and evidently the society achieved nothing more and soon disbanded. Seemingly, Brown's long campaign to transform provincial public opinion had failed.[39]

THROUGHOUT THE 1840S, ROLPH, Wilson, and Brown – and, to a lesser extent, Roaf – had conducted four essentially independent antislavery campaigns: Rolph and Wilson by working for and with the fugitives, Brown through efforts to arouse public interest, and Roaf by organizing a society. Roaf was the least successful. Having been part of the inner circle of the failed Upper Canada Anti-Slavery Society a decade earlier, he was equally unsuccessful at harnessing the enthusiasm awakened by the *Banner* and encouraged by the Stuart-Willis meetings; the nascent society was the logical instrument to spearhead provincial antislavery and to coordinate much-needed support for Wilson's educational and relief work, but it stalled after sending Roaf to New York. Rolph, despite the shadow over his Trinidad emigration scheme, brought the issue of fugitive slave safety in Canada to the attention of the British government and antislavery leaders, and unwittingly helped shape the clauses of the Webster-Ashburton Treaty that governed the extradition of fugitive slaves. Wilson's relief efforts benefited the destitute, and although his schools fostered isolation and were somewhat rudimentary, they offered the only education that hundreds received, and they afforded some former slaves experience in institutional management. But with the collapse of the 1846 Toronto society, Canadian antislavery remained leaderless and uncoordinated. If judged solely by this outcome, Brown's efforts to awaken British North American public opinion to the iniquity of slavery had little success.

However, this is a short-sighted view of Brown's impact on British North American antislavery in the 1840s. Even the failed attempt to form a society in 1846 shows that the *Banner*'s incessant editorials had influenced public sentiment to some extent since Roaf's dismal assessment three years earlier. In fact, a broader perspective reveals that the seed that Brown had patiently planted in the columns of the *Banner* began to bear fruit even before the new decade opened, with the appearance of a strong body that found an effective way to prosecute antislavery.

# 5 Land, an Interest in the Soil, and a Christian Education

Abolitionism in Britain, Canada, and the United States in the main consisted of two types of activity. Reduced to its essential element, the first concentrated on transforming public opinion in order to make slavery morally unacceptable. The other course of action was to aid fugitive slaves. In Britain, this involved sending relief and raising money for various North American projects, since very few fugitive slaves crossed the Atlantic. For Americans, it meant sheltering or even defending fugitives and speeding them on their way north. The Canadian effort was more akin to the American, for many fugitive slaves had arrived; 20,000 was a commonly cited figure by midcentury. In retrospect, this number seems high, and research currently underway strongly indicates that in 1861 a majority of blacks in Canada West (as Upper Canada had by then become) had actually been born free. Nevertheless, the public opinion was that most blacks in the province were escaped slaves, and to be an abolitionist in Canada West, where the vast majority of the escapees resided, meant receiving them and helping them to start a new life. This was as close as most British North Americans came to direct involvement in ending slavery in the United States, and it must be viewed as a salient feature of Canadian antislavery.[1]

Despite the intertwined legends of the Underground Railroad and the Canadian haven, many British North Americans did not welcome fugitive slaves with open arms, as recent studies show; in fact, as the fugitives' numbers in the province grew, there was a corresponding increase in hostility and prejudice. However, this rising opposition induced provincial abolitionists (nurtured by the *Banner's* recent campaign, which the Toronto *Globe* continued) to take up the cause of the fugitive slaves. Hiram Wilson's efforts through the Canada Mission and the British-American Institute marked the beginning of this response, though in some respects his work was not truly British North American, for it was sponsored primarily in Britain and the United States, as the institute's name symbolized. By contrast, William King, the moving force behind the Elgin Association, inspired an undertaking that was firmly rooted in British North American soil, and it achieved a large measure of success in helping the fugitive slaves to establish a viable agricultural community.[2]

The Elgin Association held significance for the antislavery movement far beyond its immediate assistance to the fugitives. In the battle over slavery, an intense debate raged about whether the slave could succeed if he was liberated. The defenders of slavery claimed that blacks, being innately inferior, would not be able to compete with whites and would become a burden on society if they were removed from an owner's supervision, and that therefore emancipation would be an unwise social policy. Abolitionists maintained, on the other hand, that educating and Christianizing slaves would enable them to succeed in American society and that they must therefore be freed. British North America, where slaves allegedly were free to achieve their maximum potential, was seen as a proving ground for these contradictory propositions. In this situation, the Buxton settlement established by the Elgin Association became the object of intense interest and attained an importance in the broader antislavery movement that was greater than its numbers warranted.[3]

WILLIAM KING CAME FROM MODEST Irish Presbyterian farming stock. In 1833 he entered Glasgow University and, judging from his "Autobiography," it was there that he first came into serious contact with antislavery. Parliamentary reform and West Indian emancipation, he noted, were matters of grave concern when he arrived at the university, "both professors and students taking a deep interest" in them. As the Scottish campaign against West Indian slavery gained momentum, two leading participants in the controversy – George Thompson and Peter Bothwick – held their famous twelve-night debate, which was presided over by Sir Daniel Sandford, the impressionable young King's professor of Greek. Thompson, on behalf of Scots abolitionists, advocated immediate emancipation without remuneration while Bothwick, representing West Indian sugar planters, called for gradual emancipation with compensation. This was the occasion, as will be recalled, when the Greek term for slave, "doulos," was "thoroughly discussed in all its meanings, in both the old and new testament" (probably by Sandford himself). Interest was so great that the hall was filled long before the debating began and hundreds were turned away night after night. Like Michael Willis, King was deeply impressed by the proceedings; fifty years later he declared, "It was my privilege to hear these discussions, and I warmly expounded the cause of the slaves."[4]

When King finished university in 1833, his family emigrated to the United States in search of better farming opportunities and purchased a section of land west of Toledo, Ohio, near the Maumee River. After seeing the family established at the new homestead, King ventured south in 1835 to take a teaching appointment near Jackson, Louisiana, at a school maintained by several families in the area. When a better position opened up nearby at Mathews Academy, the preparatory department of Louisiana College, William moved on and soon became rector. As head of the academy, he came into contact with prominent families in the region whose sons attended the school, and in 1841 he married Mary E. Phares, daughter of planter John E. Phares, and thereby gained admission to the area's social life.[5]

Establishing a household in the morally ambiguous climate of the slaveholding South was a weighty step that had troubled his conscience even before his marriage. When King had become head of the academy the retiring rector, Dr Bullen, had preached a stirring farewell sermon based on the New Testament text, "What shall it profit a man if he gain the whole world and lose his own soul?" He warned his youthful hearers against pursuing worldly pleasures so single-mindedly that they forfeited an eternal home in heaven. This sombre message struck a responsive chord within the new rector, for as a sober-minded Presbyterian he sensed the seductive dangers inherent in the position he was about to assume. There was the "prospect of wealth and a gay and fashionable world with all its pleasures spread out before me," he confessed, "including the human heart to settle down in their midst and make this world my portion – and to forget the preparation for the next." The sermon's impact on King had been intensified when Bullen, who opposed slavery, liberated his slaves in preparation for leaving the area. King had resolved to guard against too strong an attachment to Louisiana's pleasure-loving society. Now that he was likely to have children, he worried about their future in such dubious surroundings.

King believed that slavery was to blame for what he saw as the South's depravity, for the institution had thoroughly corrupted the white population. By encouraging wealth and idleness – Sodom's besetting sins, he noted – it bred strong passions, and "lust reigned there without restraint." All that was "pure and lovely" in Southern womanhood became the "sport" of Southern males, who "only lived to gratify [their] passions." Young men raised in these hedonistic surroundings would be tainted if not ruined, as he well knew, for seven of his students (two of them sons of a state senator) had died prematurely from reckless living. Moral degradation seemed to pervade all society.

As rector of the academy, King reported yearly to the state legislature in New Orleans during the first week in January. Since this was part of the annual Christmas holiday, schools were closed during this period and slaves enjoyed "high carnival" on plantations, where owners gave them "great license." In New Orleans, King mixed freely with state legislators, seeing, as he said, "a great deal that I did not like." It was a "regular saturnalia," he lamented. "The public and private morals were corrupt, they were lovers of pleasure more than of God, drinking, gambling, horse riding and dancing were common on the Sabbath. Theatres were open and brothels were licensed and established by law. there [sic] appeared to be no restraint on the people everyone seemed to act like the children of Israel when they had no King to do that which was right in their own eyes." By 1842 the young rector was a father and, with this decadent image of Louisiana society burdening his conscience, he and his wife decided to leave the region at the first opportunity so that they could raise their family elsewhere.[6]

In the meantime, King had been following the "Great Disruption" in Scotland with much interest. Like many Scots, he was against Parliament claiming the right to appoint ministers in pulpits in the Established Church of Scotland without regard for the congregation's wishes – the main point in the conflict – and he applauded the stout-hearted Presbyterians who withdrew to form the Free Church rather than submit when the House of Lords rejected their claim. King now decided to enter New College in Edinburgh to prepare for the Free Church ministry. The lump in the pudding was the remaining year in his contract with the academy. Since King was popular with both the board of trustees and the students, he felt obliged to have a good reason for resigning. This appeared fortuitously in the spring of 1843, when the trustees proposed to reorganize Louisiana College and Mathews Academy under a single head. Their choice was Dr Lacy, the rector of the college, a man King could not support because he was unpopular with the students and lacked disciplinary control over the younger boys in the academy. When the trustees hesitated to implement the change without

King's approval, this provided him with the opening he needed, and he tendered his resignation – allegedly in order to break the deadlock. The real reason was, of course, that this allowed him to escape from the clutches of Louisiana's slaveholding society and enabled him to begin theological study, which would open the door to the Free Church. He quickly put his affairs in order and departed for Edinburgh in late 1843. Meanwhile, his wife and son remained at the Phares plantation, for he did not wish to subject them to the discomfort of a late fall crossing.[7]

As planned, King returned to Louisiana for his family the following summer, but a series of events occurred that greatly altered his personal circumstances and set the stage for his eventual effort at black colonization in Canada. His son died on the trip to Scotland. Then, early in 1846, John Phares died, leaving several slaves to his daughter Mary, whose death three months later ensured that the legacy would pass to an infant daughter born in Edinburgh. When the daughter died before the year was out, King inherited the slaves. Interestingly enough, he already owned several slaves; his "Autobiography" apologetically notes that he had purchased them when it proved difficult to get reliable servants for domestic work at the academy. The slaves had been placed on a small plantation that he had bought near the home of his father-in-law, who had supervised them when he went to Scotland. Thus, when King finished his theological studies in the spring of 1846, he was the owner of a dozen or so slaves and a Louisiana farm, an awkward encumbrance for someone the Colonial Committee was about to commission as a missionary to the Free Church in Canada (a body strongly opposed to fellowshipping with slaveholders, let alone slaveholding) under supervision of the Toronto presbytery. King left Britain bound for Canada in August, but since he was an executor of Phares's estate and had his own property to care for, he went via Louisiana. While there, he evidently decided to free his slaves and take them to Canada after the estate was settled. With this course of action in mind, he went to Canada in November 1846 and took up preaching duties in the Toronto presbytery without revealing his secret.[8]

Although King was distant from his slaves in the winter of 1846–47, they were never far from his mind, for already he was considering how he might settle them in Canada. Early in the new year, he asked whether the presbytery would relieve him of his commission to begin a mission among the province's blacks. The presbytery declined but asked for a meeting with King. On this occasion, he evidently explained more fully his wish to undertake the mission, but he also intimated that private matters in the United States might require his extended absence. The presbytery again withheld its approval but appointed two presbyters to interview him about the nature of his affairs in the United States. Now King faced a thorny dilemma; either he must risk offending the presbytery by keeping his affairs to himself, a course that could jeopardize his future as a probationer, or he must reveal the unpalatable truth about his slaves and face the likelihood of severe discipline immediately. In fact, he had little choice but to inform the two ministers about his circumstances, for eventually he would have to ask them for a leave of absence to go to Louisiana, and the presbytery would be unlikely to comply without a good reason. When the church learned that he owned slaves, the news fell like a "bomb shell," King said. He was immediately suspended from further missionary work and summoned to appear. Some members of the presbytery were "greatly excited," but the mood changed when he explained that there were barriers in Louisiana law as well as entanglements in the estate that prevented him from releasing the slaves immediately and that he intended to bring them to Canada after the estate was settled. Alexander Gale and Robert Burns, two influential ministers, came to his support, assuring him that he had taken the right course of action, and this seemed to clear the air. The presbytery allowed him to resign his commission and granted a leave, with the understanding that he could resume his commission after settling his affairs in Louisiana.[9]

Having received a request from Mrs Phares, his co-executor, to come and settle the estate, King headed south, stopping at the family farm in Ohio. Here he received word of a yellow fever epidemic in Louisiana, so he delayed the trip until the more healthful fall weather had begun. He arrived in November, completed the estate business in the winter, and by May was travelling northbound on a Mississippi riverboat with fourteen slaves. He left them at his brother's farm in Ohio and went on to Canada to make arrangements to settle them permanently, arriving shortly before the synod met in June. A warm reception awaited King in the Toronto presbytery, for newspapers in the South, as well as in New York and Boston, had reported his northward journey to liberate the slaves. He was quickly reinstated.[10]

King now laid before the presbytery the plan that he had had in mind for the past eighteen months. This was a scheme by which the Free Church could aid the growing number of fugitive slaves in Canada West and, coincidentally, his slaves waiting in Ohio. He explained that he had learned much about the circumstances of ex-slaves in the province on a recent tour of their communities; presumably, this was on his way from Louisiana. Most of them were uneducated, landless, and without permanent homes, he reported, and hence they moved frequently from place to place, forming a floating element in the population. During the summer months they held a variety of menial jobs as tavern waiters, boathands, and the like, but winter found them idle, consuming their earnings. Their children were growing up in ignorance without moral development, he warned. Well-intentioned friends had opened schools for them, but these had been forced to close because the mainly American sources of support had been inadequate to maintain them. "I am convinced," King continued as he came to the heart of his case, "that the only way to improve their constition [sic], and elevate their character, is to place them on land, give them an interest in the soil, and provide them with a Christian education. To accomplish this, I propose that some suitable place be selected in the Western District, where Crown and Clergy reserve lands can be obtained on reasonable terms, on these erect a school on the manual labour system, a church and dwelling house."

Whether King contemplated a communal arrangement at this point – a "dwelling house" where the inhabitants would live while they cultivated the land in common – is not clear. It seems more likely that he envisioned making the manual labour school, which would need a central residence for students, the centrepiece of the settlement. By locating it in an area where public land was available at reasonable rates, he believed that prospective black settlers would be drawn by the twin attractions of education for their children and cheap land. If the Free Church would undertake such a project, he predicted, there would be a "large and flourishing" settlement within a few years. Its success would induce other denominations to follow suit until the "whole coloured race would be gradually absorbed in the rural districts." Moreover, there was the glorious prospect of the projected school preparing young black men for theological study, young men who at length would find their way to Africa as missionaries, and consequently the white man would at last be able to begin paying his immeasurable debt to that continent. The presbytery discussed this imaginative proposal and referred it to the general assembly, which was about to meet.[11]

The 1848 assembly endorsed King's proposal in principle, but as a spiritual body it declined to become directly involved in a matter that had such far-reaching temporal implications. Instead, it appointed an advisory committee, which consisted of Robert Burns and Alexander Gale, the two ministers who had supported King previously in the presbytery, the Rev. Henry Esson, an abolitionist professor at Knox College, and several prominent laymen. Michael Willis eventually became chairman of the committee, though he was in Scotland when it was set up. The committee's mandate was to form an association to raise the necessary funds and to contact the commissioner of crown lands in order to locate a suitable site. The assembly also agreed to request the Colonial Committee to commission King as a missionary to the black population of Canada West.[12]

The committee moved quickly. A delegation presented the plan to Lord Elgin, the governor general, who gave his support and promised the government's cooperation in obtaining lands. King toured several sites and located a well-timbered 9000-acre tract in Raleigh Township, stretching south of Chatham towards Lake Erie. From a refined plan that King presented, the committee drew up its "Prospectus," which early in 1849 invited the "Christian public" to invest in a project that would provide homesteads, land, and education for fugitive slaves. The prospectus announced that the committee intended to form an association to raise the £4000 that it estimated the necessary land would cost by selling stock at £10 per share, with 10 per cent down and the balance in nine annual instalments. When the required amount had been subscribed, a meeting of stockholders would organize the association. The intention was to reserve the land for a period of ten years exclusively for black settlers, selling it to them in lots at the lowest price that would remunerate stockholders for their outlay. The settlement's management would remain in the hands of the association's executive.[13]

King and the committee diligently promoted the scheme throughout the province during the winter. The Toronto *Globe*, a rising weekly newspaper managed by Peter Brown's son George, urged readers to support the project by claiming that they owed the fugitives a great debt, which could not be discharged merely by guaranteeing their freedom when they crossed the border:

It is true that they came to us from a people who have long ago renounced their allegiance to the British Empire, but can we forget that it was while they were British Colonists that the slaves were carried from Africa? Can we look on those poor coloured refugees without reflecting, that our grandfathers and great grandfathers stole their grandfathers and great grandfathers and mothers, and carried them into bondage, after murdering thousands and tens of thousands in the horrors of the middle passage – can we forget that Liverpool and Bristol were built up by the profits of that villainous trade?

Brown argued powerfully. By spring, 335 stockholders had under-written the necessary funds, and the Elgin Association, as the body was known, was organized in Toronto on 7 June 1849. The anti-slavery seed which the elder Brown had planted so patiently earlier in the decade had finally borne fruit.[14]

This rapid success in organizing the Elgin Association created a backlash of antiblack sentiment in the area around Chatham. Trouble first appeared early in 1849 when the Western District council, learn-ing that a black settlement might be established in its region, peti-tioned the legislative assembly to block it. Such an enclave would be "highly deleterious to the morals and social condition of the present and future inhabitants of this District, as well as its pros-perity in every other respect," the petition warned. In all likelihood, the moving force behind this was Edwin Larwill, a figure about whom little is known except that he was active in local politics in the 1840s as a member of both the Western District council and the legislative assembly, and that he was unabashedly antiblack. His name soon appeared at the head of a list of 377 signatures on a blatantly racist petition to the 1849 Free Church synod.

While professing admiration for the general assembly's lofty goals in backing King, the petition rejected Canada and especially Raleigh Township as the right place for the contemplated settlement. It ar-gued that this was an "old, well-settled" region, whose "moral, industrious, and intelligent" inhabitants during many years of hard work had established their homes, schools, and churches. Would introducing a "colony of ignorant, indolent and consequently vicious blacks" encourage the "social advancement of the present settlers?" asked the petitioners. Protecting property was a legitimate concern for every community, and the presence of such an element in Raleigh Township would depreciate its value, and "hundreds" of the region's oldest and most respected settlers would leave. "The Negro," de-clared the alarmed petitioners, was a "distinct species of the human family" that was "far inferior to that of the European. Let each link in the great scale of existence have its place. The white man was never intended to be linked with the black." The petition went on to state that "amalgamation," which it saw as the inevitable result of the proposed settlement, was "as disgusting to the eye as it [was] immoral in its tendencies and all good men discountenance it." Moreover, if the settlement got started, other organizations would sponsor similar projects, and fugitive slaves would come in "swarms" from the United States. Infected with republicanism, they would bring with them the "most wild and confused ideas about liberty." Soon they would clamour for public office. "Imagine," continued the petition, "our legislative halls studded and our principal departments managed by these ebony men." It would mean the end of the "genius of our institutions." Toronto and Hamilton might hypocritically feign support for the project to rid themselves of a nuisance and save money, but Chatham, the petition made abundantly clear, wanted none of it.[15]

This rising opposition to the project crested at an unruly meeting in mid-August, which was called by Sheriff John Wadell to take appropriate steps to prevent the "colonizing of colored people in the settled township of this district." The situation was urgent, for the Elgin Association was in place and was poised to buy land. The meeting reviewed the memorial sent to the Free Church general assembly but gave short shrift to Robert Burns's authorized reply. Nor was it in the mood to listen to King, who evidently had attended in the hope of allaying fears by explaining that only blacks who could give evidence of good character would be allowed to settle. As he was a nonresident, his right to speak was challenged, and even after gaining the floor he had difficulty making himself heard above the disorderly crowd. It was illegal, he warned, to prevent blacks from buying property in the region when they clearly had the right to do so; and if violence occurred, as seemed possible, they themselves would be held accountable. The meeting ignored King and adopted hostile resolutions. There was general acknowledgment that slavery was a great evil whose victims deserved full enjoyment of their rights, but colonizing blacks among whites, to say nothing of amalgamation and even association, was viewed with great alarm. The meeting declared that it would be impolitic of the government to sell, and unjust for any association to buy, large blocks of land in settled portions of the province in order to colonize blacks. Nor should the government offer sizable holdings to foreigners, especially "when such persons belong to a different branch of the human family, and are black." Larwill then convinced the meeting to name a vigilance committee to keep an eye on the Elgin Association. The meeting also approved an "Address" to Canadians which embodied these sentiments, warning that the time had come when they must awake from their lethargy if they wanted to avoid the "thousand curses" lurking in the Elgin project. A transcript of the proceedings was sent to the governor general, the Elgin Association, and the Kent County member of the legislative assembly.[16]

Opposition continued in the fall. Having been unable to address the Chatham meeting effectively and fearing that the *Chronicle*'s report had given readers a wrong impression of the Elgin Association's intentions, King wrote a public letter to the paper. The Free

Church synod, he explained, was not sponsoring the settlement as some believed; its only intended connection with the project was to support a mission at the site, which other churches might do as well. The other misconception he sought to clarify was the charge that the association intended to encourage a large settlement of "indolent and vicious coloured persons." The truth, declared King, was that only the "moral and industrious" would be admitted and that many who intended to settle were already British subjects of considerable means.

This failed to convince "one who was present at the meeting," who sharply retorted that if only industrious blacks were to be served in the settlement, it followed that the "ignorant, the poor, and de-graded" – those most needing the associations's assistance – would be forgotten. This anonymous correspondent insisted that the scheme was not as benevolent as it purported to be, contending that it was "purely selfish and speculative" and was "calculated to enrich its members at the expense of the labour of the coloured man." Another critic, who signed himself "Cannon," cleverly masqueraded as a black correspondent appealing to his brethren in terms that were clearly intended to alarm white opponents of the Elgin Association. Cannon asserted that the burden of guilt for the sin of slavery had at last awakened the conscience of the white man, who remorsefully was about to found a home for the slaves of North America in Kent County. To this "garden of Canada," with its health-ful climate and rich, well-watered soil that was waiting to grow bounteous crops, blacks must now invite their fellow sufferers from the United States. With access to the ballot box assured, they would form an independent political party to secure black interests as their representatives filled public offices. In a few short years, they would control the entire peninsula stretching for two hundred miles along the shores of Lake Erie. Blacks once again would rise to the position of leadership which they had occupied in antiquity when they were "courted and feared by neighbouring nations." Then, Cannon om-inously predicted, the white man would be the "emigrating party, and we be in realization of our fondest hopes and the finest land in America."

The *Chronicle*'s opposition to the scheme was more subtle. The best way to proceed, it asserted, was to appeal in a "proper spirit" to the fugitives themselves, pointing out the "many troubles and inconveniences" they would encounter in "forcing a settlement in this township." They should be told that "much contention and hard feeling will necessarily arise from the state of public opinion at pres-ent ... and their own good sense will dictate to them that their future improvement could be better consulted and more successfully carried out by locating themselves under the auspices of the Elgin Association, in a place where they would not be exposed to the interference and annoyance of the white population around."[17]

Other voices soon backed the Elgin Association. "Quid," an anonymous writer in the *Globe*, defended King as a trusted friend of blacks and scorned the Chatham meeting for the "gross partiality displayed by its chairman, the intemperance of its speeches, and the behaviour of the crowd" among whom "drunkenness abounded and obscene language and shocking oaths were bandied from mouth to mouth." Especially helpful was a public letter in the same paper signed by three justices of the peace in the Western District – Archibald McKellar, an Elgin stockholder, Thomas Williams, and George Jacobs – and by 103 others from the Chatham area; it boldly declared that a "large and respectable portion of the inhabitants of the District, offer no opposition, and take no part in such illegal proceedings."

Larwill hotly disputed the letter, claiming that nine-tenths of the signers were black men. The real attitude of the area's white majority, he insisted, could be seen from the district council's unanimous petition to the legislature the previous March, not to mention the Chatham meeting and the sentiments of the local press. He lost no time in having the council request the governor general not to sign any agreement that would convey land to the Elgin Association, and he recommended several openly antiblack policies: levying a poll tax on all blacks immigrating into Canada, accompanied by a bond that they would not become a burden on the local ratepayers; withholding the franchise; and passing a law against amalgamation. Larwill kept up his attack against the Elgin Association until the following spring, and he continued it sporadically for several years, but he was unsuccessful.

King had laid his plans carefully and was sure of the governor general's support. Before the end of October the association had purchased 4300 acres. The promotional work over the previous months had attracted numerous supporters from widely scattered communities in Canada West, and these stockholders elected an influential executive. George Skeffington Connor was chosen as president. Born and educated in Dublin, this University of Toronto law professor was a prominent member of the city's legal profession and soon to become a judge. The vice-presidents were Michael Willis and Robert Burns, both of whom were respected newcomers from Scotland and prominent names in the Free Church. James Scott Howard, a former Toronto postmaster and then treasurer of the united counties of Peel and York, was the treasurer. Nathan Gatchel, the secretary, was the only one of the leaders about whom little is known.

The association's twenty-four directors were either established or rising figures in the public life and the business and professional circles of their towns. For example, John Fisher, soon to replace Connor as president, was a prominent Hamilton iron manufacturer and the city's mayor; Peter Brown, who succeeded Fisher in 1857, had established his reputation as the editor of the *Banner* and retained close ties with the *Globe*; Andrew Taylor McCord was city chamberlain. From smaller towns came men such as Rufus Holden, the prominent Belleville physician, Edward C. Campbell, a county court judge from Niagara, and Alexander David Ferrier, the Fergus clerk of county court, land conveyancer, and future member of the legislature. In face of this sturdy middle-class widely dispersed support, Larwill's opposition seemed localized and isolated.[18]

But it was the early success and steady progress of the settlement that most effectively countered the hostility. The association divided its land into 50-acre lots that were sold to settlers on easy terms (10 per cent down and the balance to be paid with interest in nine instalments) at $2.50 per acre. This was the lowest price that would enable the stockholders to be repaid and the association to meet its costs, which, except for land acquisition, were small, since neither King nor the executive was paid. Thus, for a relatively small sum, settlers could get access to a homestead site, with the prospect of receiving title after nine years, and they quickly took advantage of the opportunity.

The Elgin Association's second annual report, which was tabled in 1851 after two years of operation, pictures a settlement that had made a promising beginning. Since the first settler moved onto the site in December 1849, more had arrived each month, spurred on, no doubt, by the passage of the 1850 Fugitive Slave Law, which greatly assisted owners in retrieving their runaways. By midsummer 1851, forty-five families had occupied 2500 acres, and ten or twelve more had made arrangements to take up land in the fall. Since about a dozen black families had also purchased land adjacent to the association's holdings, seventy families would be in the community by year's end. This rapid growth had reduced the association's land supply, so it purchased an additional 2300 adjacent acres. Some settlers had been present for more than a year and they were busily developing their holdings. On the 230 acres cleared, 218 acres were planted with corn and other grain crops, and 12 acres with tobacco. The settlers had built thirty houses according to the settlement's specifications, each house being 18 ft. by 24 ft. square and 12 ft.

high. They were situated 33 ft. back from the road that passed by each lot, and each had a front garden, which was enclosed by a picket fence for neatness. King's church and school, usually known as the Buxton Mission and sponsored by the Free Church, had been open for about a year, the latter with an enrolment of sixty.[19]

A year later the number of families had risen to seventy, giving the settlement a population of about four hundred, excluding the hundred or so people among the twenty-five families on the adjoining land. There were twenty new homes, and a post office now served the residents. Anxious to encourage cloth manufacturing, the association offered a prize for a garment made from wool that had been raised, spun, and woven on site, and two items were displayed at the annual meeting, with samples of wheat, tobacco, and maple sugar. The third annual report reflected noticeable growth in the settlement's social life. The "day school" had seventy-three students, including about twenty white children. According to King, who was a trustee of the school district, the whites were attracted by his school's "superior teaching." The district school trustees had asked whether their children might attend; as a result, the district school had closed, and the black children and white children mingled freely in the Buxton school, the former taking their share of prizes and sometimes standing at the head of the class, showing that the "young coloured children were equal to whites in learning." As a result, King noted, the "prejudice which had existed at first against both me and the coloured people was now dying away and the last vestige of it disappeared in the third year after I settled in Raleigh." The newly begun Latin class was a matter of special pride, for it opened the door to higher education, and here King was grooming "six black students" to qualify as teachers and ministerial protégés. The Buxton church had between 100 and 140 adherents, and John Straith, a Knox College student, had a thriving Sunday school. Reflecting their awakening sense of social responsibility, the settlers had formed a "court of arbitration" to handle local disputes, which had amicably resolved five cases during the year. All things considered, the directors were pleased with the first three years' achievements and were optimistic that this progress would underscore their conviction that ex-slaves could reach the "highest attainments" when given the opportunity.[20]

The settlement made steady progress throughout the decade, and by 1860 its population of 1000 to 1200 had established a firm agricultural base, which even a series of poor harvests between 1857 and 1859 did not unduly disrupt. There were 1600 acres of cleared and fenced land under cultivation, and the trees had been felled on another 300 acres. Knowing that crop failure was a potential danger, the Raleigh farmers diversified their planting to include nearly 600 acres of Indian corn, 100 acres each of wheat and oats, and 600 in other grains such as buckwheat and green crops – potatoes, peas, turnips – and a sizable area in hay to winter the growing number of farm animals. These included 100 oxen, which were vitally important in land clearing, a slightly larger number of horses, which were more useful in cultivation and transportation, 200 cows, 700 hogs, and a few sheep.[21]

The settlement's economic base extended beyond this agricultural foundation. Arriving settlers usually were short of cash, and this necessitated finding work outside the settlement for several months each year, thus removing men from their families and retarding land clearance and other improvements on their properties. King saw that if opportunities for employment within Buxton could be created by organizing local industries, the situation could be corrected. One possibility was to convert the settlement's valuable timber stands into marketable lumber, rather than wastefully burning what was not needed for building. The key was to find the capital to purchase the necessary equipment. Sometime early in the decade he called a public meeting to see what could be done, and this produced fruitful results. When numerous settlers indicated that they would use bricks to improve their houses, two men opened a brick kiln; and from the plentiful supply of good-quality clay, they produced 300,000 bricks the first year.

The prospect of erecting a sawmill drew even greater interest. In 1852, Wilson Ruffin Abbott, a wealthy black Toronto real estate investor who had moved to the settlement so that his children could attend the Buxton school, joined with a group of entrepreneurs (which included an unnamed black immigrant who had contacts in Buffalo) to form the Canada Mill and Mercantile Company. The settlers constructed the building and King bought the machinery in Detroit. The mill cut its first lumber in July 1855. By 1858 the steam-powered venture, which now included a siding machine and a shingle factory, had joined the existing wagon, carpentry, and black-smith shops in serving the local market in numerous ways. The settlers added a grist mill, since the same source of power could operate both sets of machinery, and soon it was turning the surrounding countryside's grain into flour. Wood ash, a byproduct of land clearing and the burning of unwanted timber, was another abundantly available resource. If properly prepared, it was salable. A pot and pearl ash factory was therefore added to the sawmill, and these commodities were sold, as were black salts – another byproduct of timber burning.

The sawmill's main product was the rough lumber used in frame construction, which constituted an improvement on the settlement's log structures, but King believed that Buxton's oak, beech, and hickory could be sold in Britain if suitably finished. Indeed, some was sold through a London firm in 1859, and King and Archibald McKellar, one of the directors and now a member of the legislature, visited Britain in the hope of raising £2000 to upgrade the sawmill's equipment. Thus, after ten years, the settlement's economic base included industries that increased employment and promoted stability during the poor harvests of 1857–59, and there was even a plan afoot to market lumber abroad.[22]

The settlement's social life mirrored this growing prosperity. The residents opened a savings bank, where they deposited funds until their annual instalments were due.The first Latin class finished its studies in 1856, and one of its members – Alfred Lafferty – soon became Trinity College's top student. A school each for males and females was operated in Buxton the following year with about ninety students and "highly competent" teachers, and there were additional opportunities for education in three adjoining district schools. By 1860 enrolment had risen to 180 in the settlement's three schools, one of which was known as the "classical" school at Buxton, for here students could prepare for higher education. Some adults had been taught to read in night classes, and they thus had access to the 500-volume library, which Edinburgh women had donated to supplement the London Religious Tract Society's pamphlets; they could also read the Bibles that the Buxton branch of the London and Foreign Bible Society circulated. A new brick temperance hotel graced the community, and this was soon to be joined by permanent buildings (paid for by funds that King raised on his 1860 trip to Britain) replacing the temporary log school and church.[23]

At the beginning of Buxton's second decade there was a development that was a poignant symbol, especially for William King, of the success of the Elgin Association's undertaking. This was the prospect of sending missionaries from the settlement to Africa. The notion had been in the back of King's mind from the beginning, and he had been developing a plan in conjunction with British contacts associated with the Social Science League in London. The scheme envisioned the establishment of Christian colonies on the west coast of Africa, where missionaries would show the local chiefs that there were larger profits to be made from raising cotton than from selling slaves. If this could be done, it would help to evangelize Africa and would dry up the slave trade, which the British navy had been unable to eradicate. It would also begin to pay the great debt that whites had incurred by enslaving Africans. In 1858 a young black doctor from Canada, Martin Robinson Delany, was sent to the African west coast, where he successfully negotiated agreements granting permission to settle on land. King was present when Delany reported to the Social Science League in London in 1859, and the result was the formation of the African Aid Society, which was devoted to securing these goals. King was to furnish the young men who would act as pioneers, and the London society was to provide the financial backing. By the spring of 1861, King had several volunteers who were ready to undertake the task.[24]

Thus, by 1860 the Buxton settlement had come remarkably close to fulfilling the Elgin Association's goals. More than a thousand blacks, whom public opinion assumed were fugitive slaves, had found homes in a community they had built, which rested on a firm agricultural base and also had a promising lumbering operation and several service industries. This economic activity satisfied the settlers' basic needs, saw them through a series of bad harvests, and generated enough cash to enable them to retire their indebtedness. Several churches ministered to Buxton's spiritual needs, schools provided the necessary preparation even for those hoping to enter university, and young men from the settlement were contemplating missionary work on the west coast of Africa – a move, it was believed, that would help to end slavery.

Meanwhile, rumours of the Elgin Association's success had spread among antislavery circles, creating much interest. Abolitionists soon perceived that apart from merely assisting the needy, Buxton provided the opportunity to determine whether ex-slaves would support themselves and take advantage of their liberty to achieve self-improvement – a key issue in the long debate over the feasibility of emancipation. As a result, visitors streamed to the site to see for themselves how the fugitives were faring, and antislavery periodicals eagerly published their glowing reports.

One of the earliest observers was Samuel J. May, the Unitarian minister from Syracuse. In an extensive report to the *National Anti-Slavery Standard*, the mouthpiece of the American Anti-Slavery Society, he painted a very positive picture of what he saw in the summer of 1852. The settlers had built "comfortable" log houses with "room enough for a small family," had fenced "door-yards," and had "one to two acres of ground cleared up," which were "planted with potatoes, corn, and a variety of vegetables." Some dwellings were "really picturesque," he reported. "Around their doors and windows were rose and other bushes, and various vines, and their door-yards were smooth grass plots." All who had been on their land for a year had paid their instalments and some the entire balance. The settlement was founded on the principle, May approvingly noted, that able-bodied men must provide for themselves and their families, and hence offers of food and clothing were refused; when there was illness, neighbours rallied to plant crops and tend gardens. Alcohol was banned, crime and drunkenness were unknown in the settlement, and the little government that was required was managed by annually elected committees. In these conditions, property values were rising and neighbouring farmers who once spoke of leaving the township if there was an influx of black immigrants had changed their minds. Children were doing well in school, even in the Latin class, whose skills May tested. "The boys made several blunders, but the girl not one," May enthusiastically declared. "She was 14 years old, and I never heard a child of her age construe and parse better than she did."

May's tour convinced him, he told his readers, that under the tutelage of good teachers and wise ministers for a few more years, the Elgin settlement would be an unquestioned success. He left Buxton with a "much deeper respect for this whole people than before." Thrown on their own resources and motivated by a deep sense of liberty, they were shouldering their responsibilities, he said. In fact, they reminded him of New England's founders: "Like them, they fled from the abodes of civilized men, and sought homes in the wilderness, that they might be free." Triumphantly, he added: "Who will presume to say that as great results will not come out of this expulsion of the coloured people from our country as came out of the expulsion of the Jews from Egypt or the Puritans from England." His message was clear; the fugitives had accepted the responsibilities of freedom and were thriving at Buxton. [25]

Three years later Thomas Henning, Peter Brown's son-in-law, a former schoolteacher who had joined the *Globe*, published an account of his visit to Buxton for British readers in the British and Foreign Anti-Slavery Society's *Anti-Slavery Reporter*. What he had seen at Buxton "highly gratified" him. Land clearing, logging, and the sawmill operation, together with the production of 100 barrels of pearl ash during the previous six months, had kept the ex-slaves "profitably employed, and all so happy and energetic-looking," he wrote. With 800 acres cleared and fenced, and 200 more on which the trees had been felled ready to be brought under cultivation the following season, the settlement was steadily advancing. The "encouraging character" of its development, he wrote, proved that "under proper management, the black man is as capable of success, even in agricultural pursuits, as the white one, and that the social and moral habits of the Ethiopian, when properly directed, are not inferior in any respect to those of the European."

Henning stressed that the philanthropists who had enabled King to carry out his task deserved much credit, for it was vitally important to antislavery as well as society that the fugitive slaves develop their moral and intellectual abilities while acquiring possessions. By helping them to throw off the degrading effect of slavery, he told British abolitionists, "we thereby not merely aid him in exhibiting to the world that he is fitted for freedom, but do much to hasten the day, which cannot be much longer deferred, when the bonds shall fall from the limbs of the oppressed." Henning clearly believed that the Elgin settlement was not only assisting fugitive slaves but was contributing to the ultimate task of ending slavery by destroying the proslavery claim that slaves were not fit for freedom.[26]

Those outside the antislavery movement may have questioned the objectiveness of May's and Henning's conclusions, for both were avowed abolitionists and the latter was an Elgin stockholder. But sceptics had less reason to doubt the word of the influential New York *Tribune*'s commissioner, who toured Buxton in 1857. After recounting how King came to have slaves and why he chose to liberate them by placing them on land in Canada, the commissioner's report explained that the Scottish minister was not satisfied merely to emancipate them. Instead, he wanted to "try, on a sufficient scale, the question, whether the emancipated negro would, as an agriculturist, be found self-supporting." This turned the undertaking into a "grand experiment," declared the report. After describing the size of Buxton's population, the type of dwellings the fugitives lived in, and the crops they planted, the *Tribune* noted that drunkenness, bastardy, and crime were virtually unknown in the settlement, and concluded that the "general moral standard of the community is high, and the social improvement is marked and manifest." Settlers who arrived with a little capital and some knowledge of farming did "exceedingly well, having cleared more land and made greater improvements than the great majority of white settlers" in similar circumstances. Those with neither capital nor skill had greater difficulty, admitted the paper, but even they either paid their instalments or had been given permission to put money into property improvement and defer payment. Many had already paid in full and now possessed titles, and King had assured the writer that he was confident that all would meet the nine-year deadline.

The report in the *Tribune* noted the Elgin settlement's success in comparison with two other colonization efforts in Canada West, in which the immigrants had continued to receive government aid. A group of Irish, English, and Scottish colonists at Ramsey near Brookville had dispersed altogether and a colony of Highlanders at Notowasaga had dwindled to a mere handful and had only shown improvement when the government support ended. The *Tribune*'s commissioner attributed the Elgin settlers' contrasting success partly to the fact that they had understood from the beginning that they had to be self-reliant and partly to their superior axemanship. The *Anti-Slavery Standard* recommended the *Tribune*'s "even-handed" account to those who were inclined to accept too readily the stories of poverty, crime, and degradation among ex-slaves that were circulated by the defenders of slavery. [27]

The curious came from Britain and Europe as well as from North America. For example, the Irish Presbyterian Church, in which there had been much support for the Free Church Anti-Slavery Society, sent its moderator, the Rev. Gibson, who was a professor at Belfast College; he was accompanied by William McClure, the Irish Methodist minister who was currently residing in Toronto. These two men were "strongly impressed" by what they saw. There was a similar reaction from three Englishmen – Earl Spencer, Henry Christy, and John W. Probyn, a member of parliament – who toured the settlement in 1857. They wrote glowingly that the "industry" of the settlers and "success of the experiment" showed by "practical demonstration that the coloured man, when placed in favourable circumstances, is able and willing to support himself." Christy pointedly told King, "You have there, more nearly than has yet been done, solved the problem, whether the liberated black can be linked to habits of continuous self-supporting voluntary labor."

Another visitor, the prominent French Reformed minister, Frederick Monod, declared that the Raleigh Township settlement gave "proof positive that all that the oppressed coloured race required to raise them from degradation was a fair chance." Similar sentiments echoed through the report published in 1863 by the Freedmen's Inquiry Commission, an agency established during the American Civil War to prepare for the slaves' transition to freedom. Thus, the testimony of those who visited the Buxton settlement was uniformly that the ex-slaves were thriving in Canada and were taking advantage of their newfound freedom to achieve self-improvement. Antislavery periodicals eagerly channelled the information to abolitionists in the field, and even nonabolitionist journals and government agencies publicized the reports. [28]

By 1861, as we have seen, King was planning to involve the Elgin settlement in a scheme to evangelize Africa and check slavery by planting colonies on the west coast of the continent. But this plan soon faded from his mind, for with the outbreak of the American Civil War in the spring of 1861 – an event that profoundly affected the little community – settlers turned their attention to events south of the border. The United States was their former homeland and many still had families there. A Northern victory would not only end American slavery, but in all likelihood it would also deal a heavy blow to slavery throughout the world; for, as other countries followed the American lead, the demand for slaves would fall sharply. This made the African colonization scheme redundant. The young men who had volunteered to be African pioneers now dreamed of shouldering a gun with the federal forces, though this was delayed until 1863 when President Abraham Lincoln eventually opened the Northern armies to black soldiers. Forty settlers immediately volunteered; by the end of the war, seventy men from the settlement were in uniform – a significant portion of the community's adult males. The loss of this key element in the population was not replenished by new settlers, for the outbreak of the war ended the influx of fugitives into the provinces. But even if more settlers had been available, they could not have been accommodated, for virtually all the association's land had been taken up. Those who remained continued to improve their property, and the schools and churches remained full; but the American conflict marked the beginning of an exodus from which the settlement never recovered.[29]

When the Northern victory brought peace in 1865, accompanied by the end of slavery and the destruction of the plantation system, enticing stories that cheap land was available throughout the South reached Buxton. Property seized from disloyal planters during the war had been turned over to the Freedmen's Bureau and supposedly it was for sale at low prices. This was an attractive prospect to the Elgin settlers, most of whom had paid the balance of their loans and therefore had an equity in their holdings that King estimated to be worth from $1000 to $1200 per lot. It could be used to start afresh in their former homeland, and by pooling their assets the settlers, who were now experienced in the problems of community building, might profit handsomely. With this in mind, a number of leading men in the settlement and others from elsewhere in the province approached King, stating that they wanted to purchase a block of inexpensive land and to use the cheap labour that was available in the chaotic aftermath of the collapsed plantation system to raise cotton and sugar. They hoped that King would accompany them, for now that slavery had ended, the Elgin settlement would no longer be needed as a haven. King was receptive to the idea, but before making a firm commitment to such a large undertaking, he wisely determined to get reliable information on conditions in the South by consulting appropriate figures in the American capital.[30]

The three men he consulted in Washington in the fall of 1865 all advised against the scheme. Sir Frederick Bruce, the British minister, told him that Andrew Johnson, who had become president after Lincoln's assassination, was rapidly pardoning planters and restoring their land. In fact, Bruce estimated that there were 500 then in Washington seeking the return of their property, and he believed they would get it. Neither William Henry Seward, the American secretary of state, nor Major O.O. Howard, the head of the Freedmen's Bureau, was any more encouraging. King calculated that if the Elgin settlers were to acquire the 400-to-500-acre plots their plan called for, they would need a block of 20,000 acres; but Howard explained that the available land was scattered throughout the South and could not be obtained in one piece. There was another even more serious problem: the feeling against former slaves who dared to occupy confiscated land was dangerously high. Both Seward and Howard warned King that Northern occupation forces were having difficulty controlling the lawlessness that reigned throughout the South, and they said that before order could be restored the twin problems of how to regraft the seceded states onto the Union, and what role the freemen would play in American life, must be solved.

King saw that this instability, combined with the unavailability of a large block of land, made the settlers' scheme impractical, and on his return to Buxton he discouraged it. The South was still under a volatile military occupation, and the legal status of the freedmen was unclear, he told the settlers. In his judgment, the American government was well disposed towards the freedmen and would soon grant them citizenship and civil rights. Then, even though a large block of land would still be unobtainable, they could return as individuals and they would find a "large field of usefulness ... for those now educated in the settlement to go and give instruction to their brethren in ignorance." In the meantime, they should wait.[31]

The proposed relocation of the Buxton settlement en masse to a new site in the American South never occurred. However, the postwar exodus that carried an estimated two-thirds of Canada's blacks to the United States also swept through Raleigh Township. Many of the educated and most promising young people left to serve as teachers, ministers, or social workers during Reconstruction, or to take advantage of opportunities that beckoned at such places as

Howard University, the newly established school for blacks in Washington. Some Elgin landowners rented or sold their holdings in order to try their hand in new ventures south of the border. This emigration of soldiers, young people, and landowners drained key human resources from the community; its schools became part of the district system; the sawmill failed. Yet the settlement did not disperse. Some white settlers moved into the region, and the two groups worked together with little apparent difficulty. In 1868, Buxton Mission Church replaced its original log structure with a new building, using funds that King had raised in England in 1860; the two Baptist congregations merged. By 1880, after a decade and a half of decline, the settlement reached a stability that it maintained until the First World War.[32]

IN CONTRAST TO HIRAM WILSON's efforts with the Canada Mission and the British-American Institute, King was highly successful in aiding fugitive slaves. From the beginning, the Elgin Association believed in the necessity of getting property into the hands of the fugitive slaves. This, it was felt, would end what some saw as the ex-slaves' ceaseless wandering about the province in search of work, forcing an improvident hand-to-mouth existence and lessening the chance that their children would receive schooling. By the early 1860s, the association's goals had virtually been achieved, for black settlers had acquired almost the entire 6700 acres; three lots came back because purchasers abandoned them, but when the association disbanded after submitting a final report to the Ontario legislature in 1873, there were only two with unpaid balances. Approximately 150 families had built homesteads, and in the process they had learned what it meant to borrow money and to repay it with regular instalments. The equity they established provided stability for those who remained and mobility for those who eventually went elsewhere. Nearly 700 children received a good education, while their parents gained experience in managing institutions by organizing churches and participating in the annually elected committees, which evidently helped to direct settlement affairs, although there is no record of their actions. The achievements of many in public life, business, and the professions after leaving the settlement indicate that the Elgin experience served them well.[33]

It is open to question whether, by placing the refugees on a block of land in a rural area, the Elgin Association unwisely isolated them and thus missed an opportunity to integrate them into the mainstream of Canadian life, thereby retarding the growth of interracial understanding. The *Globe*, whose proprietor's family was deeply involved with the association, was apologetic about the fact. Yet the fugitive slaves were not as isolated from white society as this criticism implies. Almost from the beginning, family heads worked for surrounding farmers and tradesmen while they were getting on their feet. Black children and white children attended school together, and by the middle of the decade white farmers ground their grain at the Buxton grist mill. At least two black settlers served together with white residents on the Raleigh Township council, and after 1865 some white settlers moved into Elgin, where the two groups coexisted with little difficulty.

Thus, although the black families were not scattered randomly throughout white communities, they were not cut off from contact with whites. Situated among others who knew the cruelty of slavery and the terror of being pursued as fugitives, they shared a bond that bound them together and provided the mutual support that was so vital for the powerless in the early days when they were establishing their homes. Once they had passed this stage and felt more secure and gradually improved their property, they were in a better position to interact with their white neighbours under conditions that were more akin to economic equality. Both groups were homesteaders who knew the problems of building log cabins in the woods, the burden of debt, and the disappointment of crop failure. In all likelihood, this promoted the growth of racial understanding and respect, which seemingly enveloped all settlers in the township after their initial fears had been overcome. Had they located in towns, the Elgin settlers would have confronted a large number of middle-class immigrants who had recently arrived from Britain, and this would have emphasized the socio-economic differences that separated them and would have complicated the development of interracial trust.

Conceivably, the Elgin Association might have used its funds to help individual families buy homes in various towns, in the hope of promoting rapid integration. However, this would have greatly complicated the task of aiding the fugitive slaves, possibly to the point of smothering it. Agents would have had to scrutinize each purchase, even if affordable housing could have been found in areas where blacks were willing to settle. To ensure that settlers could meet the necessary payments so that the association could discharge its current obligations and serve new arrivals, it would have been necessary to find suitable employment. Altogether, this would have required numerous workers, considerable travel, and much higher costs, and it would have left the question of schooling unaddressed.

The Elgin Association avoided these problems by buying a single block of land and reselling it in smaller plots to settlers, and by having just one unpaid agent – King – to supervise the exchange. The homesteaders were mainly self-employed, clearing the woods and cultivating the land to provide essentials for their families, though they supplemented what they could produce by doing casual labour for surrounding farmers and tradesmen. This provided the cash to meet their basic needs until the land could carry them. The quality education in the schools that King established enabled all to learn the basics and allowed those with the ability, interest, and inclination to pursue higher education. Thus, as far as the former slaves were concerned, the Elgin settlement was an important phase in their transition from bondsmen to householders and citizens. Having had their start in the homesteads and schools of Buxton, some settled permanently in the community while others moved on to new enterprises or entered the professions and public life.

In the larger arena of Canadian-Anglo-American antislavery, the Elgin Association performed an important if less tangible function. It apparently provided incontrovertible evidence that former slaves, when given a fair chance, would establish homesteads in which they supported themselves in modest comfort and used their newfound freedom for self-improvement, while their children benefited from education just as white children did. When international visitors to Buxton, with access to the antislavery periodical network, spread word of this, the community proved a useful source of information for abolitionists in the field who were attempting to convince a sceptical public that liberated slaves could care for themselves, and this put an end to the debate that had raged for nearly as long as the abolition of slavery had been considered. Consequently, it helped weaken one of the pillars on which slavery rested, and it advanced the cause of antislavery.

The course of the Elgin Association also reflected the important tie that linked British and Canadian antislavery as abolitionist immigrants with experience of the British antislavery movement arrived in British North America in the 1840s. King, the patriarch of Buxton, had caught the antislavery virus during the British struggle over West Indian slavery; so had Robert Burns, who had joined Michael Willis and Peter Brown in the efforts of the Scottish antislavery societies to stamp out slavery in the American South in the 1830s. All of them eagerly promoted the Elgin plan from the outset and later became association office holders, Brown being president for several years. Seemingly, King's abolitionism wavered when he married into the family of a wealthy planter, but in the long run his

Louisiana sojourn strengthened his antislavery convictions, just as his observation of the fellowshipping controversy had no doubt done when he was a seminarian in Edinburgh. The fellowshipping wrangle also influenced Willis, Burns, and Brown in various ways. However, their cooperation in the Elgin Association was only the beginning of their joint efforts in Canadian antislavery.

Samuel Ringgold Ward, agent of the Anti-Slavery Society of Canada. Frontispiece, Samuel Ringgold Ward, *Autobiography of a Fugitive Negro*, London, 1855 (courtesy of MTRL).

Rev. William King, founder of the Elgin Settlement (courtesy of the Raleigh Township Centennial Museum).

North Buxton School, Elgin Settlement (courtesy of the Raleigh Township Centennial Museum).

Isaac Riley, first resident in the Elgin Settlement (courtesy of the Raleigh Township Centennial Museum).

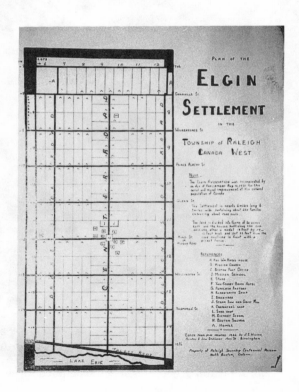

Plan of the Elgin Settlement (courtesy of the Raleigh Township Centennial Museum).

Rev. Michael Willis, President of the Anti-Slavery Society of Canada
(Archives of Ontario L147).

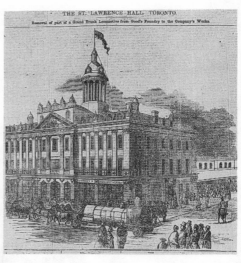

St Lawrence Hall, Toronto, where the Anti-Slavery Society of Canada frequently met. *The Daily Colonist*, Toronto, 7 Mar. 1855 (MTRL T30102).

Rev. Ephraim Evans, secretary of the Upper Canada Anti-Slavery Society (The United Church of Canada/Victoria University Archives, Toronto, P1792).

Rev. John Roaf, committee member of the Anti-Slavery Society of Canada (The United Church of Canada/Victoria University Archives, Toronto, P5525).

Rev. Robert Burns, committee member of the Anti-Slavery Society of Canada and vice-president of the Elgin Association (The United Church of Canada/Victoria University Archives, Toronto, P755).

# 6 Educating the Public

Since the American constitution made slavery a state responsibility, abolitionists had little hope of ending it through congressional action. Instead, they sought to convince public opinion that slavery was so utterly evil that the sheer weight of universal disapproval would eventually shame Southerners into emancipation. This goal energized antislavery societies and abolitionists everywhere. It enabled British and Canadian abolitionists to join their American counterparts in an effective propaganda campaign, even though they were outside the American political system.

British North Americans were slow to join this crusade. Not until the late 1830s – several years after British and American societies mobilized – did the Upper Canada Anti-Slavery Society appear, only to disintegrate, without having achieved anything of note, in the suspicion-charged atmosphere that followed the Upper Canada rebellion. John Roaf's effort to form a new society in Toronto a decade later was even more fleeting. By the middle of the century, however, forces were at work preparing the way for a new abolitionist organization. None was more important than the father-and-son newspaper team of Peter and George Brown, publishers of the *Banner* and the *Globe*. Throughout most of the 1840s, the *Banner* had kept slavery before its readers with accounts of narrow escapes by fugitive slaves and heroism on the Underground Railroad, along with frequent commentary on American political events and with criticism of churches for waffling about slavery.

When the *Banner* ceased publication in 1848, the *Globe*, in the hands of the younger Brown, continued to crusade; this was to be expected, since the elder Brown wrote for the new paper and George shared his father's hatred of slavery. The *Globe*'s early support for William King's land settlement scheme and its spirited attack on Larwill's opposition maintained public interest in slavery late in the decade. When numerous provincial residents invested in the settlement, antislavery activism (as opposed to mere verbal condemnation, on which virtually all British North Americans agreed) won increased respectability. In this way, the Browns' journalism joined the antislavery enthusiasm generated by the Elgin Association in preparing provincial sentiment to support a new abolitionist organization.

The influx of British antislavery veterans injected another vital element into the antislavery movement in Canada West in the 1840s. Peter Brown, who had been a charter member of the Edinburgh Emancipation Society, symbolized this group, but the foremost figure was Michael Willis, who had been present in Toronto since 1847 when he became principal of Knox College. Robert Burns, another recent immigrant, was an experienced antislavery hand from his days in Paisley and in the Glasgow Emancipation Society. John Roaf and Adam Lillie had been in the province since the 1830s, and like William King and William McClure, an Irish New Connexion Methodist, they brought their abolitionism from the mother country. None of them had the international antislavery reputation of Captain Charles Stuart, who had recently returned to Canada after residing elsewhere for twenty-five years, but with the exception of Peter Brown, they did not share his advanced age. Younger men such as George Brown had either been exposed to antislavery in their youth in Britain or, like Thomas Henning and James Nisbet, had been educated at Knox College under the tutelage of Willis and Burns and their abolitionist colleague Henry Esson. These men provided a pool of experienced leadership to spearhead Canadian antislavery, a resource that had largely been unavailable to the Upper Canada Anti-Slavery Society a decade earlier.

These factors ensured that British North Americans would sustain the province's third effort to form an abolitionist society, and the Anti-Slavery Society of Canada was born. Its activities combined an initially vigorous attempt to abolitionize provincial public opinion and an effort to give aid to the large number of fugitive slaves who made their way to the province in the wake of the 1850 Fugitive Slave Law. The relief work continued but, with one notable exception in 1860, the effort to shape Canadian attitudes had withered by the middle of the decade, even though the society existed long enough to celebrate the Emancipation Proclamation.

IT WAS THE PASSAGE OF THE 1850 Fugitive Slave Law in the United States that precipitated the formation of a new provincial antislavery body. The law was part of an intricate midcentury sectional compromise that Americans implemented when California's application for membership in the union as a free state threatened the balance of power between free and slave states in the Senate. It admitted California as a free state and outlawed the slave trade in the District of Columbia, in which Congress had jurisdiction. Washington assumed the Texan debt when Texas limited its western boundary in favour of New Mexico, which then organized as a territory without restrictions on slavery. To compensate slaveholders, a new fugitive slave law was passed which simplified the process of returning runaways. It created a corps of powerful officers before whom slave-catchers could bring an alleged fugitive, together with an affidavit claiming ownership. Slaves could neither testify on their own behalf nor cross-examine witnesses, and the procedure dispensed with juries. All citizens became potential slavecatchers for they could be drafted to assist in returning an escapee, and harsh penalties discouraged any interference. Free blacks as well as fugitives became vulnerable to prosecution by unscrupulous slavecatchers, and the law produced a wave of black emigration to Canada. The actual number of migrants is unknown, but the usually reliable Toronto *Globe* claimed that within eighteen months of the 1850 Fugitive Slave Law, 3000 had crossed the border.[1]

Previously, most British North Americans had opposed slavery, but few had actively advocated antislavery principles, for the majority saw slavery as a problem for Americans to settle. The 1850 Fugitive Slave Law changed this. Highly publicized accounts of captures, and the flight of vulnerable blacks across the border, stirred sympathy among British North Americans, and public opinion universally condemned the law. No provincial newspapers ventured to defend it, and many openly criticized it. Even the staunchly Tory Toronto *British Colonist*, while acknowledging the constitutionality of the law, attacked its morality. The *Globe* scornfully cried, "Shame on both the North and South," and merely summarized the terms of the legislation, contemptuously saying, "Comment is superfluous."[2]

Before the Fugitive Slave Law had been in effect for a month, Torontonians were conferring about what should be done. William McClure noted in his diary that there was a meeting at the Mechanics' Institute on 8 October, but the brief entry offers no information about other participants or the topics discussed. McClure attended another gathering on 22 February at the Rev. Geikie's Congregational church "to make arrangements for forming an antislavery society," and two days later the group reconvened in Willis's Knox College office. These sessions produced a call for a public meeting on the twenty-sixth to "express the feeling of this community on the subject of American slavery," the *Globe* joyously announced. "We are glad this meeting is to be held," the paper stated, for Canadians "should give their testimony on this question, and tell their neighbours that they feel ashamed and indignant that their common civilization, common country, and (alas!) common Christianity, should be outraged by the foulest system of iniquity to be found in the world."[3]

The *Globe*'s wish for a big turnout was fulfilled, for the "largest and most enthusiastic [crowd] ever seen in Toronto" thronged city hall. After Willis's invocation, the audience eagerly endorsed McClure's resolution proclaiming that slavery defied the laws of humanity and the Bible and that its continuance demanded the meeting's best efforts to end it. Seconding the motion, Henry Esson asserted that since slavery was the "common guilt" of the civilized world, even those beyond the United States were implicated. Reflecting the uneasiness that some Canadians felt about intervening in an American issue, Willis returned to this theme with a resolution denying that British North Americans were meddling unnecessarily in a neighbour's affair. They were only exercising the "recognized privilege of humanity," he insisted, by declaring to the world that American slavery was not the usual type of political oppression practised by some nations; it was far worse, a "forced servitude in perpetuity of the helpless poor, unaccused, untried, and uncondemned; imposed on them by a power which they cannot resist, supported by laws in which they have no voice." This, he poignantly reminded Americans – in a veiled reference to the Declaration of Independence – violated the best interest of man, whom God had endowed with the right of "life, liberty and the pursuit of happiness." He developed the point at considerable length, as did the seconder, Peter Brown. But in preparation for establishing contacts with American abolitionists, Adam Lillie and John Roaf wisely carried a resolution praising Americans who raised the antislavery banner as the "truest friends ... of their country."

The meeting then formed the Anti-Slavery Society of Canada (ASC), whose purpose was to end slavery throughout the world by dispensing "useful information and argument, by tracts, newspapers, lectures, and correspondence, and by manifesting sympathy with the houseless and homeless victims of slavery flying to our soil." Predictably, Michael Willis was chosen to head the society, a position he retained throughout its life; William McClure became secretary. Captain Charles Stuart was a logical choice for one of two corresponding secretaries, and Thomas Henning, a Toronto school teacher who was soon to be closely associated with the Browns and the *Globe*, was the other. Henning and Andrew Hamilton, the treasurer, were the only officers who had not been involved in British antislavery. The twenty-eight-member committee included several rising young men from business and professional circles in Toronto, for example, the lawyers Oliver Mowat and John McMurrich, city treasurer A.T. McCord, and various Free Church and Congregational ministers: Roaf, Lillie, Burns, and Geikie. However, with the exception of George P. Ridout, none of the city's old families was represented. Thus, two decades after British and American abolitionists had formed their antislavery organizations, Canada had at last caught up.[4]

The universal condemnation of the 1850 Fugitive Slave Law and the successful founding meeting did not mean that provincial residents were single-mindedly in favour of an antislavery society in Toronto. John Roaf had defended the Canadian society's formation by claiming that the province was like someone who heard a neighbour beating his wife; compassionate observers would intervene to protect the woman, he argued, and the ASC's intrusion into the admittedly American slave problem was similarly warranted.

A correspondent in the Toronto *British Colonist* saw the matter very differently. The offended husband should thrash the intruder, he asserted, for this sort of "meddlesome spirit" caused trouble between neighbours, and it behoved all peace lovers to abstain from such interference. Southerners feared emancipation, the writer explained, because the Jamaican experience had shown that liberated slaves would work for only three or four days a week, ruining the island's economy, and Southerners believed that they would suffer the same fate as a result of emancipation. Canadians should not presume to dictate to them on this difficult question through the medium of an antislavery society, he argued. "We who are so near the border should be especially careful of what we say or do on this question." British North Americans should avoid stirring up "hatred between the white and coloured classes in America, for by so doing we are laying a foundation for a state of things, which we may live to lament and deplore." Let Canadians provide refuge for the escapees, advised the writer, but it would be "futile," "meddlesome and mischievious [sic]" to do more.

Another anonymous correspondent declared that "high metaled" Americans might take offence at the ASC's criticism and might hold onto their slaves even more tenaciously. British North Americans should encourage compensated emancipation – an obligation America could surely afford, observed the writer cynically, for America had wasted hundreds of millions subjugating Mexico. "But, Sir, let us not take up her cause," urged this correspondent, "let her have her own 'sweet morsel,' till she is tired and sick of it – let her enact such laws as she pleases, we should not interfere." The Toronto *Patriot*, the Catholic-oriented *Mirror*, and the Anglican *Church* were similarly censorious.[5]

This criticism did not dampen the ASC's enthusiasm, for Willis and his colleagues quickly arranged a series of antislavery meetings in early April. George Thompson, the gifted British abolitionist orator, was touring New York State at the time, and the society brought him to Toronto, along with Frederick Douglass, the brilliant ex-slave and Rochester editor, and the Rev. Samuel J. May, a Unitarian abolitionist from Syracuse. The meetings were held in St Lawrence Hall, the burgeoning provincial city's new centre of civic pride, with its noble pilasters and elegant cornices surmounted by a splendid gas chandelier. The gatherings were a great success, filling the hall's 1200 seats nightly for over a week.[6]

Thompson's first speech – one of four that he made – was a powerful opening to the eight-day event. He concentrated on building enthusiasm and urging Toronto abolitionists forward. Shrewdly, he flattered his 1200 listeners, congratulating them on forming an antislavery society in their "beautiful, improving, and important city." He warmly recognized fellow campaigners from earlier days in Britain, nostalgically recalling how they had joined hands to end West Indian bondage, and he rejoiced "to find them still alive, active, and vigorous," pursuing antislavery ideals. These ideals never changed, he declared, for "if my brother be held in unjust bondage, [the] message is the same ... 'Break every yoke and let my people go free.'" They had undertaken a worthy task, he assured his audience, and there was not a nobler band of people in the world than the men and women of the ASC and their American cohorts. Slavery was a crime that had to be abolished, and he exulted in the progress towards that goal. Twenty years ago, American abolitionists had been few and despised, he recalled, but now they were numerous and respected for their "intellect ... moral courage and indomitable zeal and perseverance." To Canadians who denied having anything to do with slavery he declared:

We have to do with this question, for it lies at the foundation of your own rights as a portion of the human family ... The slave is your brother and you cannot dissolve that Union. While he remains God's child he will remain your brother. He is helpless and you are free and powerful, and if you neglect him, you are not doing as you would have others do to you, were you in bonds ... You are dwellers on the same continent with three million slaves. Their sighs come to you with every breeze from the South. Oh Haste to help them that this glorious continent may be free from its pollution and its curse.

Thompson's ear-catching phrases, wrapped in the rolling oratory that Victorians prized so highly, set the tone for the week and ensured, with one exception, a well-filled hall.[7]

The second meeting was the only one of the five that was a disappointment. Samuel May had intended to question blacks in the audience about how they were faring in Canada and what their needs were. However, there was limited attendance as a result of confusion over the place, time, and the conditions governing admission, so May used the time instead to counsel the small number of blacks who were there. He asked them to consider how they might help the growing number of fugitive slaves who were congregating south of Lake Ontario in anticipation of crossing the border. He challenged his black listeners to overcome the disabilities they faced because of antiblack prejudice in Canada, urging them to rely as much as possible on their own resources while they cultivated the "various virtues." Douglass spoke too, briefly underlining May's advice; but mainly he argued against the colonization of blacks outside the United States. He pointedly opposed the emigration of fugitive slaves to Canada, maintaining that they were needed at home to lead the fight against the Fugitive Slave Law. This could be effective, he said, if large numbers of blacks resisted to the point of making it dangerous for slavecatchers to ply their trade. To be sure, this might result in bloodshed, but they need have no more compunction about spilling slavecatchers' blood than spilling that of bloodhounds.[8]

Douglass made his main appeal the next night in a speech that rivalled Thompson's address as the high point of the week. As a former slave, he was a novelty to most Canadians and this, together with his reputation as a newspaper editor and superb speaker, gave his speech a special poignancy. American slavery was a strong force, he explained, because it was backed by a unified interest that had almost complete control over the government. The founding fathers had erred grievously by allowing the South to count three-fifths of the slaves when determining its contingent in the House of Representatives. Now this enabled a mere 150,000 slaveholders to use the government's power to protect slavery. Douglass conceded that the North lacked constitutional authority to interfere with slavery; but Northerners were not blameless in the matter, he said, for the nation's military might, which the North helped to finance and control, could be used to maintain order in the South if the slaves rebelled to win their freedom.

In American society, Douglass reminded his listeners, the slave was a piece of property to be bought, sold, and mortgaged; he was "robbed of all rights – deprived of every earthly essential to manhood – stripped of all the prerogatives of human nature, and compelled to find his companionship with the lowing ox and neighing horse, and cut off from the society of man." Douglass urged his audience to make Americans see that British North Americans regarded slavery as a "high-handed, soul damning crime against man and God." Ordinarily, he admitted, citizens of one country should not interfere in their neighbours' affairs, but slavery was a different matter. In the United States, where even the "church, press, and political parties" were identified with slavery, it was right to "bring the moral power of the world to bear upon this wrong with a view to its destruction." This, he stated, was why he had come to Toronto.[9]

May and Thompson continued the meetings the following week after Douglass's departure. The Unitarian minister warned Torontonians to be on guard against Southern efforts to use the current provincial interest in securing a reciprocal trade agreement with the United States to force their silence and inaction on slavery. Southerners, who opposed reciprocity because of its economic benefits to the North, might require Canadians to return fugitive slaves or might close their borders to them as the price of Southern support. On the other hand, May speculated, if Canadians continued to admit fugitive slaves freely, Canada West might be inundated by so many slaves that the province would be unable to accommodate them. Canadians therefore ought to "unite ... with Anti-Slavery men and women of America in with-standing" slavery and the Fugitive Slave Law. The only other choice, he said, was to "renounce humanity, deny your Saviour, and defy the Almighty." But he cautioned that if abolitionists abandoned their campaign to end slavery through moral suasion, it would soon be ended by the "awful process of servile and civil war," and he begged Torontonians to help his countrymen avoid that "horrid catastrophe."[10]

Knowing that some ASC members were still uneasy about interfering in internal American matters, Thompson again sought to allay their fears; the Canadian attack on slavery, he assured them, was a justified departure from the norms of international comity. But the major thrust of his final address was a blistering attack on Henry Clay, the author of the 1850 compromise, for a recent speech before the American Colonization Society. This society, which had been formed in 1817, believed that blacks and whites could never live together amicably, and it proposed to solve the problem by colonizing free blacks in Liberia on the west coast of Africa. This chimerical scheme had achieved only very limited success in the intervening thirty-five years, but there was renewed interest in it as a result of a slaveholder's million-dollar bequest. Some members spoke of equipping four steamers to speed the relocation effort. Clay backed the society, and his speech had invoked divine blessing on colonization, something Thompson depicted as a "cruel scheme of expatriation." Thompson scorned colonization, arguing that it made the "children of American soil outcasts, exiles and lepers" in their own country in order to "gratify the prejudice of an inhuman community calling themselves Christians!" Far from seeking to end slavery, thundered Thompson, the American Colonization Society recognized slaves as the "sacred property of [their] master" to be "eternally unmolested." Clay had argued that deportation was necessary because the high crime rates of freedmen would corrupt American society; yet he also said that it would have a glorious effect in Africa, for the freedmen would carry the blessings of civilization to their 90 million barbarous countrymen. Thompson scoffed at this reasoning: "How can the coloured people be at one and the same time the blackest and the brightest – criminals here – missionaries there? A degraded set here – an elevating race of men there." Subjected to this intense abolitionist rhetoric for more than a week, Torontonians doubtless flocked to the ASC in considerable numbers; but unfortunately no society records exist indicating how many paid the fee of two shillings and sixpence to join the ASC either at this time or later.[11]

One unexpected result of these meetings was to help the ASC chart its course in establishing ties with other antislavery groups. The American Anti-Slavery Society (AAS) and the American and Foreign Anti-Slavery Society (AFAS) invited the ASC to send representatives to their annual meetings later in the spring. This was a potentially divisive matter, as British abolitionists had learned. When Thompson, Douglass, and May had arrived in Toronto, they had discovered in private meetings with the committee that many members had strong reservations about associating with the AAS because of the unorthodox views of some of its members.

Before 1840 the AAS, led by William Lloyd Garrison, had been the only national antislavery body in the United States, but conflict had arisen over a number of matters. One faction believed that the society should abandon the single-minded reliance on moral suasion that Garrison advocated, contending that the society would have to use political techniques if it was to succeed in its aims. These political activists, who included the influential New York–based Tappan brothers, also objected to several practices of the Garrisonians: permitting women to have leadership roles and share platforms with men in antislavery affairs; mixing abolitionism with other reforms, such as women's rights; rejecting traditional Sabbath Day observance; and advocating pacifism. The disagreement became so sharp that the political activists withdrew in 1840 to form the AFAS. An unorthodox radicalism that affronted many mainstream Americans lingered over the Garrisonian wing, making some abolitionists wary of cooperating with them. [12]

The three visiting abolitionists found that these suspicions had taken root among Toronto abolitionists. Douglass reported that a "very energetic discussion" about the "different anti-slavery organizations of this country" occurred when they met with the committee. "It was evident," he said, that "some members of the Committee (perhaps all of them) had had their minds abused by misrepresentations of the character and opinions of William L. Garrison." The tongue of slander had reached beyond America's shores to discredit "one of the noblest advocates of emancipation," he wrote, and the "American Anti-Slavery Society, with its beneficent design and catholic platform, had shared in the fate of its leader. The old charges of 'ulterior objects,' 'sifting in extraneous topics,' 'infidelity,' 'socialism,' and what not, were here to be met on the threshold." May and Thompson vigorously defended Garrison and managed to separate the reputation of the AAS from the unacceptable opinions of some of its members. The closed-door discussion was "brisk on both sides and at times warm, yet good tempered," Douglass reported. Willis proved to be broad-minded, agreeing to work with anyone who sought to overthrow slavery so long as he was not required to "endorse opinions which he considered false and injurious."

This exchange helped the ASC avoid the pitfall of taking sides in the dispute between the two American bodies, and it readily accepted invitations to their annual meetings. Willis was to attend the New York meeting of the AFAS and then join Peter Brown and William McClure in Syracuse for the AAS convention. Willis spoke briefly in New York, but confusion over the date of the AAS meeting prevented a Canadian delegation from being in Syracuse. Anxious not to offend the Garrisonians, Henning carefully explained to May why the Canadians were absent, and he added significantly that as a "whole our Committee do not wish to know any party in the United States by its peculiar and distinctive features and creeds" but would "rather join all parties as fellow labourers in the great cause." Thus, as it established contacts in international antislavery circles, the ASC, guided by the visiting abolitionists' advice, avoided the potentially disruptive step of shunning the influential AAS. [13]

Circumstances also soon forced the ASC to decide whether to support the suggestion that blacks who had settled in British North America should be recolonized in the West Indies. The issue arose in August 1851 when a Baptist minister from Jamaica, the Rev. S. Oughton, visited Canada West and urged blacks to emigrate to the island, where employment supposedly was plentiful and antiblack prejudice was less evident. He consulted the committee, as well as Governor General Lord Elgin, who turned to the society for advice. A month later another Jamaican, William Wemyss Anderson, who was a member of the Jamaican legislature, appealed to participants in a black convention that was meeting in Toronto to consider re-locating in the West Indies, and he asked for the society's support. After considering the question in several meetings, the committee opposed the recommendation. Blacks had expressed no interest in making such a move, the committee's letter to the governor general stated; nor were they likely to improve their circumstances by doing so, for few of them were experienced sugar-cane growers, and Ca-nadian wages were higher than could be expected in the West Indies, even taking into consideration the extra costs that the province's colder climate brought. Moreover, since, in the committee's judg-ment, the former slaves were sober, reliable, and independent cit-izens, they should not be encouraged to depart. [14]

Having the governor general's ear on the colonization question, the committee took the opportunity to express concern about the related matter of Britain's treatment of blacks in the West Indies. The committee explained that slaves who were seized on the high seas and then liberated and sent to the West Indies, in the course of the British navy's efforts to stamp out the slave trade, were being neglected and abused in many places. In some cases, they faced forced terms of servitude for long periods and separation from their families, and some island authorities were refusing to implement the terms of agreements or investigate alleged violations. Moreover, judging by a recent Colonial Office memorandum, there was reason to believe that the British government might adopt policies that would retard the emancipation of American slaves and harm free blacks who went to British colonies in the Caribbean. The Colonial Office memorandum hinted that the British could meet the labour shortage in the West Indies by taking advantage of the desire of the American Colonization Society, as well as some states, to get rid of free blacks; Virginia, for example, was threatening to re-enslave free blacks who remained in the state for more than a year. Favourable terms might attract them to the islands.

In its letter to the governor general, the ASC warned that the presence of free blacks within the slave population was a constant inducement for slaves to escape and was the first line of help when they did. If the British government lured free blacks to the Caribbean, the committee's letter argued, this would reduce the number of slaves who fled and would therefore strengthen slavery. It pointed out that the Colonial Office memorandum envisioned attracting whole gangs of slaves and their owners from Virginia and Maryland under terms which, in the committee's judgment, would be little less than slavery itself. In the proposed plan, before leaving American shores, the slaves would have to agree to "stringent engage-ments for future service" that included losing two shillings a week from their wages for an indefinite period to pay for their freedom. Even free blacks who emigrated would be reduced to servitude for five years while paying two shillings a week to cover transportation costs. "Such proposals seem altogether at variance with the spirit of the Emancipation Act," declared the committee; they were likely to lead to "no other result, than the establishment of a new species of slavery or serfdom in British dominions, for the benefit of American slaveholders." Thus, at the outset of its existence, the ASC forth-rightly opposed the removal of blacks from Canada and warned the mother country to use care in solving the West Indian labour problem lest it inadvertently strengthen slavery and injure free blacks.[15]

In the meantime, throughout the winter and spring of 1851, large numbers of fugitive slaves had continued to flee north, and there was much concern within the ASC about alleviating the suffering of those who arrived destitute. To meet this need, the society issued an appeal for funds and supplies at the beginning of May. How the general public responded is unknown, but Toronto women quickly rose to the challenge. Within a few days they held a meeting in the Mechanics' Institute and formed the Toronto Ladies' Association for the Relief of Destitute Coloured Refugees. Although this was often referred to as the Ladies' Auxiliary, implying that it was a dependent branch of the ASC, the evidence indicates that although there was a close working relationship, the ASC and the Ladies' Association were essentially two independent bodies.

Willis opened the organizational meeting with prayer, but it was the women themselves who chose their chairperson to conduct busi-ness. The officers they elected were often closely related to leaders of the ASC, reflecting the family ties that were characteristic of the antislavery movement in general. President E. Arnold was the wife of the ASC committeeman and future vice-president, John Arnold; Agnes Willis was treasurer; the secretary, Isabella Henning, was Peter Brown's daughter and Thomas Henning's wife. Nevertheless, the Ladies' Association raised its own funds and steered its own course. To raise the money required to implement the relief program, which was their primary objective, the ladies organized an early June concert at St Lawrence Hall. This was so successful that they held another the following January, netting a total of nearly £100 from the two events. Combined with membership fees and incidental donations, this enabled them to carry out their assistance efforts. Careful stewards, the women appointed a weekly visitors' committee that investigated all requests for aid; in this way, they assisted more than one hundred families during the first year.[16]

After sponsoring the three abolitionists in April, the ASC held no further public meetings until fall. The fall meetings were prompted by the appearance in Toronto of a figure who was to make a large contribution to the society's work during the next two years. Samuel Ringgold Ward was the son of Maryland slaves who had escaped to New York. He had been educated by Quakers as a boy and became a teacher in black schools. Later, as a Congregational minister, the energetic young man served two white charges in the state, as well as engaging in many other activities; he used his electrifying rhetorical skill in the temperance cause and as an agent for the AAS and the Liberty party, and he also tried his hand at newspaper editing.

Ward's career changed abruptly in the fall of 1851 when an impromptu speech he made outside the Syracuse jail implicated him in the rescue of the captured fugitive slave, Jerry Henry. Fearing arrest under the 1850 Fugitive Slave Law, Ward fled to Canada. He had met John Roaf some years earlier in New York, and the affable Roaf greeted him warmly and introduced him to the ASC committee, who invited him to address a public meeting in late October. Ward spoke for more than an hour, describing the life of American blacks and the prejudice they faced, and concluding with an "interesting and amusing" account of the Jerry Henry rescue and his part in it. The audience listened with "marked attention" to this "man of intelligence and great abilities as a popular speaker," one newspaper noted, and the ASC spied an opportunity in the making.[17]

The speech's favourable impression, together with a strong endorsement from Samuel J. May, evidently convinced Willis and the committee that Ward could be a powerful force in arousing provincial antislavery sentiment. They encouraged him to lecture for the cause, and he responded to their challenge, possibly with the committee's financial support. In mid-November the *Voice of the Fugitive* jubilantly announced that Ward would travel west after completing his current tour through villages north of Toronto, which ended with lectures at two ASC meetings in Knox Church. Willis was so convinced of Ward's potential that early in the new year he asked the British and Foreign Anti-slavery Society for aid to enable the ASC to retain Ward's services; he compared Ward's abilities as a "speaker and pleader" with those of Frederick Douglass, and he hinted that Ward might be useful in Britain in the future.

It is unclear whether the British society sent funds, but somehow the Toronto committee found the means to employ Ward as its agent until April 1853. By late February the busy campaigner, who was also teaching at the ASC's night school for adults in Toronto, reported that he had travelled widely in York County during the winter, speaking to good audiences in Vaughan, Etobicoke, Markham, and Pickering townships and in the village of Newmarket. In March he concentrated on the western part of York, as well as Peel and Halton counties, and wherever he went the "public mind [was] literally thirst[ing] for the truth, and honest listeners, and anxious inquirers [would] travel many miles, crowd our country chapels and remain for hours, eagerly and patiently seeking the light." He predicted that if the widespread ignorance about slavery could be met with "fair and full discussion, and open and thorough investigation," the apathy about it would soon disappear. [18]

When the ASC gathered at St Lawrence Hall in March 1852 for the annual meeting, there was much satisfaction with its first year's activities. There had been numerous abolitionist meetings in the city, and Ward had carried the torch into a growing number of the province's towns and villages with considerable success. A resolution praised the Ladies' Association for helping more than a hundred needy families find shelter, clothing, and employment, and the annual report noted that illiterate adult fugitives now had the opportunity for elementary education in the society's night school. Anxious to be known in the larger Anglo-American antislavery world – a matter that the Upper Canada Anti-Slavery Society had neglected – the secretary had systematically corresponded with other abolitionist bodies; this ensured an avenue for cooperation, exchange of information, and access to antislavery literature. The committee published 1500 copies of the report.

Other achievements of the society were described at this annual meeting. It was explained that venturing into international antislavery had required Canadian abolitionists to decide whether to associate with the radical American Anti-Slavery Society, some of whose members were tainted for having advocated unpopular social reforms; and that Willis and the committee had wisely decided to cooperate with all opponents of slavery but to avoid endorsing the questionable reforms. This shielded the ASC early in its life from the divisive controversy that the Garrisonians had caused in Britain and the United States. Asked to support recolonization of black settlers in the Caribbean, the committee had refused, and the meeting supported this decision with a resolution that roundly condemned the American Colonization Society as a body "founded, and chiefly supported ... by slaveholders – the worst enemies of Freedom." The meeting was also informed that the committee had boldly warned Britain that the government's eagerness to meet the West Indian labour shortage might retard the antislavery cause in the United States and might even result in the rebirth in the Caribbean of a form of bondage akin to slavery. This, too, was well received. In fact, the only criticism of the first year's achievements heard at the annual meeting was a comment on the treasurer's report. Robert Burns was disappointed that the society had raised only £81, a sum scarcely more than half the revenue of the Ladies' Association. He said that friends of the association would wonder why the amount was not much larger.[19]

During the second year, the ASC gave much less attention to cultivating public interest in Toronto. A close examination of city newspapers reveals only a single public meeting of the society between the first and second annual meetings. This occurred in mid-December 1852 when the featured speakers were John Scoble (the former secretary of the British and Foreign Anti-Slavery Society, who had emigrated to Canada), Henning and Ward. Perhaps the committee believed that, after the previous year's meetings, enough effort had been devoted to educating the city about slavery in order to retain its support. In any case, the society directed its main effort at influencing public opinion in the outlying regions of the province, where Ward continued his work of reducing antiblack prejudice and arousing abolitionist sentiment by holding public meetings. In following this course, Willis was no doubt relying on the strategy that he had seen employed so successfully in the late stages of the British emancipation campaign, when the Agency Committee sent Charles Stuart, George Thompson, and others into the English countryside. By the year's end, the busy agent had delivered 108 lectures.[20]

This resulted in local societies springing up in the wake of Ward's meetings. In some cases they were organized after he left. For example, Ward had held numerous meetings around Windsor in late

August, but it was not until mid-October that the residents, many of them black, organized. They passed the usual resolutions condemning slavery, and then those who were prepared to pay the two-shilling membership fee formed the Anti-Slavery Society of Windsor because, as they said, they were "bound by the law of God and humanity to do all in [their] power" to secure emancipation. Declaring itself to be an auxiliary of the ASC, it planned to hold monthly committee meetings and to sponsor an annual course of lectures on slavery "to meet prevalent fallacies on the question, opposed to scripture as well as humanity." Henry Bibb, editor of the *Voice of the Fugitive* and Windsor's leading black citizen, became president; and a committee of seven, including the spirited Mary Ann Shadd, who was about to launch the province's second black newspaper, was named to assist him. The society soon met again to consider the prospects for fugitive slaves in Canada, and it directed the executive to develop a plan for aiding needy fugitives when they arrived. Beyond this, little is known about how long the society existed or what its other activities were.[21]

At London, Ward participated in forming a society. Near the beginning of his western tour in August 1852, he had preached at the London Methodist New Connexion church of William McClure, whose conference had recently moved him from Toronto. Perhaps his sermon was a particularly effective abolitionist plea, but the mere fact that a black minister of Ward's ability had preached for McClure would have drawn much interest. He returned for two antislavery meetings in early September and spoke with "much eloquence and power," according to London's *Canadian Free Press*, doing "great good" among those who were sceptical about the "mental development" of blacks and doubted the wisdom of trying to educate them, for he was a "living example of what education and mental culture would do for that long despised people." The London Anti-Slavery Society was organized as a branch of the ASC. McClure, who had quickly established ties with the black population, was its president; and Robert Boyd, a Baptist minister recently emigrated from Stirling, Scotland, was named secretary-treasurer. Reportedly, the society occupied itself with measures to rescue slaves and assist arriving fugitives; but as with the Windsor body, there is virtually no concrete evidence about its duration or its work.[22]

Even less is known about three other branches that Ward's efforts spawned. A Hamilton society was organized in March 1853 at a packed city hall meeting at which Ward delivered the main speech, supplemented by the efforts of several area ministers. After passing vague resolutions expressing thanks for the success of the British and Foreign Anti-Slavery Society and the "prospects for usefulness before the Anti-Slavery Society of Canada," the meeting declared that it was "expedient" to form a society in the city, and it forthwith elected officers. However, the *Spectator*, claiming to speak for most Hamiltonians, lamented the "folly and uselessness" of forming the society, and there is no evidence that it ever met again. The Kingston society evidently shared the same fate, although the Rev. R.V. Rogers, the incumbent at St James Anglican Church in the town, served on the ASC committee in 1852. The Grey County Society, although attributed to Ward's efforts, probably received as much encouragement from Charles Stuart, who had recently settled nearby at Lora Bay. It published at least one annual report, although no complete copy of this has come to light. The Anti-Slavery Society of the Town and Neighbourhood of Barrie predated the ASC, but there is no record of its work except for a letter to the secretary of the London [England] Anti-Slavery Society.[23]

While Ward laboured in the townships, the ASC learned that rumours were circulating in Britain and the United States to the effect that Canada West was unsuitable for blacks because of its hostile physical and social climate. Fearing that these "erroneous statements" would create a false impression about the province's abolitionism, the committee sought to counteract them by publishing a statement about the conditions blacks faced in Canada. It claimed that after passage of the Fugitive Slave Law, a wave of 4000 to 5000 uprooted blacks had crossed the line. As was to be expected, many arrived destitute and faced hardship, especially those who came in the fall months without provisions and clothing for winter. The committee's statement asserted that interested parties – slaveholders and their agents – were exaggerating these difficulties in order to discourage slaves from gaining their freedom. In reality, claimed the ASC, employment was plentiful and wages were high enough to enable the healthy who were ready to work to enjoy a modicum of comfort once the initial discomfort of relocation was past. The claim that Canadians were hostile to blacks and that Toronto was a "city of cribs and pens, harsh exemptions, and cruel exclusions" was a "deliberate falsehood, and an atrocious libel." The committee declared that as soon as a slave stepped on Canadian soil, he was forever free and "on a level, in regard to every political and social privilege, with the white man." Blacks voted, freely used transportation facilities, and schools were open to their children, although they might choose to establish their own; they generally had their own churches but could worship with whites if they wished, for there were no barriers to pews or special seats at the communion table. The society insisted that blacks had no cause for grievance in Canada. The only question was whether British North Americans had a good antislavery record, and the committee's answer was an emphatic yes. Many British North Americans, the statement said, had campaigned against slavery for years before leaving Britain, and their philanthropy in Canada West had helped fugitive slaves win homesteads in the Elgin settlement. The ASC and the Ladies' Association had cooperated to raise $1100 the previous year to aid needy arrivals. The committee circulated this spirited defence to several British and American journals.[24]

Willis had also encountered harsh criticism of American abolitionists while travelling in Britain during the year, and as president of the ASC he attempted to deflect it, since it injured the antislavery movement. It was the old charge hurled at the Garrisonians – that many leading abolitionists held unorthodox views and were tainted with infidelity. Speaking in Edinburgh, Glasgow, Belfast, Dublin, and elsewhere, he declared that it was a "libel on America – a grievous misrepresentation" to claim as some did that antislavery agitation was virtually indistinguishable in American circles from opposition to "regular government," Sabbath observance, and the Christian religion. Some of the "best and holiest" men in America, he assured his listeners, were leading the antislavery movement, and to say that most abolitionists were "libertine or infidel" was indefensible. To be sure, a few people in the movement might entertain such ideas, but this was no reason to draw back from the entire cause, for antislavery was the "common interest of humanity, which even an infidel might justly" advocate.[25]

While Ward sought to ignite the hinterland and while the committee wrestled with destructive rumours, the Ladies' Association continued its work. Fewer destitute escapees arrived during the second year, after the first wave of fugitives from the 1850 law had subsided, but relief was still necessary. During the year, the women helped many refugees move from the city to farms in the west of the province, especially to those at Buxton. The women also attempted to influence public opinion. Inspired by a petition sponsored by the Duchess of Sutherland and other British women, the Ladies' Association appealed to American women, in an open letter, to use their influence to end slavery. The letter said that since Canadian women were situated near the border, they could not avoid seeing daily the "bitter fruits" of slavery as fugitives crossed the border. As "sisters, daughters, and as mothers," they implored their American counterparts to end this horrible system, which "deprives its victims of the fruits of their labours; which substitutes concubinage for the sacred institution of marriage; which abrogates the relations of parent and child, tearing children from the arms of their parents, and parents from each other." Recalling the slave trading of their British forefathers, they denied writing in a "spirit of self-complacency" or in order to injure sensitive feelings, insisting that their only purpose was to awaken womanly sympathies with those who were suffering. They begged American women to use the "quiet seclusion of domestic privacy" to "soften the harsh and cruel – to remonstrate with the unfeeling and unjust – to confirm the wavering and encourage the timid." Many slaveholders knew that slavery was sinful, the Canadian women believed, but they lacked the moral strength to act on their convictions; tender words might guide them to the path of virtue. Above all, American mothers should prayerfully instruct their children in the great truth that God had made all nations from one blood. Wielding "great power," the letter declared, American women bore great responsibility, and it pleaded with them to win the "imperishable honour" of ending slavery on American soil.[26]

The society met in March 1853 for the second annual meeting. It recorded resolutions praising the Ladies' Association's relief work and its letter to American women. The previous year's criticism of the 1850 Fugitive Slave Law and the American Colonization Society was renewed. Another resolution severely censured American churches; the continuation of slavery in the United States, it claimed, was "chiefly attributable" to the "unfaithfulness" of the churches in refusing to condemn the institution openly. There was much satisfaction, however, with the publication of *Uncle Tom's Cabin*, for the appearance of this forceful abolitionist book had stimulated renewed interest in Europe in the antislavery movement. The highlight of the meeting was the committee's report on Ward's tours through Canada West. Under his inspiration, antislavery had broadened its appeal in the province, and now the door seemed open for productive cooperation between the parent and its auxiliary bodies. But instead of building on this foundation, the committee decided to take steps to raise funds for the "moral elevation" of the fugitives in Canada. British abolitionists wanted the ASC to send someone to explain to the British public the ex-slaves' situation in the province. The committee, eager to raise money, was glad to respond, and it recommended that Ward undertake a British lecture tour. The annual meeting endorsed the idea.[27]

Ward arrived in Liverpool in mid-April 1853 and contacted various reform societies that might be able to assist his cause, presenting the letters of reference he carried. His acceptance was as rapid as it had been in Toronto, and within a month he was speaking at the annual meetings of several groups, including the British and Foreign Anti-Slavery Society, which was convening in London's Exeter Hall. Soon he was well known to the English public and the object of a friendly press. Sympathetic supporters, headed by the Earl of Shaftesbury, organized a committee to promote his speaking engagements and to handle funds. Ward travelled widely in England, gave at least ten lectures in Scotland, and spent twenty days in Ireland. Initially, his purpose was to spread information about the "antislavery cause in Canada, and the actual condition" of ex-slaves in order to raise funds to "abolitionize" the province and assist destitute fugitives. But British audiences were more interested in aiding the needy than in "abolitionizing" British North Americans, and this became the focus of his speeches. His immense popularity made the tour a resounding financial success. When the Shaftesbury committee met the following April to review Ward's work, it reported that he had raised nearly £1200. When the ASC met in June, it had received £400 from London. Part of this went to pay Ward's costs and to aid refugee relief, and the balance was kept in reserve.[28]

Seemingly, Ward's British tour was the ASC's main activity during the third year, for Toronto newspapers and the abolitionist journals that usually reported such information were silent about antislavery meetings in the city. The 1854 annual report was destroyed with the society's accumulated records when fire swept through a section of Toronto that included secretary Henning's house. Henning's oral report at the annual meeting on 21 June made no mention of any meetings during the year. In fact, after devoting most of his remarks to Ward's tour and acknowledging the Ladies' Association's ongoing relief efforts, Henning confessed that except for unspecified "correspondence and publication," the committee's work had been mainly of a "preparatory character." Now the committee's task, he stressed, would be to decide how to use the newly available British funds.

This inactivity undoubtedly explains why the committee took such care to create interest in the annual meeting. To ensure good attendance, it was timed to coincide with the sitting of the Free Church synod in Toronto, when numerous ministers, laymen, and their wives would be present. Moreover, the Ladies' Association collaborated with the Rochester Anti-Slavery Society to hold a two-day bazaar on 21 and 22 June in St Lawrence Hall to raise money for the Rochester-based *Frederick Douglass' Paper*. Some goods had been donated by English women to a Rochester Anti-Slavery Society bazaar, but they remained unsold, and Julia Griffith, secretary of the American society, brought them to Toronto. The sale netted $230. Douglass, who was present to promote the affair, added his lustre to the annual meeting and remained to give two lectures, filling St Lawrence Hall on both nights.[29]

Despite the flurry of enthusiasm around the 1854 annual meeting, the ASC was no more active in its fourth year than it had been in its third. An unusually severe winter brought a need for more relief, and both the men's and women's groups alleviated a considerable amount of suffering. The women's association had carried on most of the year's work, Henning told the May 1855 annual meeting, even though the men also had adopted the weekly visitation system. There had been no public meetings during the year, and only a "very small amount of local contributions" had come in, Henning admitted, since the committee had been too busy to canvass the city. This did not handicap the society, however, for Ward's tour had brought nearly £1100 to the treasury. Nevertheless, as Henning reminded the society, these funds were earmarked for the fugitives; if the ASC hoped to continue its other efforts – circulating antislavery tracts, sending occasional representatives to encourage other societies, and bringing noted abolitionists to evangelize the province – British North American contributions would have to increase. The society's only new initiative during the year had been to open an antislavery office on King Street. Managed by J.B. Smith, a black Baptist minister from the United States, it was intended to serve as an antislavery clearing house, where arriving slaves could seek aid and get word of friends and relatives; where well-intentioned people who wished to aid or employ the needy might find them; and where those looking for abolitionist information could obtain it. However, Smith left the post after a few months, and the committee closed the office.[30]

Always conscious of political events that affected slavery, the meeting denounced the 1854 Kansas-Nebraska Act. This act repealed the section of the Missouri Compromise barring slavery from the upper portion of the Louisiana Purchase, thereby opening the new territories of Kansas and Nebraska to the institution. Proslavery forces, it seemed, had triumphed once again. But it was the silence of American churches and religious organizations that received the meeting's strongest censure. Willis called American Baptists, Presbyterians, Episcopalians, and Methodists "cold on this great moral interest, or worse than cold – perverse." As well, he applauded those who demanded "stricter principles from Tract Societies" that skirted the slavery question in their publications, and he urged that ties with them be severed unless they abandoned the "faithless compromising policy by which they effect to serve God, in the way of hiding part of his truth, and suppressing testimony against a great national enormity." The secretary's report praised a new York antislavery society for demanding that organizations withhold support from missionary or religious publishing societies that did not openly rebuke slavery. Robert Burns presented these sentiments in a resolution shaming American churches and religious organizations for a policy of not speaking out for freedom, saying that, in effect, this made them advocates of slavery. He specifically cited the American Tract Society for removing all references to slavery from its publications; he said that instead of ignoring this great evil in order to avoid offending slaveholders, the tract society and its sister bodies should lift their testimony against slavery, just as unabashedly as they did for other sins. The committee, despite its full treasury, offered no new plans for the coming year; the women's association's relief work would continue, but by 1855 the frequent public meetings of the early months had tailed off, and meetings were held far less often. After four years, the enthusiasm marking the ASC's formation was waning.[31]

In fact, after the fourth annual meeting, held in the spring of 1855, the full society did not meet again for two years. Seemingly, the only matter the committee dealt with in the intervening period was an unsavoury incident marking the end of its connection with Samuel Ringgold Ward. He had terminated his employment with the committee sometime in the winter of 1854–55, but he remained in England writing his memoirs. In the meantime, John Candler, a Chelmsford Quaker who was greatly impressed by Ward's lectures, had given him 50 acres of land in Jamaica with an option to buy considerably more. Ward accepted the offer, but before going to the West Indies in the fall of 1855, he borrowed £140 from William Baynham, a London tradesman. Evidently, the agent had convinced Baynham that he had £5000 invested in Canada and had promised to repay the loan as soon as Baynham emigrated to the province. The trusting artisan arrived penniless in Toronto with his wife and six children in December, only to learn that Ward had gone to Jamaica.

When the ASC heard the story and discovered that Baynham actually had Ward's promissory note, Henning wrote to Louis A. Chamerovzow, secretary of the British and Foreign Anti-Slavery Society (BFAS) explaining the situation. He inquired if Ward had given the impression while in Britain that he was a man of property, and whether there would be any chance of recovering the sum from the person who had donated the Jamaican land. While denying that the ASC had any responsibility for Ward's action, Henning nevertheless reminded the British secretary that both societies, as well as the antislavery cause in general, would suffer if the information was found to be true. There is no record of Chamerovzow's reply, but evidently it confirmed Henning's fears, for Henning told the British secretary that the Canadian committee would soon meet on the matter. The Toronto abolitionists apparently decided that it was wiser to remain silent than to risk adverse publicity, for Ward was left undisturbed in Jamaica, where he pastored a Baptist church and cultivated his land, dying in poverty in 1866.[32]

Although the committee's interest flagged after resolving the Ward affair, its conscientious secretary remained at his post. Educated at "The Institution" in Belfast, Henning had emigrated from Portadown in northern Ireland to Quebec City about 1842. He intended to study for the ministry at Divinity Hall, Queen's College, in Kingston; but the "Great Disruption" occurred before he enrolled and, having cast his lot with the Free Church wing of Canadian Presbyterianism, he went to Knox College instead. While a student there in the late 1840s, he also taught at Toronto Academy, a preparatory school briefly sponsored mainly by Free Churchmen, and he remained at the school after graduation, staying until 1852 when the academy closed and he joined the *Globe* staff, having married Isabella Brown.

Henning wrote a series of reports on the ex-slaves in the province which appeared in the *British Anti-Slavery Reporter* during 1855–56. The first of these detailed the growth of the Elgin settlement, emphasizing its purpose of discovering whether ex-slaves could prosper as free men if they had access to land. The founding of the Dawn settlement (together with an incisive explanation of its failure) and a description of the black population in the southwestern part of the province near Amherstburg and Malden were examined in succeeding reports. The series concluded in the fall of 1856 with an analysis of the black community at St Catharines and the tireless work of Hiram Wilson.

These articles kept the ASC in contact with the BFAS, even though the Canadian society was not meeting, and informed British abolitionists about the ex-slaves' progress. The other consideration that doubtless prompted Henning's writing was the question about Canada's desirability as a haven for fugitive slaves which had arisen earlier in the decade in Britain. At the time, the ASC had issued a reassuring statement and had directed Ward to address the matter on his tour. Henning's reports, which were probably authorized by the committee, continued this policy.[33]

While the society's well-supplied treasury was no doubt one factor in the committee's decreased activity at mid-decade, there are grounds for speculating that internal friction was also a factor. The evidence is incomplete, but differences of opinion within the committee surfaced over which American religious organizations were at fault for their positions on slavery. In turn, this raised questions about whether Canadian organizations could legitimately maintain ties with them and retain their integrity in the eyes of abolitionists.

A glimmer of dissension appeared at the 1855 annual meeting when Robert Burns, an ASC vice-president, introduced the resolution charging American churches and religious bodies with not denouncing slavery adequately; he stated that the American Foreign Mission Board could be "considered sound upon the question," for at a recent meeting it had rejected a law of the slaveholding Choctaw Indians, among whom it had a mission, which prevented missionaries from teaching black children to read. Moreover, the board, an umbrella group representing several prominent evangelical churches, had endorsed a letter from one of its secretaries, Mr Treat, which described the system of slavery as sinful. However, this did not exonerate the board in secretary Thomas Henning's eyes, and although he seconded Burns's motion, he sharply disagreed with the minister's assessment of the board. Henning welcomed its decision to ignore the Choctaw law barring black children from learning to read; but he saw no reason to congratulate the board for affirming Treat's declaration that the system of slavery was sinful, for Treat's letter also had stated that not every act of slaveholding was necessarily sinful. Nor did Treat believe that the New Testament expressly condemned slavery. This was a crucial oversight on Burns's part, contended Henning, for it meant that the board essentially believed that "slaveholding in itself [was] not sinful," – that only "overt acts" of cruelty towards slaves were sinful – and consequently that slaveholders should not necessarily be excluded from church membership. Such doctrine, Henning declared, "is not and cannot be satisfactory to the consciences of anti-slavery Christians."

Henning emphasized his concern by citing several other examples of American religious bodies' faithlessness on slavery: the Episcopal Methodist press printed 4000 volumes a day 300 days a year, but not a single word against slavery; the Sunday School Union had published a million dollars' worth of books in 1853, but not a line on slavery; and the record of the American Tract Society was even worse. To underline the iniquitous behaviour of the American board, whom Burns had certified, Henning stated that it had just invited the Rev. Nehemiah Adams of Boston, author of the proslavery book *South Side View of Slavery*, to preach to a forthcoming board meeting. Burns did not rise to refute Henning, but the incident showed a difference between the two men, and it must have produced a tense moment at the ASC annual meeting as Henning administered a stinging rebuke to his former Knox College professor.[34]

Had Henning let the matter rest with this speech, there would be less reason for suspecting that it became an issue in ASC inner circles. However, he took the matter to a wider audience in November 1855 with three articles in the *Globe*, which were republished as a pamphlet the following year by John J.E. Linton of Stratford. Linton had no ASC ties, but he was in the midst of his own one-man campaign to rid Canadian churches and societies of their alleged ties with "pro-slavery" American groups. Henning reiterated his indictment of the American Board of Foreign Missions, adding the damning fact that there were twenty slaveholders whom the board had admitted to membership in the Choctaw Mission churches. This proved beyond a doubt, his articles claimed, that the board's seemingly high-sounding 1854 principles were indistinguishable from the mainstream American churches' shoddy practices on slavery. Henning also attacked the American Tract Society and the Sunday School Union, asserting that their literature condemned every sin in the decalogue without saying a word against slavery. They even suppressed and altered the writings of those who ventured to criticize slavery, he said: "Wherever the word 'slavery' occurs, it is struck out, and 'intemperance,' or 'dancing,' or 'novel-reading' or the 'use of tobacco'" was substituted. Canadian Christendom should become better acquainted with slavery in the United States, he declared, so that ties with any religious bodies and mission societies that appeared to sanction slavery or even to view it with indifference could be "studiously" avoided. He concluded by pointedly urging leaders of Canadian "Tract and Missionary Societies to ponder well their actions, whether indeed they may not even in a remote degree be by their silence on the question, encouraging sin and retarding" the day when slavery would end.[35]

Although Henning did not mention it by name, he must have had in mind the Upper Canada Tract Society. In 1854 this Toronto-based organization had appointed an agent, the Rev. Yates Hickey, to establish a provincial colportage system to distribute religious literature. Hoping to employ some twenty agents who were working in Canada for the American Tract Society, the provincial group believed that Hickey would be especially useful because of his close tie with the American body. To promote its efforts and publicize the opening of its Yonge Street distribution centre, the Upper Canada Tract Society held a corportage convention in the city in September, which eighteen agents attended. Thus, by the middle of the decade, the Upper Canada Tract Society had seemingly entered into an informal alliance with the American Tract Society and was systematically circulating – to individuals as well as churches – religious literature that included the suspect publications of both its American associate, the Sunday School Union and the American Board of Foreign Missions. Although Henning had refrained from naming names, Linton's editorial on Henning's articles warned the "Religious Book and Tract Societies of Canada, including the Bible Societies," to "take heed." Linton also denounced Canadian Wesleyan Methodists for their ties with the American Methodist Episcopal Church, and he upbraided Free Church Presbyterians for using material from the Philadelphia publishing house of the discredited Old School Presbyterians.[36]

By challenging Burns at the 1855 annual meeting and by casting a shadow over the Upper Canada Tract Society in his articles, Henning created an embarrassing dilemma for several ASC committee members, since they were also officers of the tract society. Burns, Adam Lillie, and John Roaf, all long-time abolitionists and major figures in the antislavery society, were vice-presidents of the tract society and the Upper Canada Bible Society. Their ASC associate, the Methodist Episcopal clergyman James Richardson, was president of the tract society for a decade, and A.T. McCord was its secretary-treasurer for thirty years. Linton, with whom Henning was associated by the publication of the tract, sharpened the division by also questioning the behaviour of the Presbyterian Free Church and the Congregational Church, both of which were well represented in the ASC. A public dispute was avoided, but the controversy must have created much tension within the ASC, and this may help to explain why there were no meetings of the society for nearly two years after 1855.[37]

From the report the committee submitted when the society met for its next annual meeting in April 1857, it is apparent that except for dealing with the Ward affair, and except for Henning's articles on the progress of the ex-slaves, the ASC had been relatively inactive. The bulk of its work – aiding some 400 to 500 fugitive slaves – had been carried on mainly by the women's association with £450 supplied by the committee. There had been no public meetings, and the committee had not attempted to raise any additional money, since there was still nearly £250 left in the treasury from Ward's tour. If the need for more funds arose, the committee believed that the citizens of Toronto would quickly supply it.

The meeting passed routine antislavery resolutions, the most stirring of which limply stated that it was imperative to continue exerting moral influence for emancipation in order to strengthen the hands of American abolitionists. If the question of Canadian organizations using literature from American societies with unacceptable policies on slavery was still causing friction, it was carefully concealed. There were no references to the Upper Canada Tract Society and its dealings with the American Tract Society, the Sunday School Union, or the American Board of Foreign Missions; instead, in language broad enough to allow people of either the Henning-Linton or the Burns persuasion to read into it their own meaning, British and Canadian churches were abjured to have no dealings with "ecclesiastical organizations" in the United States that were not "walking orderly" on the slavery issue. This may have been a compromise between two factions that could not otherwise resolve their differences, or possibly the Upper Canada Tract Society had had time enough to correct the situation by obtaining its material from British sources.[38]

After this meeting, the ASC was virtually dormant until 1860, when an incident involving the possible return of a fugitive slave jolted it into action. In 1853, John Anderson was sold by his owner, Moses Burton of Howard County, Missouri, for refusing to be whipped after being away from the plantation without permission in order to visit his wife. Rather than being sent "down the river" away from his family, he fled. A neighbouring planter, Seneca T.P. Diggs, chanced to meet Anderson and, suspecting that he was fleeing, tried to apprehend him. Anderson killed the planter in the ensuing struggle. He made his way to the Windsor area where, as a result of his efforts to have his family join him, the Diggs estate located him; but its efforts to have him returned failed, and Anderson lived quietly as a stonemason in the area after 1854. However, his seemingly successful relocation in Canada was interrupted in the spring of 1860, when a fellow black to whom Anderson had told his story became angry for some unknown reason and reported Anderson to the Brantford magistrate William Mathews, who jailed him. Word of this reached a detective firm in Detroit, which contacted the Diggs estate (for it still hoped to retrieve Anderson) and began extradition proceedings. The American secretary of state, Lewis Cass, requested extradition under article 10 of the 1842 Webster-Ashburton Treaty, making this request through the British ambassador, Lord Lyons – who, surprisingly, regarded the matter as routine. Evidently, the British foreign secretary, Lord Russell, did too, for he instructed the Canadian governor general to take whatever steps Canadian law warranted to deliver up Anderson.

In the meantime, Canadian abolitionists had learned of the affair. But although John Scoble managed to secure Anderson's release, it was only to see him rearrested within a week. This time, Samuel B. Freeman, a Hamilton lawyer known for his concern for ex-slaves, won Anderson's release after threatening to bring a charge of wrongful arrest against Mathews, who was so intent on retrieving the fugitive that historians speculate he stood to profit if the extradition took place. Anderson was jailed for a third time, at Brantford in September 1860, when the affidavits for his extradition arrived from Washington. Both Mathews and Attorney General John A. Macdonald believed that there was sufficient evidence of Anderson's guilt of murder to extradite him; however, Macdonald evidently was unwilling to accept responsibility for advising the governor general to return the slave, and he decided to allow Anderson's lawyer to take the case to court and let the judges decide.

Before the case was heard in the Court of Queen's Bench on 24 November, most people in Canada West had paid little attention to it, believing that the government would not extradite Anderson and that he would be discharged. Only the black citizens of Toronto were concerned; they took up a collection for Anderson's counsel. In court, Freeman took the line that if Anderson was to be returned, the judges would have to decide that he would have been found guilty of murder if the act had been committed in the province; and since slavery was not recognized by Canadian law, they must surely conclude that Anderson had acted in self-defence because someone had sought to deprive him of his liberty. At the most, he was guilty of justifiable homicide, which was not an extraditable offence under the 1842 treaty. Therefore, Freeman claimed, Anderson should be discharged.

Initially, Anderson's supporters were optimistic that he would be freed. But when the three judges who heard the case delayed announcing their decision for several weeks, and when the *Globe* hinted that the chief justice, who sat on the case, as well as the attorney general favoured extradition, some concern was expressed. It was during this interval before the decision was announced – a time when the widespread discussion of the case by the provincial press began to sound a note of anxiety – that the long-silent ASC committee stirred into life. It issued a public statement strongly deprecating Anderson's return to Missouri. Such a course of action, the committee declared, would amount to applying the American slave code to Canadian territory, a policy that was "in every sense unBritish, disastrous to the sacred rights of human beings, and irreconcilable with any fair exposition of international law." The authorities must act in the "spirit" of the 1842 treaty, the committee asserted, rather than relying on "what may appear technically to be a possible reading of its letter"; otherwise, "thousands of fugitives" in the province would be in jeopardy. The committee also rejected the notion that Britain had entered into an agreement that intended to "include under the definition of murder, or anything more than homicide (which is not one of the cases for rendition contemplated by the treaty), the violent resistance by a slave, of the attempt to spoil him of what no law under heaven could make to be any other's property but his own." The committee hoped that the court's decision would be "in unison with the dictates of the higher law," and it defiantly announced that "neither the disposition nor the power" would be lacking to "exhaust by appeal from court to court, if necessary, the means of obtaining a righteous verdict."[39]

When, on 16 December, the judges finally announced their decision not to discharge Anderson, Freeman gave notice of intention to appeal, and the ASC swung into action. Henning immediately wrote to Chamerovzow, sending him details of the case, which had been published in Toronto papers, and requesting help. He asked the secretary of the British and Foreign Anti-Slavery Society (BFAS) to find out whether there was any truth to the rumour that the British government, because of its wish not to offend the United States while civil war hung in the balance, was behind the Canadian court's decision, warning that if Anderson was surrendered, Canada would "become a hunting ground [for slaves] equally with the Northern States." The committee then called a public meeting of the ASC. It was as large as any ever held in St Lawrence Hall and lasted for nearly four hours. Willis explained that they had considered calling a meeting for more than a month but had hesitated, not wanting to give the impression of trying to pressure the court. Now, however, the fugitive slaves in the province could be endangered because of the decision to return Anderson, and the committee therefore believed that it was absolutely necessary to declare its feeling on the matter.

The meeting brought together people from a wider spectrum of Toronto society than usually attended ASC functions. For example, Daniel Wilson (a noted professor at the newly organized University of Toronto who, with George Brown thirty years earlier, had been a steward at an Edinburgh Emancipation Society reception for abolitionist George Thompson) offered a resolution the essence of which had echoed and re-echoed in halls from Glasgow to Toronto whenever Canadian abolitionists declaimed. Slavery was "unscriptural and a violation of the fundamental principles of the law of nature," Wilson declared, and it was unjust to call the violence that slaves had to use to defend their own liberty murder, as the court had done in Anderson's case. A resolution presented by John Scoble, whose voice was sure to be recognized in Britain because of his long affiliation with the BFAS, asserted that the British government had never intended the Webster-Ashburton Treaty to be used to extradite fugitive slaves who were charged with crimes committed while in pursuit of their liberty. The meeting ended with an appeal to the administrator of the government to withhold his warrant to deliver up Anderson and to discharge the unfortunate man. Henning wrote to Chamerovzow again after the meeting, stating, "You are alive to the importance of the subject I have no doubt." To underline the urgency of the case, he added that the meeting had warmly applauded the suggestion that the extradition of Anderson "might cause Britain the loss of this province." He enclosed the resolutions for Chamerovzow's use as he saw fit, but asked that Lord Brougham, a leading abolitionist in the House of Lords, be fully informed.[40]

As soon as Chamerovzow received Henning's letter, he convened the BFAS committee. It sent a memorial to the colonial secretary, the Duke of Newcastle, outlining the history of the case and explaining that if Anderson was returned to Missouri, it would place the other 40,000 fugitive slaves in Canada West in jeopardy. The 1842 treaty, the committee declared, had never been intended to facilitate the return of fugitive slaves who were charged with crimes committed while striving to secure their liberty. The memorial ended with a strong appeal to the British government to stand fast for British principles of justice.[41]

Shedding the nonchalance that Russell had displayed earlier, the British government moved quickly. After receiving the BFAS memorial dated 4 January, it sent the first of several "cautionary" dispatches to the acting Canadian governor general, Sir Fenwick Williams, reminding him that Anderson could be extradited only under the governor's warrant and not merely by "action of the law." Anderson's case was of the "gravest possible importance," Newcastle warned, and he doubted whether the Toronto court's action conformed to the British government's view of the 1842 treaty. Williams was instructed not to extradite Anderson until the British government had considered the case further, and he was told to keep the home government fully informed.[42]

Uncertain how the memorial would be received, and unaware of Newcastle's instructions to Williams, Chamerovzow searched for an alternate way to ensure that Anderson would not be returned to Missouri. Legal advisers speculated about using a writ of habeas corpus from an English court to force the case to be heard in England, but they were uncertain whether there were precedents for such a step. When an English barrister found a serviceable precedent and offered to take the case, Chamerovzow informed Newcastle of how he intended to proceed. The government cooperated, since the BFAS had, in the meantime, mounted an effective campaign to inform the public about the case; Lord Chief Justice Cockburn of the Court of Queen's Bench quickly issued a writ ordering the sheriffs of Brant and York counties to deliver Anderson to the British court. Cockburn justified his action by saying that the case affected a treaty that was the mother country's responsibility. This apparently ensured that Anderson's case would be transferred to England if Canadian legal authorities recognized the British court's jurisdiction. In fact, there was no doubt that they would, for York sheriff Fred Jarvis, into whose custody Anderson would be delivered when he was transferred from the Brantford jail at the time of his appeal before the Court of Common Pleas in Toronto, was "heavily with us," Henning informed Chamerovzow, and had given his word. On 12 January a mailboat left for Canada, and Henning had the document in Toronto before the end of the month, in time to give it to Jarvis before Anderson's appeal on 9 February.[43]

Even before the people of Canada West learned of Cockburn's writ, there were complaints about officious British interference in Canadian affairs. However, these were counteracted by the joint efforts of the ASC and the *Globe*. The society held a second mass meeting at St Lawrence Hall in mid-January, at which Gerrit Smith, the New York abolitionist, spoke. While introducing him, Willis reminded Canadians that they had been criticized for interfering in American matters when they spoke out against slavery; but, believing that it was a world question, they had continued to do so; and now Smith had come to speak of the great "question of humanity." Willis implied that British North Americans should see the Anderson issue in the same light and not be too sensitive about British action in the case. Smith reiterated the point indirectly in his two-hour speech, claiming that he was not meddling in Canadian affairs, for in this instance, he said, they were "my concerns as well as yours" and, by implication, Britain's. The *Globe* kept the affair before its readers by reporting the daily developments and by publishing a series of articles from British journals, which argued that Anderson must not be returned, in order to show how much attention the case was getting in Britain. When the *Globe* finally broke the story of Cockburn's writ, explaining that it would take the issue out of Canadian hands by sending the case to England for trial, the newspaper admitted that this would be hard for Canadians to accept, but argued that it was infinitely better than seeing Anderson returned to Missouri, which might be the outcome if the Canadian courts had their way.[44]

When the final act in the Anderson drama unfolded, the writ did not occupy centre stage. The Court of Common Pleas heard the appeal on 9 February, and Henning served the writ two days later, evidently acting on the advice of Anderson's three counsels, whom the ASC probably provided; but when the decision was announced on the sixteenth and the judges discharged Anderson, the document became redundant. The court based its decision on technicalities, the most important being that Anderson was charged with felonious homicide rather than murder, which the 1842 treaty and Canadian law required for extradition. He was freed without the judges deciding on the merits of the case.[45]

The ASC's important role in helping to free Anderson was its last significant contribution to antislavery. When the society met again in 1863, the Civil War had been underway for nearly two years. The influx of needy fugitives had slowed to a trickle, greatly reducing the Ladies' Association's caseload, and there had been no new appeal for funds. After the Anderson affair the committee had had little to do, for events in the United States did not require any special attention. In fact, the 1863 meeting seems to have been called largely to celebrate the progress that had been made towards ending slavery throughout the world, especially in the United States, during the two previous years. Freed by the absence of the once pervasive proslavery influence of the seceded South, Congress had abolished slavery in the District of Columbia and had prohibited it in the territories. The attorney general, in disregard of the U.S. Supreme Court's decision in the Dred Scott case, had recognized the citizenship of blacks, and the administration had negotiated a treaty with Britain that provided for cooperation in controlling the international slave trade. The crowning achievement was Lincoln's Emancipation Proclamation of 1 January 1863, which declared slaves to be free in the still-unconquered Southern states. The military contest still had not been decided, Willis admitted, but Lincoln's proclamation meant that slavery's days were numbered. A resolution called on all friends of freedom to reject the "oppression of caste" that prevented blacks from "rising in the community according to their talents, industry, and moral character," sometimes even on British soil; the committee was directed to convey these sentiments to President Lincoln. Before adjourning, the society elected new officers, but there is no record that the ASC met again.[46]

THE PATIENT ANTISLAVERY JOURNALISM of the Browns and the presence of British antislavery veterans had combined to secure the formation of the ASC when the 1850 Fugitive Slave Law forced large numbers of escaped slaves to flee to Canada West. At the outset, the committee wisely avoided the danger of dividing the young society over whether to cooperate with the radical Garrisonians by affirming its willingness to work with all opponents of slavery. It also rejected the temptation to support the recolonization of fugitives in the West Indies, viewing with scepticism the suggestion the ex-slaves would face less discrimination and have better working conditions there than in British North America. Instead, the ASC enthusiastically started a two-front abolitionist campaign that envisioned providing assistance for destitute fugitive slaves and capturing public opinion for the antislavery cause.

Initially, the effort to win the support of public opinion was successful, with the large public meetings in Toronto and with Ward's tours through the countryside, which led to the formation of several local antislavery organizations. This prepared the way for cooperation between the parent and auxiliary societies; for instance, antislavery celebrities who were brought to evangelize Toronto audiences could travel the circuit under joint sponsorship; and when women's groups modelled on the Ladies' Association were organized, the two-front offensive that worked so well in Toronto could be applied throughout the province. Ward's success with the local committees made him the logical person to coordinate such a program, and in retrospect the decision to send him to Britain appears to have been a tactical error. Evidently, the committee believed that his example would have a beneficial impact on the aspiring slaves; it would also promote antislavery, for by exhibiting a black man of Ward's unquestioned ability, the ASC could undercut the belief that it was pointless to try to educate blacks. Then, too, there was the money that could be raised by his tours. All this was undoubtedly true, but the committee failed to see the potential risks.

Ward's mission drew the ASC's attention away from the auxiliary bodies, and the financial success of the venture in Britain reduced the necessity of holding public meetings – which were vitally important to maintaining public interest – in order to enlarge the membership and replenish the treasury. The committee was able to drift, comfortable in the knowledge of its success during the first three years, while the fledgling regional bodies withered on the vine for want of nourishment from the parent society, which did not keep them well provided with abolitionist speakers to build local interest. Public antislavery meetings virtually ceased after 1855. Moreover, being under stress, in all likelihood because of conflicting views about maintaining ties with American religious bodies whose views on slavery were suspect, the committee lapsed into relative inaction after the middle of the decade, and the momentum of the early stages of the campaign to shape public opinion subsided.

The efforts of the Toronto abolitionists to ease the suffering of the arriving fugitives were more constant. The Ladies' Association, relying on its own funds as well as on the money that Ward had raised in Britain, kept the second front alive throughout the decade. By 1863, when the ASC ceased to function, more than a thousand fugitive slave families had benefited from this work.

Despite being virtually invisible (if not completely inactive, except for the relief work) for more than three years, the ASC quickly mobilized its force in response to the Anderson crisis in 1860. The meetings and public statements, together with the *Globe*'s numerous articles – some of which were certainly written by Henning, who worked for the paper – aroused a lethargic public opinion on the issue and clearly shaped the environment in which the court made its decision. Moreover, Henning's urgent appeal to Chamerovzow helped to awaken a seemingly indifferent British government to the seriousness of the case, with the result that it instructed Williams not to extradite Anderson without Newcastle's approval. Unaware of the Colonial Office instructions, and determined to do all possible to prevent Anderson's extradition in view of the grave Canadian plea, Chamerovzow secured the writ of habeas corpus, which Henning had an important hand in implementing and which would have been invaluable if the appeal had gone against Anderson.

Having played a central role in Anderson's release, the ASC evidently believed that its work was essentially finished by the time of Lincoln's proclamation. The society celebrated the event and elected a new slate of officers, giving the impression that its efforts would go on. But the committee offered no new plans in 1863 and was apparently oblivious of the fact that the rapidly rising number of freed slaves in the continuing Civil War meant that there was still much work to be done.

# 7 The Church and Antislavery

The church was a force to be reckoned with in nineteenth-century Canada, and it undoubtedly played a larger role in determining thought patterns, in shaping behaviour, and influencing political affairs than the church does today. Society took the church's centrality for granted, indirectly recognizing its position in various ways; for example, the nominal census data listed religious affiliation for each person, assuming that church association was virtually universal. Widespread participation in the life of the church in effect made it a microcosm of the larger society: its attitudes and responses to issues and events both shaped and reflected the values and behaviour of the people of Canada West. Consequently, an analysis of the church's reaction to antislavery can reveal much about one of the main influences that shaped the Canadian response to the movement, as well as providing a cross-sectional image of provincial thought on the subject.[1]

IN EARLY 1852, SAMUEL RINGGOLD WARD wrote that, on the issue of antislavery in British North America, "Catholics, Episcopalians, and Kirkmen, with some rare and brilliant exceptions, walk by on the other side after the most approved manner of modern Pharisaism." Ward probably arrived in Canada too late to know of the work of the Roman Catholic layman, Thomas Rolph (unless he counted the English doctor as one of the "brilliant exceptions"), but his graphic metaphor accurately depicted the Catholic church's response to the issue of slavery. There is no evidence that the church issued episcopal pronouncements on antislavery or took any action to aid the fugitive slaves. Its usual spokesman, the Toronto *Mirror*, mentioned neither the Stuart-Willis antislavery meetings nor John Roaf's concurrent efforts in 1846 to form an antislavery society in the city. However, four years later, the *Mirror* did condemn the Fugitive Slave Law, if somewhat apologetically. Ordinarily, declared the paper, it was "scarcely legitimate" for Canadian journals to comment on so delicate an American issue as slavery; but when confronted with such an abomination as the 1850 act, "all national distinctions must give way" and one must exercise the "right to speak and write, not as the subject or citizen of any particular country, but as a member of the human family." While insisting on his deep respect for American political life, the editor declared this "peculiar institution of slavery we do detest."[2]

The *Mirror*'s indignation had cooled noticeably by the time the Anti-Slavery Society of Canada (ASC) organized, for it questioned whether Canadians should even raise the issue of slavery. A "mixed" audience crowded city hall when the society was formed, the paper disdainfully reported; Methodist and Presbyterian clergymen lined the platform, and a few ladies were present, but the "great bulk of our respectable citizens were absent, not caring, we presume, to take part in a movement that had the aspect of direct interference with the internal institutions of a government with which we are on most friendly terms." Certainly, slavery was an evil of the "gravest kind" whose end must be prayed for and vigorously encouraged, but since it was so firmly entrenched, any "sudden bursting of the chains" could bring even "greater evils than those which it might seek to remedy," and therefore emancipation must be handled carefully. Liberation must come gradually, the paper declared, through "more culture and Christian influence" rather than by immediate release, as abolitionists desired. Slavery was deeply rooted in man's interests and ideas, as St Paul had recognized, and that was why he had treated it so "guardedly." Canadians should take heed.[3]

The *Mirror* gave George Thompson a chilly reception after his antislavery lectures in Toronto in the spring of 1851. Thompson and his followers were unwise to encourage slaves to escape and citizens to disregard the Fugitive Slave Law, the paper stated, for they were placing their opinions above the combined wisdom of society's duly constituted laws. This would undermine the very cornerstone of civilization and bring anarchy. Moreover, if Canadians counselled others to break American laws, regardless of how evil the laws were, this might establish precedents that they would live to regret. Canadians did more harm than good by remonstrating against slavery, the editor believed, for such criticism only made slaveholders more defensive. "Let us take care that our benevolence is not converted into an instrument of torture," the *Mirror* cautioned, "wherewith to scourge the slave – that our sympathy is not made an excuse for imposing heavier burthens upon his shoulders." The paper took no further notice of ASC activity throughout the decade.[4]

AT MIDCENTURY, ANGLICANISM in Canada West was centred in the Diocese of Toronto, headed by Bishop John Strachan. In 1851 the diocese was empowered to sit as a synod to discuss policy and conduct church business. The church's other important arm was the Church Society of the Diocese of Toronto, which had been organized in 1843. Sanctioned by the bishop, this annually elected body of clergy and laymen met monthly to handle a wide variety of church matters, including distribution of religious literature, missionary work among Indians and remote settlers, and assistance for clergy and their widows and orphans, and for theological students. Strachan opposed slavery and was personally well disposed towards blacks. As a young teacher in Kingston early in the century, he had written against racial prejudice and had even volunteered part of his salary to help organize a school for black children when discrimination barred them from common schools. But his opposition to slavery and prejudice did not translate into a broad policy of support for abolitionism by Canadian Anglicans. Not once before the end of the Civil War did the synod or the Church Society discuss antislavery or assistance to the fugitive slaves, although these bodies dealt with numerous other social issues.[5]

The silence and inaction of the synod and the Church Society left it to the *Church* – the voice of high Anglicanism, published by the diocesan press in Toronto – to speak for the denomination on antislavery. This journal clearly attacked slavery and opposed discrimination against fugitive slaves. For example, in early 1850 it berated the Toronto *British Colonist*'s criticism of the Canadian government for selling land to the Elgin Association. No grounds existed for the government to refuse the transaction, the *Church* declared: "Black skin and thick lips were merely physical flaws," and they did not disqualify fugitive slaves from acquiring land any more than a "club foot or hare lip" barred other men from acquiring land. One of the glories of the British constitution, claimed the editorial, was that it protected "Anglo-Saxon and Hindoo – the Hottentot of Africa and the Redmen of North America" without distinction. Had the government succumbed to the demands of the western opponents of the Elgin Association, the *Church* declared, it would have been no better than the Spanish Inquisition. With "Scots, Irish, French, and German settlements" in the province, the paper asked, "Why may we not have an African settlement?"[6]

Although it demanded fair play for the fugitives, the *Church* was unsympathetic to abolitionists. An inkling of this appeared in late 1849 when Ohio abolitionists aroused the journal's ire. An Oberlin antislavery convention had passed a resolution rejoicing at the alleged decline of religion among the "popular churches" of the United States as reflected in the diminishing number of revivals and seminary enrolments. This was a blessing, the resolution claimed, for these same churches had long frustrated the slaves' hope of liberty by refusing to condemn slavery and by continuing to fellowship with slaveholders. The convention welcomed the churches to a "speedy and ignominious grave," saying that their passing would make way for true churches to sound a clear signal against slavery and would hasten the day when man no longer shackled his fellow man. These "satanic sentiments" outraged the *Church*, which stated that only infidels would welcome the decline of churches with such "demonic glee." The journal's reaction seems to have been an attempt to discredit abolitionists by associating them in the public mind with infidelity.[7]

The *Church* held its fire while the ASC organized but broke silence when Douglass, Thompson, and May appeared at the Toronto antislavery meetings in April 1851. It agreed with the *Patriot* and *British Colonist* that Canadians had no mandate to concern themselves with American slavery, and, like the *Mirror*, declared that Canadian interference would do more harm than good. Forming an antislavery society in the province was "utterly uncalled for," the editorial stated; the slaveholder would not be cajoled into freeing his slaves by the "remonstrances of a junto of foreigners who brand him as an insatiable blood-hound" and advocate treating him as a "beast of prey [to be] done to death like a wolf," as Douglass had called for. Such "anti-Christian ravings" in the province were a disgrace, transforming noble Britannia, the symbol of "virtuous liberty," into a "savage gore-soaked thug."

The *Church* also ridiculed Thompson's claim that Canadians were morally obliged to denounce slavery, since their opposition was already well known by the fact that every slave who reached Canadian territory was automatically free. This "silent, standing protest" would be more effective in reaching the slaveholder's conscience than the "violent and outrageous" denunciations heard at Canadian antislavery meetings. The slaves had "no sterner enemies," declared the *Church*, than the abolitionists who advised them to ignore the law in pursuit of emancipation, for this would promote "pandemonium" and the collapse of society. Let Canadians "strain every nerve" to aid fugitive slaves by giving them employment and serving their spiritual needs, urged the journal; they might even establish a fund to compensate slaveholders for emancipating their bondsmen, although the *Church* doubted that it would be of any practical value. At all events, British North Americans should avoid any further involvement with abolitionism or interference on the American side of the question.[8]

Anglicans heard no more on slavery from their paper for a year. However, in August 1852 the journal, renamed the *Canadian Churchman*, published a letter from "Alpha" calling on the church to advance the fugitive slaves' moral improvement. The letter pointed out that many of the fugitives arrived in the province untutored, yet, except for a few isolated cases, their religious training came from "perverted sources" because Anglicans ignored them, even though the Anglicans had missions to the Indians. If the Church Society would take up the challenge, Alpha predicted, church services and Sunday schools for blacks would spring up in the larger cities; Alpha even envisioned the day when blacks would take holy orders in the church. The *Churchman* supported Alpha's plea. It was not enough, claimed the journal, merely to open the church's privately owned pews to the newcomers; the fugitives' special needs cried out for help, and Torontonians should build a chapel for them. A dozen devoted individuals could raise the sum in a week. Endowing support for a minister might be more difficult, but there were hundreds of Anglicans who believed that the church was "signally to blame" in the matter and were anxious to remove the stigma. The *Churchman* joined Alpha in urging the Church Society to rise to the challenge.[9]

The answer to slavery, in the *Churchman*'s view, lay in providing just compensation for the owner. It made this point when Canadian women, following the Duchess of Sutherland's lead, sent their public letter across the border in 1853 asking American women to use their influence to end slavery. Surprisingly, the *Churchman* approved of this step, but it tempered its plaudits by expressing regret that the address had not called for compensation. This had been the fatal error of abolitionists all along, said the journal. With "burning eloquence" and "withering sarcasm" the abolitionists described the slaves' suffering and the owners' cruelty; but their ill-considered denunciations overlooked the injustice of asking slaveholders to relinquish property without remuneration. The ladies' letter had repeated the mistake, the *Churchman* stated, for in effect it asked Southern women to accept "patrimonial ruin." Yet Southerners could no more afford to sacrifice their holdings than the Duchess of Sutherland could be expected to abandon the rent from her Scottish estates. Canadian women should therefore correct the error and should give their letter credence in Southern eyes by recalling and amending it to advocate just compensation.

This insistence on remunerated emancipation brought Anglicans into conflict with some Canadian abolitionists who opposed compensation. In the latter's view, compensation would legitimize the slaveholder's claim to the right of holding property in the form of another human being. Hence it was unacceptable.[10] The *Churchman* also disagreed with most Canadian abolitionists on the question of fellowshipping. As we have seen, the ASC was in principle opposed to the retention of ties with churches and other bodies that did not openly denounce slavery. The *Churchman* did not directly attack the ASC on this issue, but it derided J.J.E. Linton's antifellowshipping campaign, saying that his claims, that churches maintaining ties with denominations who welcomed slaveholders were actually proslavery, were largely "imaginary." In the journal's opinion, American Episcopalians had followed the right course; by remaining "far from the division and angry strife" that enveloped antislavery, they had preserved denominational peace and harmony.[11]

Although in 1852 the *Churchman* had reminded Anglicans that they should serve the spiritual and educational needs of the fugitives, nothing concrete was done for two years. Then, under the inspiration of the Rev. Marmaduke Dillon, the West London Ladies' Association (England), whose husbands included some prominent British antislavery men, asked the Colonial Church and School Society to evangelize the ex-slaves in Canada West. It was proposed that this missionary wing of the Anglican church in Britain would organize three schools, with male and female teachers for each, and appoint two missionaries to travel among the people. The estimated cost of £2000 for the first year and from £1000 to £1500 annually thereafter was to be carried by the Ladies' Association. The society backed the idea and proceeded with the project in early 1854. It hired Dillon, a missionary experienced in Antigua, to implement the scheme, and he brought with him a black layman named R.M. Ballantine and two black teachers, Mary Anne and Sarah Titré. This team arrived in Toronto in August and, after receiving warm encouragement from Governor General Lord Elgin and Bishop Strachan, presented its plan to blacks in the city. Initially, there was some hostility from black leaders because they objected to the establishment of a school exclusively for blacks. However, when Dillon decided to locate the mission in London and open the school to all children, the opposition dissipated.[12]

The project moved forward rapidly. The first school was opened in November 1854 in a large room at the London artillery barracks, with the Titré sisters in charge under Ballantine's supervision. Within a week, fifty children were attending, whites as well as blacks, the community having accepted the racial mixing of students and the idea of having black teachers for white children. A second school opened in January, when older children were sent to a room provided by Benjamin Cronyn, the rector of St Paul's Church. These children were under Sarah Titré's management; sixty-one appeared on the first day, and the room soon reached its capacity. There was so much interest in the two schools that Dillon shortly reported that there were 430 applications for only 250 places. Two more teachers soon joined Dillon and his assistants: John Hurst, a master at the society's Central School in Newfoundland, and Miss J. Williams, who was from the society's training facility in England. To cooperate with the mission and find more space, Cronyn organized a local committee that recommended erecting a brick building at a cost of £1200; but this became unnecessary when the military authorities released more rooms at the barracks and the local committee raised money to equip them. These changes enabled the mission to accommodate 450 students.[13]

At the peak of its operations, the London mission workers carried a heavy load, which included separate schools for young children and for older boys and girls, a school for adults, a Sunday school requiring nearly thirty teachers, weekly sessions for adult females, and cottage lectures. In these circumstances, it was not surprising that Dillon, whose health had been poor before he came to Canada, soon showed signs of physical exhaustion. The trouble began at the end of 1855 when the parent committee cautioned Dillon to reduce expenditures because the treasury was low, and he unwarrantedly accused the sponsors of criticizing his work. Matters worsened when friction developed between Cronyn and Dillon after the London rector's son suddenly purchased a prime site on which Dillon had hoped to build a permanent school. In the midst of these developments, the exhausted Dillon exhibited questionable behaviour that led to charges of profanity and drunkenness. An investigation by a commission that Bishop Strachan appointed cleared the beleaguered missionary of these charges, but he resigned pleading poor health. At the same time the Titré sisters, unaccustomed to the harsh Canadian climate and doubtless weakened by overwork, contracted tuberculosis and were sent back to Antigua under a physician's orders. Despite these serious setbacks, the Colonial Church and School Society's mission to the fugitive slaves carried on until 1858, when the London common schools were opened to all without discrimination. [14]

On balance, mainstream Anglicans, while advocating fair play and some assistance for the fugitive slaves, had little use for antislavery. However, there was an evangelical Low Church faction that identified with abolitionism. Its mouthpiece was the *Echo and Protestant Episcopal Recorder*, published in Port Hope in the early 1850s by William Furly, and later in Toronto. "SIGMA," an anonymous correspondent to the periodical who was almost certainly an evangelical Anglican, claimed to have helped organize the Anti-Slavery Society of Canada (ASC), and at least two evangelical Anglican clergymen – Alexander Sanson, the incumbent at Trinity Church in Toronto, and R.V. Rogers, the minister at St James Church, Kingston – were board members. Unlike the *Church*, the *Echo* lionized George Thompson as an "eloquent advocate" of slaves' rights, and it similarly praised Frederick Douglass. The ASC under Willis had done "much good," the *Echo* claimed, and it believed that Samuel Ringgold Ward's lectures would contribute solidly to antislavery. The journal kept its readers informed of Canadian abolitionist affairs early in the decade, printing sympathetic accounts of events such as the Ladies' Association's fund-raising concerts and giving a summary of their first annual report. It attacked the U.S. Supreme Court's decision in the 1857 Dred Scott case, which denied citizenship to blacks, and hoped that this would spur abolitionists to redouble their efforts and cause hitherto reticent American clergymen to denounce slavery fearlessly from their pulpits. Unfortunately, because of discontinuous files, it is impossible to determine whether the *Echo* carried on its antislavery editorials later in the decade. [15]

IF WARD'S ASSERTION THAT THEY "walked by on the other side" required some qualification in the case of Anglicans, it was not far from the truth in the case of the Presbyterian Church in Canada in Connection with the Church of Scotland, or the "Kirk" as it was commonly known. The senior branch of Presbyterianism in the Canadas had become largely autonomous in 1831 when a Canadian synod was formed consisting of four presbyteries: Quebec, Glengarry, Bathurst, and York. From 1831 to the end of the Civil War, the *Acts and Proceedings of Synod* did not apparently mention slavery even once. Two Kirk ministers, William Rintoul and David Ferguson, were associated with the Upper Canada Anti-Slavery Society before its collapse, but at least one of them left the denomination during the "Great Disruption." For a short while in the late 1830s, the *Christian Examiner* was published in Niagara to represent the church interest. It contained one lone item on slavery – an imaginary converstion between two friends attempting to show that slavery contradicted biblical doctrine; however, the article made no mention of American slavery or abolitionism.[16]

The other main group of Presbyterians in the province in the 1830s sprang from the United Associate Synod of the Secession Church in Scotland. In 1834 it organized as the Missionary Presbytery of that body in Canada, and in 1843 became an autonomous synod with three presbyteries – London, Flamboro, and York – which Canada East (Quebec) joined the following year. The name was changed in 1847 to the Synod of the United Presbyterian Church in Canada in Connexion with the United Presbyterian Church in Scotland. By the mid-1850s the United Presbyterians, as they were generally called, had about 7000 members and an average attendance of just under 14,000 among their 93 congregations. They were strongly voluntaristic and counted many Irish and Americans among their adherents.[17]

United Presbyterians attacked slavery in their synod and in their denominational monthly, the *Canadian United Presbyterian Magazine*. In 1853 the synod declared its "unqualified and unmitigated abhorrence" of slavery as being "repugnant in the light of reason, the principles of natural justice, and the spirit and precepts" of Christianity. It deplored the fact that some American denominations "connived" at slavery, virtually giving it their approval by allowing "church members and even office bearers" to participate in the practice; but the resolution praised churches that excluded slaveholders, asserting that United Presbyterians considered it an honour to cooperate with such bodies in their stand against slavery. The following year, when the Upper Canada Tract Society established its colportage system in partnership with the American Tract Society, the *United Presbyterian* voiced strong disapproval. It pointed out that the American organization had a record of suppressing antislavery sentiments by removing all allusions to slavery from its publications, and it said that the Canadian society should not tolerate this "connivance and obsequiousness" with slavery. Such "abominable conduct" would ruin any praiseworthy project in a British province, the magazine warned; the Upper Canada Tract Society ought to steer clear of this danger, for it would wreck the organization's otherwise laudable work and all "right-hearted men" would be bound to cheer. [18]

The United Presbyterian sharply attacked slavery again in 1861, when it commented on recent statements by three American clergymen. The first, an anonymous Southerner of alleged distinction, had proclaimed that the South must preserve slavery as a duty to the civilized world and in the "cause of God and religion." "Shame!" cried the magazine. "Woe awaits that land whose people could listen to such sentiments with approbation or even with tolerance." A Buffalo minister, John Lord, provoked the journal's scorn for defending the founding fathers' compromise on slavery in the constitution, when the prevailing belief had been that slavery would gradually die out. Lord preached that slavery served a useful purpose in the short run as a means of introducing "inferior and indolent races" to civilization, and he maintained that it would disappear when it was no longer needed to perform this task. In these circumstances, slavery was beneficial, he said, the Fugitive Slave Law of 1850 was necessary, and immediate abolition would be harmful. The United Presbyterian's reaction was to state that such views might be "somewhat" satisfactory if there was any hope that slavery would end from natural causes, but this was wishful thinking; it contended that these "moderate views" were "essentially proslavery" and were utterly unworthy of a "clear-headed man, and faithful minister of the gospel." [19]

Even more revealing of the United Presbyterian's antislavery attitude was its response to the temporizing of the Princeton theologian and editor of the influential Princeton Review, Charles Hodge, in an 1861 article. Hodge had praised the wisdom of the Fugitive Slave Law and he begged Southerners not to leave the Union, pleading with them to see that not all Northerners were dangerous abolitionists as the Southerners seemed to believe. This caused the United Presbyterian to express its grief that America's leading theological review – not to mention its Presbyterian identity – could voice such rankly proslavery sentiments. It cited a critique of Hodge's article by Dr Guthrie, a respected Edinburgh minister, which flayed Hodge and the American churches for not attacking slavery openly and called them "rotten at the core." Guthrie's response to Hodge's plea to the Southerners was to say that he would gladly see the Union split, however unwelcome this might be, if it brought an end to slavery. It was true, he admitted, that most Northerners, including religious newspapers, were not abolitionists, but that was no cause for hope, as Hodge had implied. Among the nation's entire 3000

Old School Presbyterian clergymen – supposedly the "very sound Presbyterian clergymen" – Guthrie doubted that there were even a dozen abolitionists. The magazine's agreement with Guthrie shows how fully United Presbyterians shared the antislavery beliefs that were characteristic of Canadian abolitionists.[20]

A third important branch of Presbyterianism appeared in Canada West at the time of the "Great Disruption," when in 1844 nearly one-quarter of the Kirk membership followed the example set in the homeland and seceded. They formed the Presbyterian Church in Canada, commonly called the Free Church. This aggressive new body grew quickly to become the second largest Presbyterian communion in the province. In 1861, when the Free Church and the United Presbyterians joined together, the former had 140 ministers to the latter's 70, and it nearly equalled the Kirk in size.

In addition to being voluntary and evangelical, the Free Church was strongly antislavery virtually from its inception. As already noted, the Free Church *Banner* began campaigning against slavery in 1843. In the spring of 1845 the new synod received an overture on the subject from the Toronto presbytery. Almost certainly Robert Burns was the guiding hand, for he had just arrived in Toronto from Paisley to fill the pulpit at Knox Church, and he presented the proposal to the synod in a long antislavery speech, which he accompanied with several resolutions. After several other ministers had given speeches, the resolutions were referred to a committee for revision and for the drafting of a letter that would accompany the resolutions when they were sent as a remonstrance to the general assembly of the Presbyterian Church (Old School) in the United States.[21]

The resolutions protested that 3 million human beings were enslaved in the United States by slaveholders who claimed the right to buy and sell them as pieces of property. In the process, the owners regularly split families, dividing husbands from wives and parents from children. The "rearing of slaves" for market was a common practice. Injustice and cruelty always attended slavery, and cases of kindness by a few individuals did not mitigate that fact. Some states barred citizens from teaching slaves to read, thereby withholding from them knowledge of the scriptures, in direct contradiction of the Bible's injunctions and the right of conscience, and imposed heavy penalties on offenders. The church must protest these evil practices and must advocate their removal, the resolutions stated, but many American churches, "particularly the Presbyterian, [had] manifested a sinful apathy in regard to these evils." The synod's indictment specifically cited the general assembly of the Presbyterian Church (Old School) for its action in May 1845, when by a nearly unanimous vote, the assembly had declared that it was not its duty to take any action on slavery, since the church had been founded on the assumption that slaveholding was no bar to communion, and since discussion of the issue threatened to divide the denomination.

These resolutions, especially the fledgling Canadian synod's willingness to rebuke such a prestigious fellow Presbyterian body, reflect the strength of the Free Church's abolitionism. There is no record of the general assembly's response, but it could not have been satisfactory, for the synod returned to the antislavery issue in 1851 with continued criticism of the American churches. Michael Willis, who like Burns was a veteran of British antislavery, introduced an overture with an antislavery speech. His resolutions attacked slavery for ignoring the right of contract and for violating the slave's natural rights and reducing him to mere chattel, thereby dishonouring the Creator. Willis contended that by interfering with the "natural relationships of domestic life," the slaveholder contemptuously arrogated to himself absolute power over the conscience of his bondsman, whereas Christian doctrine made each individual responsible to God. As God's earthly spokesmen, said Willis, Christians and churches were called to witness against a system that so obviously violated divine commands; failing to do so would incur a "large share of the responsibility and guilt" for the effects of such practices. The synod resolved to appeal to American churches again in the hope of encouraging those seeking to redress this "crying oppression" and of bringing conviction to those who were "otherwise minded"; it appointed Willis to the committee to handle the correspondence.[22]

Willis's committee presumably sent these resolutions with a covering letter to the American general assembly, as the synod directed; but from the resolutions he offered when reporting in 1853, it is not clear that a reply was received. His motion at the time regretted that American churches generally refrained from forthrightly denouncing slavery, and it alluded to the "inadequate effect" that British and Canadian responses had had on them. Seeking to avoid being a "partaker in other men's sins," the synod now charged its ministers and churches to take every opportunity to awaken the consciences of "professing Christian slaveholders" but to avoid communing with "ministers and congregations avowing or known to be supporters and defenders of this national iniquity." Thus, while it heartily rejoiced with "Christian societies and individuals in the American

Union, who [had] perseveringly contended against slavery," the synod severed ties with offending churches. Notices to this effect were published in Canadian and American newspapers.[23]

As well as asserting its hatred of slavery and ending ties with churches that failed to do so, the Free Church was at the centre of efforts to assist fugitive slaves as they settled in the province. The Toronto presbytery, it will be remembered, supported William King's plan to found a settlement for fugitive slaves in Canada West on his return from Louisiana in 1848, and encouraged him to present it to the synod. As an ecclesiastical body, however, the synod believed that such an undertaking was outside its proper sphere of activity, but, favouring the plan, it appointed a committee to help King publicize the scheme. The *Ecclesiastical and Missionary Record*, the denomination's journal, cooperated, and the result was the formation of the Elgin Association, which succeeded in implementing King's plan. In addition, the Free Church contributed to the successful venture by establishing the Buxton Mission at the Raleigh Township site in order to meet the settlers' spiritual and educational needs.

In the spring of 1849, just after the Elgin Association had been organized, William King reported to the synod on the progress of his venture and asked it to assist by establishing a mission in the settlement. The synod consented and appointed a committee, on which Willis and Burns served, to superintend the mission and guide King's educational and religious activities. Services began in King's house at the Buxton Mission, as the station was called, in December, concurrent with the arrival of the first settlers. A Sunday school opened at the same time with both black and white children attending. During the winter the mission erected a school building, and a day school was opened in June 1850 with sixteen students. By mid-1851, when King again reported to the synod, there were between one hundred and one hundred and fifty people attending the church and between thirty and forty at the Sunday school, and enrolment at the day school was fifty-six. A year later, when there were approximately ninety families in the settlement, church attendance was unchanged, but numbers had risen to fifty-three at the Sunday school and seventy-three at the day school. The *Record* reported that fifty-two day-school students sat for the semi-annual examination in late 1853; and to prepare students for college entrance King added the Latin class in the fall in 1852.[24]

In 1851 the synod had transferred responsibility for the supervision of Buxton Mission, together with the added duty of providing funding in cooperation with the presbyteries, from the temporary committee formed when the mission was organized to the Home Mission Committee. Raising buildings had been expensive, the mission still needed a church house, and there was the ongoing cost of salaries for King and a teacher, and for supplies for the school. King and Burns had undertaken a fund-raising trip, primarily to Presbyterian churches in Pittsburgh, in late 1850, and they returned with $400 and a quantity of books, as well as a bell for the mission, which had been provided by the city's black residents. A year later King made another money-raising tour, visiting Illinois and Michigan, but it was less successful. Clearly, continued reliance on such undependable sources of income could jeopardize the mission (as Hiram Wilson had learned). By 1853 the accumulated debt was £250. Meanwhile, the synod had been urging presbyteries to support the mission, and in 1852 all congregations were asked to take a collection for Buxton. This became an annual affair, and it enabled King to build a temporary church house and to retire the debt in 1854. The Latin class had its first graduates ready for college in 1856, and two years later ninety students were attending the day school. Placing Buxton Mission under the control of the Home Mission Committee and instituting the annual collection signified that the mission had moved from the periphery into the mainstream of the church's concerns. Resting on this stable foundation, by mid-decade Buxton Mission was able to achieve its goal of providing spiritual nurture for the ex-slaves and Christian education for their children. [25]

METHODISM TOOK ROOT IN CANADA as a result of missionary efforts by groups in the United States and Britain. Americans began their work in Upper Canada in 1791, and the area was soon organized as a district by the Genesee Conference of the Methodist Episcopal Church. In 1824 it became a separate conference called the Methodist Episcopal Conference in Canada. Nine years later this body joined the British Wesleyan Methodist Church to form the Wesleyan Methodist Church in Canada, the province's leading Methodist body and largest denomination, and it grew to have about 25,000 members by midcentury. [26]

The annual conference (the Wesleyan Methodist governing body) had previously taken no notice of the slavery issue, but in the early 1830s the *Christian Guardian* (the church weekly, published in Toronto) began to show concern for the British emancipation campaign. It briefly reported the 1831 annual meeting of the British Anti-Slavery Society, commenting that the society's activities were "worthy of Christians and Philanthropists," and stating that clergymen participated in them without fear of being charged with meddling in politics. As the British emancipation campaign heated up in the summer of 1833, the *Guardian* published antislavery items regularly: an account of how Wilberforce, Sharp, and Clarkson had awakened to the evils of the slave trade in the 1780s; Colonial Secretary Stanley's announcement that the government would soon introduce measures to end slavery; and speeches by key antislavery figures at a London meeting. After the House of Commons passed the British government's emancipation package, the *Guardian* asserted that all good men hoped that this would end the cruel bondage in which Britain, a nation "professing to be governed by the pure, just, and merciful principles of Christianity," held its slaves. If the government succeeded, declared the *Guardian*, it would win an "imperishable memorial throughout all generations." With the paper voicing these strong antislavery sentiments, it seemed that the Methodist church was about to adopt abolitionism; but, surprisingly, the annual conference remained silent on the issue throughout the decade.[27]

The *Guardian*, as we have seen, nevertheless played a key role in events leading to the formation of the Upper Canada Anti-Slavery Society (UCAS) in 1837. Through its editorial columns, Ephraim Evans aroused public opinion to the urgency of helping to end slavery in the United States. He became secretary of the society, and several other Wesleyan clergy and laymen (John Ryerson, Joseph Stinson, M. Lang, and J.N. Lawrence, for example) figured prominently in the organization. Yet the UCAS collapsed quickly in the turmoil and suspicion that surrounded the Upper Canada rebellion. Wesleyan Methodists were not officially committed to abolitionism, and having aligned themselves with the Tory constitutionalists in provincial politics since 1833, they seemingly wanted to avoid offending their political allies by continuing to proclaim the abolitionist principles that the constitutionalists opposed. Moreover, there was the unresolved matter of funding for their new school at Cobourg which the mother country had promised but the provincial government had not yet delivered. In the recrimination-charged atmosphere of the post-rebellion period, as Canadians looked for scapegoats and as Bishop Macdonell publicly fingered Methodists and Presbyterians, Wesleyan Methodists evidently believed that it was best to lie low, even if this meant the demise of the UCAS.[28]

While these considerations forced Wesleyan Methodists to handle the slavery question with great care, their actions were also influenced by a desire to maintain good "connexional" relations with their American Methodist Episcopal brethren. Since many American Methodists were opposed to abolitionism, association with the movement held considerable potential for disrupting the fraternal tie, as Canadian Wesleyans discovered in 1838. As we have seen, the Methodist Episcopal conference in 1836 was hostile to antislavery. When British Methodists reprimanded American Methodists for failing to denounce slavery, the conference defensively replied that Englishmen would have been less critical had they understood the complexities of dealing with slavery in the American setting. The conference also disciplined two members for participating in a recent Cincinnati antislavery meeting, disavowed any intention to interfere with the master-servant relationship, and openly opposed "modern abolitionism" (immediatism). This temporizing policy offended some American Methodist abolitionists, and the Black River conference in New York called an antislavery convention to meet at Utica in the spring of 1838, a step that most Episcopal Methodists regarded as schismatic. The Utica convention created an awkward situation for Canadian Methodists, for it sent a delegate, the Rev. Luther Lee, to the annual conference in Kingston. Receiving him in this capacity would have offended the American general conference, and to avoid this the Canadian conference welcomed Lee as a delegate of the Black River conference rather than the Utica convention. Recognizing the threat that the antislavery issue posed to the good "connexional" relationship between the churches, the conference replaced Evans, the outspoken abolitionist *Guardian* editor, with Egerton Ryerson, the denomination's leading minister, who was committed to maintaining good relations with the American church. Antislavery immediately disappeared from the *Guardian*'s columns, and the Wesleyan Methodists drew back from supporting antislavery at the end of the 1830s.[29]

Predictably, the abolitionists were soon at Ryerson's heels. *Zion's Watchman and Wesleyan Observor*, the mouthpiece of abolitionist Methodist Episcopal dissidents in New York, had previously regarded Ryerson as a fellow worker, but now it attacked him. Not only was the *Guardian* silent on all matters pertaining to slavery, charged the *Observor*, but Ryerson was deleting references to any discussion of the topic from the minutes of Methodist conferences that he published for Canadian circulation. Moreover, according to the *Observor*, he had uttered sentiments at the Methodist Episcopal conference at Baltimore in 1840 that were completely unacceptable to abolitionists. Ryerson had told the conference that the Wesleyan Methodist Church in Canada agreed with the Methodist Episcopal general conference in opposing "modern abolition" and "all connection with or sympathy for the antislavery conventions, societies, and irregular proceedings in the United States on this subject." These were the views that he was committed to as editor of the *Guardian*, he had stated, explaining that he had accepted the position only on the condition that the church would support him in not attacking American institutions. When John Scoble, secretary of the British and Foreign Anti-Slavery Society, learned of this, he sent the *Observor*'s report of Ryerson's remarks to the *British Anti-Slavery Reporter* for publication, charging that they amounted to "support of the peculiar institutions of the southern states." Ryerson rejected Scoble's charge that he had defended slavery or had even said "one word in palliation" of it, insisting that the *Observor* had reported his comments erroneously. However, he did not deny that he and the Wesleyan Methodists opposed "modern abolition," and his explanation did not satisfy Scoble.[30]

Unfortunately, the charge of defending slavery did not deter the annual conference or the *Guardian* from their policy of silence on antislavery. For two decades the journal virtually ignored the topic. It never mentioned the Stuart-Willis antislavery meetings in Toronto in 1846 or John Roaf's concurrent effort to form an antislavery society. Organization of the Anti-Slavery Society of Canada (ASC) in 1851 received a scant nine lines in which the paper, though admitting its aversion to slavery, disparaged interference in American affairs. The *Guardian* raised the same objections to George Thompson's appearance at the ASC's week-long antislavery meeting in the spring of 1851, and it vilified his attack on American churches and religious journals for their handling of slavery, saying that Thompson had mixed a "good deal of hyperbole" with "much painful, naked Truth" in order to "win applause, or round a period."[31]

In the meantime, Wesleyan Methodists had retained their connexional tie with American Episcopal Methodists, and this prompted criticism from some Canadian abolitionists in the mid-1850s. This was the period, as will be recalled, when J.J.E. Linton and Thomas Henning were hounding Canadian churches and religious organizations for their ties with American bodies that had questionable records on slavery. Differences of opinion over policies on slavery had caused the American Methodist Episcopal church to divide into Northern and Southern wings in 1844, but several border state conferences had remained within the Northern church, even though there were some slaveholders among their numbers. In his newspaper campaign, Linton charged that this remnant of slaveholders in the Northern church meant that it "countenanced" slavery, and he imputed shared guilt in this sin to Canadian Wesleyan Methodists for retaining the tie. The *Guardian* rejected this inference, protesting that the mere presence of a few slaveholders in the border state conferences did not signify approval of slavery by Northern Methodists. The very opposite was true, the *Guardian* insisted, as could be seen by examining the developments at the 1844 general conference, where the division had occurred. The crisis had arisen after Bishop Andrew of Baltimore had inherited some slaves. Methodist Episcopal practice barred the episcopacy from owning slaves, and consequently the Northern Methodists introduced a motion requiring Andrew to desist from carrying on his duties. The Southern phalanx at the conference then objected, and it withdrew when the measure passed. The *Guardian* claimed that the Northern vote requiring Andrew's withdrawal showed how strongly the Northern wing was opposed to slavery, even if circumstances left a few slaveholders within its wall.

In an extended public correspondence with the *Guardian*'s editor, Thomas Henning questioned this conclusion. The 1844 conference, he pointed out, had not debated the fundamental issue of slavery or questioned its sinfulness. Rather, Northern Methodists had acted on the basis of precedent and expendiency to remove a slaveholding bishop whose ministrations would have been disruptive in the North, where episcopal duties were likely to take him. The *Guardian*, however, insisted that the Northern Methodists had not acted out of expediency; it said that they knew that requiring Andrew to step down would divide the church. Moreover, argued the paper, the Northerners could have side-stepped the issue by delaying action until Andrew had disposed of his slaves. Thus, Northern Methodists, the *Guardian* concluded, had unmistakably opposed slavery rather than taking the easy way out, and by implication Canadian Methodists remained untarnished in retaining the tie.[32]

In 1856 the *Guardian* used this exchange with Henning to explain where it stood on antislavery. If asked whether it was abolitionist, it said, the answer would be no, for abolition was not the best way to deal with slavery. Abolition had had the effect of "increasing the weight and riveting more firmly the fetters of the slaves, and [had] deferred their emancipation for at least a quarter of a century." However, the paper insisted that its opposition to abolition did not mean that it was any less opposed to slavery; any inference that it defended slavery was "gratuitous slander." Slavery would not be abolished, continued the *Guardian*, by the most

terrific denunciation of its infamy and wrongs, and ... those who most loudly declaim against the system and summarily hand over its abetters to perdition, are not always the best friends of the slave. The shallow philanthropy of some noisy abolitionists justifies this remark. If denunciations of slavery could have accomplished the freedom of Africa's unhappy children, every chain would long ere this have been shivered to atoms, and the day of universal jubilee have been ushered in without a cloud. But a system so deeply rooted, in the civil institutions of the country, and so vigilantly guarded by human avarice, cannot be overthrown by the breath of indignation. It will require a more practical agency, and sacrificing benevolence.[33]

For the rest of the decade, the Wesleyans adhered to their policy of maintaining ties with Episcopal Methodists in the United States and treating slavery as an American question. In 1859 the Congregational *Northern Independent* deplored the annual conference's failure to admonish the Methodist Episcopal general conference for its slavery policy, again implying that Canadian Methodists sanctioned slaveholding in the church. The *Guardian* replied that Canadian Methodists did not presume to dictate to their American brethren on such a complex question, which puzzled wiser men than themselves. Sanctimoniously, the paper cited a passage from Proverbs which stated that one who "meddleth with strife not belonging to him is like one that taketh a dog by the ears." American Methodists were fully aware that Canadian Methodists unequivocally opposed slavery whether in or out of the church, the *Guardian* reminded its critics, and reiteration of this point would constitute malicious repetition. Fifteen months later, after a long editorial categorizing the positions of various American civil and religious groups on slavery, the *Guardian* still insisted that its course was "uncompromising hostility to evil" but "Christian tolerance to those who sincerely differ[ed]" from it.[34]

The Wesleyan Methodists showed some signs of softening their policy of not discussing slavery when the outbreak of the Civil War was imminent. Uncharacteristically, the *Guardian* attacked the Nashville *Advocate* (a border state Methodist newspaper) for criticizing Northern Methodists for suddenly making slavery a sin when neither the Methodist discipline nor the scriptures did so. The *Guardian* stated that Canadians viewed slavery as the "sum of all villainies" and berated Southerners for defending it. The Nashville editor might complain that this was meddling in a neighbour's affair, stated the *Guardian*, but "slavery interests all the world; and the moral aspect of it is such that all Christians ought to have sound opinions upon it, and ought to express their opinions." This seemed to signal a change of policy by Wesleyan Methodists, but the annual conference remained silent on abolition, and the *Guardian* went no further than to applaud the Methodist Episcopal general conference of 1864 for at last forbidding members to hold slaves.[35]

Among the four smaller branches of central Canadian Methodism, two openly supported abolition. When in 1833 the Episcopal Methodists and British Wesleyans had joined to form the Wesleyan Methodist Church in Canada, a remnant of the former group had rejected union and retained the name Methodist Episcopal Church in Canada. In 1844 its annual conference divided into the Bay of Quinte and Niagara conferences, and the Ontario conference was added twenty years later. It became the province's second-largest body of Methodists, with about 9000 members in 1851.

Unlike the Wesleyan Methodists, the Episcopal Methodists did not avoid the issue of slavery. Through the *Canada Christian Advocate*, their weekly newspaper, they were informed about events relating to it: a St Louis woman's arrest for sending slaves to Canada; the 1845 action of the Old School Presbyterians that condoned slavery; the existence of Christian slaveholders in the United States. Initially, the *Advocate* merely reported these matters with little comment, but after 1850 it clearly backed the abolitionists. It rejoiced at the formation of the Anti-Slavery Society of Canada in 1851, "ardently" wishing it success. "It is time for the Christian world to speak out on this subject," it declared, and to "record its sense of gross outrage perpetrated upon the rights of our common humanity by the system of Southern slavery." An antislavery society in Toronto would not directly affect American slavery, the paper admitted; but "if all the friends of freedom and humanity throughout the world could be induced to adopt the course taken by the people of Toronto," the result would certainly be great.[36]

The *Advocate* readily discussed the actions of American Methodists, something the Wesleyans avoided. In 1853 it applauded the East Genesee conference for passing resolutions that called slavery a crime against God and man, that said its continuation in the church was a "burlesque" on holiness, and that demanded revisions in the discipline to exclude slaveholders from membership. The *Advocate*'s criticisms, however were usually directed at the Southern wing of the church. A Methodist paper in Texas was attacked for arguing that slavery, like the relationship between husband and wife or parent and child, was a divinely sanctioned institution that was necessary for social order. The *Advocate* also noted that throughout the South the priceless treasure of free speech was being lost, since people were silenced by intimidation or even death for speaking against slavery. In fact, it said, the whole section seemed to be infected with a common insanity on the topic. For example, some Southerners claimed that slavery was the natural state of all labourers regardless of colour, while others decried the impact of free public schools on labourers' children and even asserted that the claim of the Declaration of Independence, that all men were created equal, was a self-evident lie. Conditions might not have deteriorated so far, the paper ventured, had the church continued to witness against slavery. But it had steadily retreated from the historic position enunciated by Wesley himself – that slavery was the "sum of all villainies" – a position enshrined in the Methodist discipline in the declaration that slavery was a "great evil." This had been the church's position not twenty years earlier, said the paper. But in the meantime, Southern Methodists had opened the episcopacy to slaveholders, had split the church, and had removed sanctions against slavery from the discipline and were now defending it. If only they had maintained a faithful witness, the hearts of slaveholders might have been softened and the system ended.[37]

The *Advocate* emphasized that Episcopal Methodists disagreed with the Wesleyan view that those who attacked American slavery were interfering improperly in a neighbour's business. Instead, they believed that Canadians had a duty to let their sympathy with those suffering and dying under slavery be known. They rejected the claim of Anglicans and Wesleyans that calling on Americans to end slavery would make matters worse. On the contrary, declared the *Advocate*, if Canadians, the British, and Europeans condemned slavery adamantly enough, the Southerners might heed their voices. But if not, one still had a duty to witness against the evil. The paper also warned of dire consequences for Canada if slavery was not stamped out in the United States: aggressive Southerners, who had managed to gain the extension of slavery into the trans-Mississippi territories where it once was excluded, might succeed in re-establishing it in the North. Then slavery would be entrenched along the Canadian border and hundreds of thousands of fugitive slaves would flee North, almost certainly bringing war as their owners attempted to retrieve them.

Unfraid of meddling in a neighbour's affairs, the *Advocate* openly avowed abolitionism and attacked Southern Methodists for compromising on slavery, even though it seldom chastised Northern Methodists for their equivocation. Surprisingly, given the stance of the *Advocate*, the annual conference took no action on slavery or on abolition until 1863, when concern over rising sympathy in Canada for the Confederacy during the Civil War prompted action. The Bay of Quinte conference formed a committee on slavery, which reported that it was necessary to make the church's view on the matter clearly known at the time, since there were people in Canada West who sympathized with the Confederacy's social system. In the committee's view, the Confederacy had waged war to defend and extend slavery, a system that was a "sin against God," a "violation of the spirit of the Gospel," and a "monstrous injustice" to the slaves by subjecting them to the absolute will of the owner. The Ontario conference adopted a similar position in 1863, but the Niagara conference did nothing until 1865, when it announced its sympathy for American Methodists (because of the difficult times they had experienced with the war and because of Lincoln's assassination) and expressed joy that slavery was finally broken.[38]

The smallest of the three Methodist bodies in the province to declare a position on slavery had its roots in an amalgamation of splinter groups. British New Connexion Methodists sent missionaries to Lower Canada in 1837 and soon made contact with a faction that had separated from the original Methodist Episcopal Church in Canada in 1828 under Henry Ryan. The Ryanites and the New Connexion Methodists united in 1841 under the name Canadian Wesleyan Methodist New Connexion Church. The Protestant Methodists, a group in the Eastern Townships of Lower Canada who had American roots, joined in 1843, and the denomination's name was changed in 1865 to Methodist New Connexion Church of Canada. Its membership had reached about 4000 in 1850.[39]

The New Connexion annual conference was strongly antislavery and repeatedly expressed its sentiments on the topic. In 1851 it adopted resolutions declaring its "utter abhorrence" of slavery and its repudiation of ministers who attempted to justify slavery from scripture. The conference also voiced sympathy for fugitive slaves who had fled to the province for protection. Three years later, it prepared to open a mission among the black residents of Colchester, who had asked for recognition by the New Connexion Methodists, and the 1855 conference requested the Canadian government to appropriate funds to educate the province's blacks. Reaffirming its hatred of slavery, the meeting denounced Christians who in any way participated in the evil. On this occasion, the church also declared that it would break fellowship with Christian bodies that tolerated slaveholding among their members, and it praised faithful church members who were valiantly labouring to excommunicate the offenders. The American Tract Society and the American Sunday

School Union were sharply repudiated for their "false position and temporizing policy" in practising "studied and guilty silence" by refusing to circulate antislavery material in their literature.

The conference reiterated these declarations in 1856, adding, in a statement that espoused abolition, its prayer that the "present agitation of the question in the Northern United States" would bring freedom to the slave. There is no record that the new Connexion Methodists officially endorsed the Anti-Slavery Society of Canada (ASC), but denominational leaders, both clerical and lay, were influential members of the society. The Rev. William McClure, as has been noted, was a moving force in organizing the society and became one of its secretaries, and when he moved to London he organized an ASC auxiliary; the Rev. J.H. Robinson and the Toronto merchant R.H. Brett served the church in numerous capacities and were ASC committee members.[40]

There were two additional small Methodist communions in Canada West at this time: the Primitive Methodist Church and the Bible Christian Church. The annual conference of the former took no action on antislavery, although at least one of its ministers – the Rev. Edward Barras – was an ASC vice-president. However, the Bible Christians seemingly paid no attention to the question.


CONGREGATIONALISM HAD MADE ITS APPEARANCE in Upper Canada by 1820, but slow growth – there were about 3500 members with an average attendance of about 9800 in 1859 – inhibited the rise of a central structure until almost the middle of the century, when the Congregational Union of Canada organized. In the early period, individual clergymen such as John Roaf and Adam Lillie identified with the antislavery cause. Roaf, who arrived in Toronto just after the Upper Canada Anti-Slavery Society had been organized, quickly joined it and, as we have seen, promoted abolition in Toronto in the 1840s and was a founder of the ASC. Lillie signed a public petition on behalf of the imprisoned Jesse Happy in 1837, assisted blacks at Brantford, and eventually participated in the ASC, as did the Toronto minister Francis H. Marling and numerous laymen such as Peter and Patrick Freeland and John F. Marling.[41]

Determining the policy of the denomination as a whole on antislavery is more difficult. Evidently, there are no surviving minutes of the yearly meetings of the Congregational Union before 1860; and files of the *Canadian Independent*, the church's magazine, are very incomplete for the same era. Yet those that remain make it clear that the Congregational church was strongly antislavery and, unlike Wesleyan methodists and High Church Anglicans, had no inhibitions about speaking out on the question. In 1846 the Congregational Union condemned slavery, and eight years later it passed a resolution censuring the American Tract Society for its "studied silence" on the "great sin of American slavery," and for removing all references to the topic from its publications. The *Independent* believed that Congregationalists "to a man" deplored the "sad subserviency" of the tract society and "most of the great religious organizations in the United States to the Southern slave influence." This "cringing sycophancy of Northern men and Northern Christians," the journal asserted, was worse than Southern slavery, for it was a slavery of the "soul." It was the true foundation on which slavery rested, making Northerners the "real slaveholders" for tamely doing the "bidding of their Southern masters, in keeping the bondsmen chained." The church repeated its charges against the American Tract Society the following year, and it warned "Brother Nall" (an agent of the Upper Canada Tract and Book Society, who attended the meeting) to inform his organization of the Congregational Union's strong conviction that while denouncing other sins, the "manifold and intolerable abominations of slavery should be set forth and condemned with unsparing fidelity by such an organization."[42]

The *Independent* felt so strongly about the equivocation of the American Tract Society that it conducted a long public correspondence on the question with J.T. Byrne, a Congregational minister at Whitby, east of Toronto. Byrne had attended a colporteur convention at Rochester in 1855, and the American Tract Society's agent there had apparently convinced him that the society was not evading the slavery issue. On his return, Byrne wrote a series of letters to the Whitby *Commonwealth*, defending the society. He claimed to be satisfied with the agent's explanations and cited examples showing that the society's literature did include negative comments on slavery. The American Tract Society, eager to counteract the criticism that Linton and Henning were then making and to smooth the way for continued circulation of its material in the province, reprinted and circulated the letters. The *Independent* rejected Byrne's claim that the "general influence of all their publications is to destroy slavery," arguing that the evidence did not support him. It was surprising that a "British Congregational minister should be satisfied with anything short of a thorough denunciation of the whole system," insisted the *Independent*, and it lamented the "probable influence [that] approval spoken from such a source" would likely have. This brisk exchange continued for three months, with Byrne finally admitting that the American Tract Society's policy on slavery was not as forthright as it should have been. It clearly identified the Congregational church with the hard-line Linton-Henning abolitionist position in the American Tract Society–antifellowshipping controversy that arose within Canadian antislavery in the mid-1850s.[43]

LIKE CONGREGATIONALISTS, CANADIAN BAPTISTS had a strong tradition of local autonomy, permitting each congregation to follow its own conscience. It is therefore impossible to specify a single Baptist position on slavery and abolition in the province. Among Regular Baptists, small regional associations were formed and several of these adopted antislavery positions. For example, in 1841 the Ottawa Baptist Association passed resolutions supporting the American Baptist Anti-Slavery Convention, and it denied communion to slaveholders. The Niagara Association denounced slavery in 1856, calling it a "monstrous evil and a crying sin, and one, the commission of which dishonours God by trampling on his laws," and the Haldimand and Western associations followed suit. Another group, called the Union Baptists, passed motions in 1845 and 1847 abhorring slavery and deprecating its existence in all forms in all countries, and after 1848 they established ties with the strongly abolitionist Free Will and Free Mission Baptists in the United States. The Toronto minister, Robert Dick, a leader of this group, was an ASC committeeman; he also published the *Gospel Tribune*, sometimes wrongly identified as the group's journal, which was adamantly antislavery. Dick attacked the Kansas-Nebraska Act, predicting that Northerners would not endure much longer the "blackening, poluting [sic] scourge" that was extending slavery into their region. The *Tribune* hailed Linton for his energy and endurance in the anti-fellowshipping controversy, and applauded the Toronto branch of the Young Men's Christian Association for ending its affiliation with the American body after the national convention in 1855 refused membership for blacks. The Toronto editor also severely reprimanded Bethany College, a Northern school, for banning discussion of slavery on its campus after an unauthorized antislavery lecture had created serious friction between Northern and Southern students.[44]

BY THE FIRST DECADE OF THE NINETEENTH CENTURY, the Society of Friends had organized in several Upper Canadian locations under the authority of the Genesee and New York yearly meetings. English and American Quakers had long been known for their opposition to slavery, but Upper Canadian Friends showed much less interest. The West Lake Monthly Meeting in Prince Edward County in 1830 entertained a request for money to help North Carolina Quakers, who were cooperating with the American Colonization Society, to remove slaves from that state. But interest in antislavery among most monthly meetings was low. The Canada Half-Yearly Meeting (orthodox) briefly showed concern in 1835 when it appointed a committee to examine the slavery question. It recommended sending a memorial to Congress on the "oppressed condition of our American Brethren and Sisters of colour held in slavery" and adopting a "Minute of Advice" to local meetings; the directive asked Quakers to do all in their power to help relieve the slaves' suffering, and specifically asked fellow churchmen to consult their consciences about using articles made by slave labour. The Half-Yearly Meeting adopted the committee's proposal but did no more.

Occasionally, individual Quakers showed interest in the physical or spiritual condition of refugee slaves. For example, in 1849 Henry Widderfield secured the Yonge Street Monthly Meeting's approval for a "religious visit" to Ancaster Township and the Queen's Bush settlements, where there were many black settlers. Several years later, the West Lake Monthly Meeting gave its blessing to Jane Young when she proposed a similar mission to the "people of colour in Canada West." But Upper Canadian Friends remained aloof from the province's antislavery societies and did not participate in the efforts of the Elgin Association. As a body, the Society of Friends took no action to support antislavery in the province or to assist fugitive slaves. It seems that Canadian Quakers were content to let the Genesee and New York yearly meetings, to whom they contributed, deal with the matter.[45]

The position of Lutherans, Mennonites, and Jews in the province on antislavery is unclear. Except for two Jewish stockholders in the Elgin Association, representatives of these groups were noticeably absent from the major abolitionist organizations and seemingly took little interest in the matter.[46]

WHILE VIRTUALLY ALL CANADIAN CHURCHES opposed slavery, there were wide variations in the way they responded to antislavery. The Roman Catholic attitude was that slavery was a problem for Americans to solve, and that Canadian intervention would only worsen the slave's lot and retard emancipation by hardening Southern hearts. The Canada Half-Yearly Meeting of the Society of Friends recorded its hatred of slavery but never went beyond memorializing Congress on behalf of the slaves and asking its local meetings to consider boycotting slave-grown produce; and Quakers as individuals avoided joining provincial antislavery organizations. Anglicans were divided, the majority being decidedly cool towards abolition. High Churchmen agreed with Roman Catholics that slavery was an American problem; hence, they rejected antislavery activism and shunned the ASC. Evangelical Anglicans, on the other hand, were sympathetic to abolitionists and cooperated with the ASC. The High Church mainstream felt that breaking the fraternal tie with slaveholding churches in order to advance the demise of slavery was unwise, for it could endanger church unity, as the experience of some American churches had shown. Slavery would only end, they believed, if planters were adequately compensated for releasing slaves, a solution that some Canadian abolitionists rejected since it implied recognition of the slaveholder's right to own human property. Despite their hostility to abolition, High Churchmen stood for fair play for the fugitives, advocating that the church should assist the ex-slaves in finding work and should look to their moral improvement by providing chapels and education. However, neither the synod nor the Church Society took concrete steps to achieve these goals. The mission to the fugitive slaves at London was organized, funded, and staffed by the Colonial Church and School Society in England, with minimal support from the local committee in Canada West.

Like Anglicans, Presbyterians divided into conservative and evangelical camps on antislavery. With few exceptions, Kirkmen ignored the matter; United and Free Church Presbyterians, both notably evangelical, supported abolition. Through their synod and church journal, United presbyterians forthrightly condemned slavery and denounced churches and religious societies that wavered in their opposition to it. The Free Church commitment to antislavery was more comprehensive and continuous. The *Banner* raised the antislavery standard in the early 1840s when few other provincial antislavery voices were to be heard. The synod backed the cause in 1845 with an uncompromising declaration and appealed to American Presbyterians to stand firmly against slavery; these steps were repeated and eventually led the church to break ties with those American churches that ignored its plea. The Free Church also aided fugitive slaves by providing a church and schools at Buxton Mission. Numerous Free Churchmen, moreover, were leaders in the Elgin Association and the ASC. John Fisher, Peter Brown, Michael Willis, and Robert Burns were presidents and vice-presidents of the former, while Thomas Henning became the association's treasurer and William King its founding manager; Willis, Burns, and Henning were president, vice-president and secretary, respectively, of the latter. Many of their co-religionists sat on the boards of both groups. The Congregational stance on antislavery, except for the absence of a program to aid the fugitives, was almost a mirror image of the Free Church position.

Methodists, too, failed to find common ground on antislavery, but unlike Anglicans and Presbyterians, they did not separate along the conservative-evangelical axis, for all followers of John Wesley considered themselves to be evangelicals. Through the *Guardian* and through participation in the Upper Canada Anti-Slavery Society, Wesleyan Methodists initially led the abolition movement; but as a result of political considerations exacerbated by the Upper Canadian rebellion, coupled with the fear of alienating American Methodists, they drew back from the movement at the end of the 1830s, and this led to the collapse of the antislavery society. They remained virtually silent on the subject until the Civil War ended. Episcopal Methodists supported abolition, welcomed the ASC, and discussed American churches and their policies on slavery. Most of their critical comments, however, were directed against Southern Episcopal Methodists rather than against Northern Methodists, with whom they maintained a connexional tie. The smaller Methodist New Connexion denomination was unreservedly abolitionist; it unequivocally denounced slavery, participated in the ASC, and broke ties with slaveholding bodies.

Some churches obviously played important roles in promoting Canadian antislavery. In most cases, it was association with evangelicalism that determined whether a church group supported abolition. Congregationalists, United and Free Church Presbyterians, and Episcopal, New Connexion, and Primitive Methodists, as well as Low Church Anglicans, backed abolition. High Anglicans, the Kirk, and Roman Catholics, all outside evangelicalism, opposed it. The one group that does not fit this pattern was the Wesleyan Methodist church, the province's largest denomination; it rejected the antislavery movement because cooperating with it would have endangered the tie with American Methodists, which it was anxious to maintain. But the Wesleyans had another reason for opposing abolition; like High Anglicans and Roman Catholics, they were conservative in their political loyalties, and supporting abolition would have offended their political allies. Episcopal and New Connexion

Methodists, on the other hand, like Free Church Presbyterians and Congregationalists, were reformist in their politics and supported the movement. These considerations indicate that it was not religious influences alone that shaped the Canadian response to anti-slavery.[47]

# 8 A Question of Identity

The historian's traditional sources and tools have yielded a wealth of insight into how Canadian antislavery evolved from the early 1830s to the end of the American Civil War. Tracing the formative experiences of the movement's leaders has shown that their abolitionism was rooted in British antislavery soil. Analysing their speeches, editorials, and other writings has uncovered the ideas and convictions that moved them. The actions of the organizations they led have revealed their methods. Yet our image of Canadian abolitionists is still quite fragmentary even after traversing this diverse historical terrain, stretching from Britain in the 1820s to Canada West at midcentury. A systematic examination of their identity, focusing on their socio-economic characteristics, will enlarge the picture of those involved in Canadian antislavery and will enhance our understanding of the entire movement.

Two groups central to Canadian antislavery invite analysis. The 132 identifiable officers and committee members of the Upper Canada Anti-Slavery Society (UCAS), the Elgin Association, and the Anti-Slavery Society of Canada (ASC) were the leaders of the movement. As they were relatively prominent people, considerable data is available on them in such areas as national origin, age, time of arrival in the province, religious and political affiliation, benevolent activity, prior involvement with antislavery, race, and various factors reflecting their socio-economic status. Unfortunately, there are no extant membership lists of either the UCAS or the ASC from which to reconstruct a comparable roll of the Canadian antislavery rank and file. This leaves the 335 stockholders in the Elgin Association as the best available facsimile of those who were the foot soldiers of Canadian abolition. As the "followers" of Canadian antislavery, they tended to be less prominent socially than the leaders. Consequently, data was gathered in five areas: national origin, age, religious affiliation, race, and occupation. By assembling this information on the two groups, a general picture is provided of Canadian abolitionists – a group biography, in current methodological terminology.[1]

MANY OF THE 132 CANADIAN ANTISLAVERY leaders shared British roots. Of the 96 whose birth country was identified, 80.2 per cent were British-born (table 1), although British-born residents were only 35.1 per cent of the Canada West population in 1851 (table 2). Among the remainder of the leaders, 9.4 per cent were American-born and 8.3 per cent were born in British North America; these two groups constituted 4.6 and 58.7 per cent, respectively, of the provincial population. For the 71 whose place of education could be established, 57.7 per cent were schooled in Britain, 21.1 per cent in British North America, and only 8.5 per cent in the United States (table 3). Among the 92 whose birth year was known, 64.1 per cent were born between 1800 and 1819 (table 4). The rising tide of British hostility to slavery during the first three decades of the nineteenth century could scarcely have failed to shape the antislavery thought of this large portion of future Canadian abolitionist leaders who were born and educated in Britain during this era. Granville Sharp, William Wilberforce, and Thomas Fowell Buxton – the great leaders of British antislavery – in all likelihood were well-known household names. Some of the future Canadians would have been old enough to remember the British government's ineffective "amelioration policy" in the 1820s; and most would at least have been young adults when the Agency Committee led the final triumphant assault that brought emancipation throughout the British Empire in 1834.

It was possible to establish the emigration year of 68 of the provincial antislavery leaders. Since 58.9 per cent left during the 1830–49 period, they emigrated after British emancipation was won but while the British movement to end slavery in the United States (symbolized by the organization of the Edinburgh Emancipation Society and the Glasgow Emancipation Society in the 1830s) was at flood-tide (table 5). Table 1 shows that 77 of 96 Canadian antislavery leaders came from Britain; of these, 42 were from Scotland alone, and only 20 and 15 were from England and Wales, and from Ireland, respectively (table 6). Thus, 43.8 per cent of all Canadian antislavery

Table 1
Birth Country of Canadian Antislavery Leaders

| Country | Frequency | % | Valid % |
| --- | --- | --- | --- |
| British North America | 8 | 6.1 | 8.3 |
| United States | 9 | 6.8 | 9.4 |
| Britain | 77 | 58.4 | 80.2 |
| West Indies | 2 | 1.5 | 2.1 |
| Unknown | 36 | 27.3 | – |
| Total | 132[1] | 100.1 | 100.0 |

[1]Valid cases 96, missing cases 36

Table 2
Place of Birth of Canada West Population in 1851

| Location | Frequency | % |
| --- | --- | --- |
| Britain | 334,473 | 35.1 |
| United States | 43,732 | 4.6 |
| British North America | 558,634 | 58.7 |
| Other | 15,165 | 1.6 |
| Total | 952,004 | 100.0 |

Source: Censuses of Canada. 1665 to 1871, 4:182–3

Table 3
Country of Education of Canadian Antislavery Leaders

| Country | Frequency | % | Valid % |
| --- | --- | --- | --- |
| British North America | 15 | 11.4 | 21.1 |
| United States | 6 | 4.5 | 8.5 |
| Britain | 41 | 31.1 | 57.7 |
| Britain and BNA | 7 | 5.3 | 9.9 |
| BNA and United States | 2 | 1.5 | 2.8 |
| Unknown | 61 | 46.2 | – |
| Total | 132[1] | 100.0 | 100.0 |

[1]Valid cases 71, missing cases 61

leaders came from Scotland. This preponderance of Scots implicates the two Scottish antislavery societies as key forces that awakened and nurtured the antislavery convictions of future Canadian antislavery leaders and provided them with guiding models that were useful after they arrived in British North America. The London-

Table 4
Birth Decade of Canadian Antislavery Leaders

| Birth Decade | Frequency | % | Valid % |
|---|---|---|---|
| 1770–79 | 1 | 0.8 | 1.1 |
| 1780–89 | 3 | 2.3 | 3.3 |
| 1790–99 | 11 | 8.3 | 12.0 |
| 1800–09 | 28 | 21.2 | 30.4 |
| 1810–19 | 31 | 23.5 | 33.7 |
| 1820–29 | 16 | 12.1 | 17.4 |
| 1830–39 | 2 | 1.5 | 2.2 |
| Unknown | 40 | 30.3 | – |
| Total | 132[1] | 100.0 | 100.1 |

[1]Valid cases 92, missing cases 40

Table 5
Emigration Decade of Canadian Antislavery Leaders

| Emigration Decade | Frequency | % | Valid % |
|---|---|---|---|
| 1810–19 | 5 | 3.8 | 7.4 |
| 1820–29 | 6 | 4.5 | 8.8 |
| 1830–39 | 25 | 18.9 | 36.8 |
| 1840–49 | 15 | 11.4 | 22.1 |
| 1850–59 | 9 | 6.8 | 13.2 |
| 1860–69 | 1 | .8 | 1.5 |
| Born in BNA | 7 | 5.3 | 10.3 |
| Unknown | 64 | 48.5 | – |
| Total | 132[1] | 100.0 | 100.1 |

[1]Valid cases 68, missing cases 64

Table 6
Birth Country (Including England, Scotland, and Ireland) of Canadian
Antislavery Leaders

| Country | Frequency | % | Valid % |
|---|---|---|---|
| British North America | 8 | 6.1 | 8.3 |
| United States | 9 | 6.8 | 9.4 |
| England and Wales | 20 | 15.2 | 20.8 |
| Scotland | 42 | 31.8 | 43.8 |
| Ireland | 15 | 11.4 | 15.6 |
| West Indies | 2 | 1.5 | 2.1 |
| Unknown | 36 | 27.3 | – |
| Total | 132[1] | 100.1 | 100.0 |

[1]Valid cases 96, missing cases 36

Table 7
First Pre-BNA Antislavery Affiliation, in Britain and the United States, of Canadian Antislavery Leaders

| Name | Britain | United States | None | Born in BNA | Total |
|------|---------|---------------|------|-------------|-------|
| | | | 112 | 7 | 119 |
| EES | 2 | | | | 2 |
| GES | 1 | | | | 1 |
| Paisley AS meetings | 1 | | | | 1 |
| AAS | | 1 | | | 1 |
| Agency Committee | 2 | | | | 2 |
| Liberty party | | 1 | | | 1 |
| Lane Seminary rebels | | 1 | | | 1 |
| U. Glasgow AS debates, 1831 | 2 | | | | 2 |
| Wolverhampton AS meetings | 2 | | | | 2 |
| Total | 10 | 3 | 112 | 7 | 132 |

Table 8
Second Pre-BNA Antislavery Affiliation, in Britain and the United States, of Canadian Antislavery Leaders

| Name | Britain | United States | None | Born in BNA | Total |
|------|---------|---------------|------|-------------|-------|
| | | | 118 | 7 | 125 |
| GES | 2 | | | | 2 |
| BFAS | 1 | | | | 1 |
| AAS | | 1 | | | 1 |
| FCAS | 1 | | | | 1 |
| Oberlin College | | 1 | | | 1 |
| Liberty party | | 1 | | | 1 |
| Total | 4 | 3 | 118 | 7 | 132 |

based British and Foreign Anti-Slavery Society did not emerge until the late 1830s, and only 20 of the Canadian leaders came from England.

Since many Canadian antislavery leaders had witnessed British emancipation and were contemporaries of the great British antislavery societies, it was to be expected that some would have been connected with the antislavery movement before their arrival in British North America. In fact, at least 13 were in this category, 10 of whom had previous abolitionist connections in Britain and 3 in the United States (table 7). Moreover, 7 of these had more than one such tie, 4 of them in Britain and 3 in the United States (table 8). Altogether, among the 132 Canadian antislavery leaders, there were

Table 9
Occupation of Canadian Antislavery Leaders' Parents

| Occupation | Frequency | % | Valid % |
|---|---|---|---|
| Financier/broker | 1 | 0.8 | 2.7 |
| Trade/transportation | 9 | 6.8 | 24.3 |
| Manufacturing | 3 | 2.3 | 8.1 |
| High-status professions | 8 | 6.1 | 21.6 |
| Low-status professions | 9 | 6.8 | 24.3 |
| Agriculture | 7 | 5.3 | 18.9 |
| Unknown | 95 | 72.0 | – |
| Total | 132[1] | 100.1 | 99.9 |

[1]Valid cases 37, missing cases 95

Table 10
Occupation of Canadian Antislavery Leaders, 1849–65

| Occupation | Frequency | % | Valid % |
|---|---|---|---|
| Rentier | 1 | 0.8 | 0.9 |
| Financier/broker | 5 | 3.8 | 4.5 |
| Trade/transportation | 26 | 19.7 | 23.4 |
| Manufacturing | 4 | 3.0 | 3.6 |
| High-status professions | 56 | 42.4 | 50.4 |
| Low-status professions | 9 | 6.8 | 8.1 |
| Skilled trades | 3 | 2.3 | 2.7 |
| Agriculture | 1 | 0.8 | 0.9 |
| Retired | 4 | 3.0 | 3.6 |
| Deceased | 2 | 1.5 | 1.8 |
| Unknown | 21 | 15.9 | – |
| Total | 132[1] | 100.0 | 99.9 |

[1]Valid cases 111, missing cases 21

20 pre–British North American antislavery affiliations, 14 in Britain and 6 in the United States. This provided a corps of experienced antislavery figures among the leaders, with the majority of their experiences having been gained in Britain.

Their socio-economic status, to the extent that it may be determined from such indicators as occupation, education, and size and type of dwelling, situates the antislavery leaders in the middle ranks of society. They came from middle-class families. Parental occupation could be identified in 37 cases; of these, 24.3 per cent were in trade/transportation, 21.6 per cent had high-status professions, 24.3 per cent had low-status professions, and 18.9 per cent were in agriculture (table 9). By the period 1849–65, when the Canadian

Table 11
Detailed Analysis of Occupation of Canadian Antislavery Leaders

| Occupation | Frequency | % | Valid % | |
|---|---|---|---|---|
| Rentier | | | | 0.9 |
| landlord | 1 | 0.8 | 0.9 | |
| Financier/broker | | | | 4.5 |
| banker | 3 | 2.3 | 2.7 | |
| land agent | 2 | 1.5 | 1.8 | |
| Trade | | | | 23.4 |
| wholesaler | 14 | 10.6 | 12.6 | |
| retailer | 9 | 6.8 | 8.1 | |
| accountant | 2 | 1.5 | 1.8 | |
| hotelkeeper | 1 | 0.8 | 0.9 | |
| Manufacturing | | | | 3.6 |
| heavy | 3 | 2.3 | 2.7 | |
| household | 1 | 0.8 | 0.9 | |
| High-status professions | | | | 50.4 |
| judge | 1 | 0.8 | 0.9 | |
| attorney | 7 | 5.3 | 6.3 | |
| minister/missionary | 30 | 22.7 | 27.0 | |
| physician | 4 | 3.0 | 3.6 | |
| college president/professor | 4 | 3.0 | 3.6 | |
| government official | 10 | 7.6 | 9.0 | |
| Low-status professions | | | | 8.1 |
| journalist/editor/publisher | 5 | 3.8 | 4.5 | |
| apothecary | 1 | 0.8 | 0.9 | |
| lecturer/reform agent | 3 | 2.3 | 2.7 | |
| Skilled trade | | | | 2.7 |
| clerk/bookkeeper | 1 | 0.8 | 0.9 | |
| confectioner/baker | 1 | 0.8 | 0.9 | |
| shoemaker | 1 | 0.8 | 0.9 | |
| Agriculture | | | | 0.9 |
| farmer | 1 | 0.8 | 0.9 | |
| Retired | | | | 3.6 |
| pensioner | 4 | 3.0 | 3.6 | |
| Deceased | 2 | 1.5 | 1.8 | 1.8 |
| Unknown | 21 | 15.9 | – | – |
| Total | 132[1] | 100.3 | 99.9 | 99.9 |

[1]Valid cases 111, missing cases 21

antislavery movement was at its peak and most of the leaders had established themselves in the province, the group had moved up somewhat from its parents' position. Among 111 anti-slavery leaders, 50.4 per cent were in high-status professions (27.0 per cent ministers, 9.0 per cent government officials, 6.3 per cent lawyers, and 8.1 per cent physicians, judges, and college presidents/professors); and 8.1 per cent were in low-status professions. There were

Table 12
Educational Level of Canadian Antislavery Leaders

| Level | Frequency | % | Valid % |
|---|---|---|---|
| No college | 23 | 17.4 | 41.8 |
| Some college | 7 | 5.3 | 12.7 |
| College graduate | 12 | 9.1 | 21.8 |
| Postgraduate degree | 10 | 7.6 | 18.2 |
| No formal education | 3 | 2.3 | 5.5 |
| Unknown | 77 | 58.3 | – |
| Total | 132[1] | 100.0 | 100.0 |

[1]Valid cases 55, missing cases 77

Table 13
Canadian Antislavery Leaders' Dwelling Size

| Size | Frequency | % | Valid % |
|---|---|---|---|
| Single storey | 4 | 3.0 | 10.3 |
| Two storey | 24 | 18.2 | 61.5 |
| Three storey | 8 | 6.1 | 20.5 |
| Four storey | 3 | 2.3 | 7.7 |
| Unknown | 93 | 70.5 | – |
| Total | 132[1] | 100.1 | 100.0 |

[1]Valid cases 39, missing cases 93

23.4 per cent employed in trade, mainly as wholesale or retail merchants. Finance/brokerage, manufacturing, and the skilled trades each had less than 5 per cent, and agriculture had only 0.9 per cent. Thus, the antislavery leaders were deeply rooted in the professional and business sectors, with ministers and merchants being the predominant occupational groups (47.8 per cent), followed by government officials and lawyers (tables 10 and 11).

The leadership enjoyed a high level of schooling, another badge of middle-class status, as the educational attainment of 55 shows. Only 5.5 per cent had no formal education; 41.8 per cent had formal schooling but no college training, while 52.7 per cent had either some university training or an undergraduate or graduate degree (table 12).

As a rule, they occupied spacious and substantial housing; 82.0 per cent lived in either two- or three-storey houses (table 13). Of the 46 whose type of house is known, none lived in rough cast

Table 14
Canadian Antislavery Leaders' Dwelling Type

| Type | Frequency | % | Valid % |
|---|---|---|---|
| Frame | 14 | 10.6 | 30.4 |
| Brick | 29 | 22.0 | 63.0 |
| Stone | 2 | 1.5 | 4.3 |
| None (deceased) | 1 | 0.8 | 2.2 |
| Unknown | 86 | 65.2 | – |
| Total | 132[1] | 100.1 | 99.9 |

[1]Valid cases 46, missing cases 86

Table 15
Age at Which Canadian Antislavery Leaders Joined ASC

| Age | Frequency | % | Valid % |
|---|---|---|---|
| 20–29 years | 6 | 4.5 | 9.4 |
| 30–39 | 23 | 17.4 | 35.9 |
| 40–49 | 18 | 13.6 | 28.1 |
| 50–59 | 12 | 9.1 | 18.8 |
| 60–69 | 5 | 3.8 | 7.8 |
| Unknown or never joined ASC | 68 | 51.5 | – |
| Total | 132[1] | 99.9 | 100.0 |

[1]Valid cases 64, missing cases 68

or log buildings; 30.4 per cent inhabited frame and 63.0 per cent brick structures (table 14).

A few of the antislavery leaders were very young men still in their twenties, and somewhat more were over 50, but the majority were between 30 and 49 when they joined the ASC and the Elgin Association. Among 64 leaders of the ASC whose ages are known, 35.9 per cent were between 30 and 39, and 28.1 per cent were from 40 to 49 (table 15). The leadership of the Elgin Association was slightly younger, with 42.1 per cent in the former category, and 28.9 per cent in the latter, in the case of 38 subjects (table 16). On the whole, they were in their prime years and were probably still rising in their careers.

Church ties were widespread within Canadian antislavery leadership, with evangelicals in general, and Free Church Presbyterians and Congregationalists in particular, playing large roles. One hundred and three of the 132 antislavery leaders had a religious affiliation; 81.6 per cent were evangelical and only 3.9 per cent

Table 16
Age at Which Canadian Antislavery Leaders Joined Elgin Association

| Age | Frequency | % | Valid % |
| --- | --- | --- | --- |
| 20–29 years | 3 | 2.3 | 7.9 |
| 30–39 | 16 | 12.1 | 42.1 |
| 40–49 | 11 | 8.3 | 28.9 |
| 50–59 | 5 | 3.8 | 13.2 |
| 60–69 | 3 | 2.3 | 7.9 |
| Unknown or never joined Elgin Association | 94 | 71.2 | – |
| Total | 132[1] | 100.0 | 100.0 |

[1]Valid cases 38, missing cases 94

Table 17
Canadian Antislavery Leaders' Affiliation with Evangelicalism

| Affiliation | Frequency | % | Valid % |
| --- | --- | --- | --- |
| Evangelical | 84 | 63.6 | 81.6 |
| Nonevangelical | 4 | 3.0 | 3.9 |
| Had religious affiliation but whether evangelical unknown | 15 | 11.4 | 14.6 |
| Unknown | 29 | 22.0 | – |
| Total | 132[1] | 100.0 | 100.1 |

[1]Valid cases 103, missing cases 29

nonevangelical (table 17). Denominational ties were determined in 102 instances; the Free Church and the Congregationalists led the way with 32.4 per cent and 21.6 per cent, respectively. The Anglican church supplied 8.8 per cent, and the Wesleyan Methodists, the province's largest communion, only 7.8 per cent, the same portion as the much smaller Baptists and only about 1 per cent more than the New Connexion Methodists (table 18).

Predictably, since religion was important to Canadian antislavery leaders, they were involved in numerous benevolent concerns. There were 65 among the 132 who were engaged in philanthropic work other than antislavery; 81.5 per cent belonged to at least one formal group (table 19), and 36 had an interest in a second benevolent cause outside antislavery, with 80.6 per cent holding formal membership (table 20). This affiliation with nonabolitionist philanthropy was more than merely a matter of membership. In the 64 instances where there was one non-antislavery tie, 92.2 per cent of the leaders were office holders or committee members in these organizations

Table 18
Denominational Affiliation of Canadian Antislavery Leaders, 1849–65

| Denomination | Frequency | % | Valid % |
|---|---|---|---|
| Anglican | 9 | 6.8 | 8.8 |
| Church of Scotland | 2 | 1.5 | 2.0 |
| United Presbyterian | 3 | 2.3 | 2.9 |
| Free Church Presbyterian | 33 | 25.0 | 32.4 |
| Methodist New Connexion | 7 | 5.3 | 6.9 |
| Wesleyan Methodist | 8 | 6.1 | 7.8 |
| Episcopal Methodist | 2 | 1.5 | 2.0 |
| Congregational | 22 | 16.7 | 21.6 |
| Baptist | 8 | 6.1 | 7.8 |
| No membership, but evangelical | 1 | 0.8 | 1.0 |
| Black Wesleyan Methodist | 2 | 1.5 | 2.0 |
| Primitive Methodist | 1 | 0.8 | 1.0 |
| African Methodist Episcopal | 1 | 0.8 | 1.0 |
| Methodist (branch unspecified) | 1 | 0.8 | 1.0 |
| Not applicable | 2 | 1.5 | 2.0 |
| Unknown | 30 | 22.7 | – |
| Total | 132[1] | 100.2 | 100.2 |

[1]Valid cases 102, missing cases 30

Table 19
Canadian Antislavery Leaders' Participation in Philanthropy
other than Antislavery, 1849–65

| Participation | Frequency | % | Valid % |
|---|---|---|---|
| Had concern for specific cause | 9 | 6.8 | 13.8 |
| Subscriber to cause | 3 | 2.3 | 4.6 |
| Formal membership | 53 | 40.2 | 81.5 |
| Unknown, not applicable | 67 | 50.8 | – |
| Total | 132[1] | 100.1 | 99.9 |

[1]Valid cases 65, missing cases 67

(table 21). There were 34 second non-antislavery benevolent ties; of these, 11.8 per cent were memberships and 88.2 per cent were office-holding and committee obligations (table 22). Thus, the Canadian antislavery leaders were deeply involved in benevolent causes other than antislavery. The type of nonabolitionist philanthropy ranged widely, from temperance to aid for homeless children and church founding, but it was concentrated (77.3 per cent in 66 cases) in educational work, distribution of religious literature, temperance work, and mission work (table 23).

Table 20
Canadian Antislavery Leaders with Two Philanthropic Affiliations
other than Antislavery, 1849–65

| Affiliation | Frequency | % | Valid % |
|---|---|---|---|
| Had concern for specific cause | 4 | 3.0 | 11.1 |
| Subscriber to cause | 3 | 2.3 | 8.3 |
| Formal membership | 29 | 22.0 | 80.6 |
| Unknown, not applicable | 96 | 72.7 | – |
| Total | 132[1] | 100.0 | 100.0 |

[1]Valid cases 36, missing cases 96

Table 21
Nature of Canadian Antislavery Leaders' First Philanthropic Affiliation
other than Antislavery

| Type | Frequency | % | Valid % |
|---|---|---|---|
| Member | 4 | 3.0 | 6.3 |
| Office holder/committeeman | 59 | 44.7 | 92.2 |
| Affiliation but nonmember | 1 | 0.8 | 1.6 |
| No affiliation, not applicable | 68 | 51.5 | – |
| Total | 132[1] | 100.0 | 100.1 |

[1]Valid cases 64, missing cases 68

Table 22
Nature of Canadian Antislavery Leaders' Second Philanthropic Affiliation
other than Antislavery

| Type | Frequency | % | Valid % |
|---|---|---|---|
| Member | 4 | 3.0 | 11.8 |
| Officeholder/committeeman | 30 | 22.7 | 88.2 |
| No affiliation, not applicable | 98 | 74.2 | – |
| Total | 132[1] | 99.9 | 100.0 |

[1]Valid cases 34, missing cases 98

The antislavery leadership had a substantial interest in public life
as well as private benevolence. Forty-five held one elective or ap-
pointive public office during the 1849–65 period (table 24). At least
7 were members of the legislative assembly, the province's highest
elective office, while 14 were city, town, or municipal officers

Table 23
Type of Non-Antislavery Philanthropy in Which Canadian Antislavery
Leaders Participated

| Type | Frequency | % | Valid % |
|------|-----------|---|---------|
| Educational | 8 | 6.1 | 12.1 |
| Dist. of religious literature | 21 | 15.9 | 31.8 |
| Temperance | 11 | 8.3 | 16.7 |
| Missions | 11 | 8.3 | 16.7 |
| Political reform | 2 | 1.5 | 3.0 |
| Poor relief | 5 | 3.8 | 7.6 |
| Aid to immigrants | 1 | 0.8 | 1.5 |
| Church founding | 1 | 0.8 | 1.5 |
| Separation of church and state | 2 | 1.5 | 3.0 |
| Sunday school | 1 | 0.8 | 1.5 |
| Sabbatarianism | 1 | 0.8 | 1.5 |
| Aid to homeless children | 1 | 0.8 | 1.5 |
| Black self-help | 1 | 0.8 | 1.5 |
| Unknown, not applicable | 66 | 50.0 | – |
| Total | 132[1] | 100.2 | 99.9 |

[1]Valid cases 66, missing cases 66

Table 24
Public Office Holding of Canadian Antislavery Leaders, 1849–65

| Office holding | Frequency | % | Valid % |
|----------------|-----------|---|---------|
| Held elective or appointive office | 45 | 34.1 | 100.0 |
| No office, unknown | 87 | 65.9 | – |
| Total | 132[1] | 100.0 | 100.0 |

[1]Valid cases 45, missing cases 87

(table 25). It was possible to identify the political affiliation of 34; of these, 73.5 per cent were Reform and 23.5 per cent Tory (table 26). Thus, Reformers outnumbered Tories in the upper levels of the movement by a factor of three.

Racial identification was ascertained in 121 cases. Whites were 90.1 per cent and blacks 9.9 per cent of the group. Blacks therefore constituted a considerable portion of the 132 antislavery leaders (table 27).

Several trends evident among antislavery leaders surfaced in the rank and file, as represented by the 335 Elgin Association stockholders, but there were also noteworthy differences. Among 180 stockholders, 60.5 per cent were born in Britain, 27.2 per cent in the

Table 25
Type of Public Office Held by Canadian Antislavery Leaders

| Office Type | Frequency | % | Valid % |
|---|---|---|---|
| Member of legislative assembly | 7 | 5.3 | 15.6 |
| City, town, municipal officer | 14 | 10.6 | 31.1 |
| Court officer | 5 | 3.8 | 11.1 |
| University officer | 3 | 2.3 | 6.7 |
| School inspector | 2 | 1.5 | 4.4 |
| Customs official | 1 | 0.6 | 2.2 |
| Two or more offices | 13 | 9.8 | 28.9 |
| Unknown | 87 | 66.0 | – |
| Total | 132[1] | 99.9 | 100.0 |

[1]Valid cases 45, missing cases 87

Table 26
Political Affiliation of Canadian Antislavery Leaders

| Affiliation | Frequency | % | Valid % |
|---|---|---|---|
| Reform | 25 | 18.9 | 73.5 |
| Tory | 8 | 6.1 | 23.5 |
| Not applicable | 1 | 0.8 | 2.9 |
| Unknown | 98 | 74.2 | – |
| Total | 132[1] | 100.0 | 99.9 |

[1]Valid cases 34, missing cases 98

Table 27
Racial Identity of Canadian Antislavery Leaders

| Race | Frequency | % | Valid % |
|---|---|---|---|
| White | 109 | 82.6 | 90.1 |
| Black | 12 | 9.1 | 9.9 |
| Unknown | 11 | 8.3 | – |
| Total | 132[1] | 100.0 | 100.0 |

[1]Valid cases 121, missing cases 11

United States, and 11.1 per cent in British North America (table 28). Thus, like the antislavery leaders, a large majority of the rank and file were born in Britain, but a considerably larger proportion of the followers were American-born (table 1).

There were notable differences also between the occupations of the antislavery leaders and those of the rank and file. The vocation

Table 28
Country of Birth of Elgin Association Stockholders

| Country | Frequency | % | Valid % |
|---|---|---|---|
| England | 15 | 4.5 | 8.3 |
| Scotland | 72 | 21.5 | 40.0 |
| Ireland | 22 | 6.6 | 12.2 |
| United States | 49 | 14.6 | 27.2 |
| British North America | 20 | 6.0 | 11.1 |
| Other | 2 | 0.6 | 1.1 |
| Unknown | 155 | 46.3 | – |
| Total | 335[1] | 100.1 | 99.9 |

[1]Valid cases 180, missing cases 155

Table 29
Occupation of the Elgin Association Stockholders

| Occupation | Frequency | % | Valid % |
|---|---|---|---|
| Gentleman/landlord | 4 | 1.2 | 2.0 |
| Financier/banker | 2 | 0.6 | 1.0 |
| Trade/transportation | 51 | 15.2 | 25.0 |
| Manufacturing | 8 | 2.4 | 3.9 |
| High-status profession | 32 | 9.6 | 15.7 |
| Low-status profession | 19 | 5.7 | 9.3 |
| Skilled trades | 51 | 15.2 | 25.0 |
| Unskilled trades | 13 | 3.9 | 6.4 |
| Agriculture | 23 | 6.9 | 11.3 |
| Other | 1 | 0.3 | 0.5 |
| Unknown | 131 | 39.1 | – |
| Total | 335[1] | 100.1 | 100.1 |

[1]Valid cases 204, missing cases 131

of 204 followers was identified. Of these, 25 per cent, virtually the same portion as in the case of leaders, were in trade/transportation. However, only 25 per cent were professionals, less than half the figure for the leaders. Moreover, among the stockholders, 25 per cent came from the skilled trades and 6.4 per cent from the unskilled, while 11.3 per cent were farmers (table 29). There were virtually no representatives from the trades or agriculture among the antislavery leaders. Altogether, 42.7 per cent of the Canadian antislavery rank and file, as represented by the Elgin Association stockholders, came from the skilled, unskilled, and agricultural sectors of society.

The racial composition of the Elgin stockholders helps to account for some of these differences. Among the 193 whose racial identity

Table 30
Racial Identification of Elgin Association Stockholders

| Race | Frequency | % | Valid % |
|------|-----------|---|---------|
| White | 149 | 44.5 | 77.2 |
| Black | 44 | 13.1 | 22.8 |
| Unknown | 142 | 42.4 | – |
| Total | 335[1] | 100.0 | 100.0 |

[1]Valid cases 193, missing cases 142

could be established, 77.2 per cent were white and 22.8 per cent black (table 30). Thus, blacks constituted nearly one-quarter of the Elgin stockholders whose racial identity is known. Since many of them doubtless were either fugitive slaves or free blacks from the United States who preferred to live in the province, in most cases they would have been American-born. They help to account for the larger number of stockholders (27.2 per cent as compared to 9.4 per cent of the leaders) who were born in the United States. Moreover, some would have brought with them skilled and unskilled trades, and others would have come from agricultural backgrounds, but only a relatively small number would have arrived as professionals or would have been in the province long enough to have moved into that group. This helps to explain why fewer professionals but a relatively large number of working-class people participated at the membership level in Canadian antislavery.

It was possible to establish the ages of 172 of the stockholders who invested in the Elgin Association; of these, 37.2 per cent were from 30 to 39 years old, and 28.5 per cent were from 40 to 49 (table 31). Thus, 65.7 per cent of the stockholders were between 30 and 49 years old when they joined the association; comparable figures for the leaders of the ASC and the Elgin Association are 64.0 per cent and 71.0 per cent, respectively. What distinguished the stockholders was that 18.6 per cent were from 20 to 29 years old, while only 9.4 per cent and 7.9 per cent of the ASC and the Elgin Association leaders were in this younger age group (tables 15 and 16).

Like the antislavery leaders, the abolitionist rank and file had strong church ties and, with one notable exception, they were similar to the church connections of the leaders. In 181 cases, Free Church Presbyterians constituted 39.8 per cent, Anglicans (whether evangelical could not be determined) 12.7 per cent, and Baptists 10.5 per cent. Predictably, only 7.2 per cent were Wesleyan Methodists. Surprisingly, however, given the fact that 21.6 per cent of the leaders

Table 31
Age at Which Stockholders Joined Elgin Association

| Age | Frequency | % | Valid % |
|---|---|---|---|
| Under 20 years | 1 | 0.3 | 0.6 |
| 20–29 | 32 | 9.6 | 18.6 |
| 30–39 | 64 | 19.1 | 37.2 |
| 40–49 | 49 | 14.6 | 28.5 |
| 50–59 | 18 | 5.4 | 10.5 |
| 60–69 | 6 | 1.8 | 3.5 |
| 70–79 | 2 | 0.6 | 1.2 |
| Unknown | 163 | 48.7 | – |
| Total | 335[1] | 100.1 | 100.1 |

[1]Valid cases 172, missing cases 163

Table 32
Denominational Affiliation of Elgin Association Stockholders

| Denomination | Frequency | % | Valid % |
|---|---|---|---|
| Anglican | 23 | 6.9 | 12.7 |
| Church of Scotland | 4 | 1.2 | 2.2 |
| United Presbyterian | 4 | 1.2 | 2.2 |
| Free Church Presbyterian | 72 | 21.5 | 39.8 |
| Presbyterian (unspecified) | 17 | 5.1 | 9.4 |
| Wesleyan Methodist | 13 | 3.9 | 7.2 |
| Episcopal Methodist | 3 | 0.9 | 1.6 |
| Methodist New Connexion | 1 | 0.3 | 0.6 |
| Methodist (unspecified) | 12 | 3.6 | 6.6 |
| Baptist | 19 | 5.7 | 10.5 |
| Congregational | 6 | 1.8 | 3.3 |
| None | 1 | 0.3 | 0.6 |
| Protestant (unspecified) | 6 | 1.8 | 3.3 |
| Unknown | 154 | 46.0 | – |
| Total | 335[1] | 100.2 | 100.0 |

[1]Valid cases 181, missing cases 154

were Congregationalists, they represented only 3.3 per cent of the stockholders (see tables 32 and 18).

From this body of information a general profile of those involved in Canadian antislavery emerges. The vast majority, leaders as well as followers, were born in Britain during the first two decades of the nineteenth century. The former, and almost certainly most of the latter, had been socialized in a society in which antislavery ideals and actions were intensifying. Many had witnessed British emancipation and, later, the vigorous efforts of the British antislavery organizations (especially the Scottish societies, in which some served) to end slavery in the United States. These memories were still vivid when they emigrated, arriving in British North America in the late 1830s and 1840s as relatively young men. It was the memory of these experiences, spurred on by an unquenchable hatred of slavery, which, when confronted with the reality of rising numbers of needy fugitive slaves, energized their efforts to rekindle a Canadian antislavery movement that was dispirited and in disarray.

When the leaders assumed direction of Canadian antislavery, they were aspiring professionals and businessmen – mainly ministers, government officials, lawyers, and merchants – who were seeking to establish themselves in a new setting. Most had not yet reached the pinnacle of their careers. Ministers arriving from the mother country were in great demand, for generally they had better credentials than those trained in the limited facilities of the province; they were quickly put into positions of leadership in the churches and elsewhere, and their status was secure. For local clerics, as well as for other struggling professionals and merchants, the path was more difficult. Participation in benevolent organizations doubtless offered men seeking to make their way in new surroundings a means of becoming known. It also gave them the opportunity to establish contact with others who shared their background and their religious and humanitarian concerns, and to meet those who might incidentally be helpful professionally or in business. Moreover, as newcomers to Canadian society, lawyers and merchants tended to be outside the circle of power. Identification with Reform politics was a means of helping to redistribute power and open the doors of influence to them.

Nevertheless, the religious element was clearly the key factor for those involved in antislavery, as the large role that ministers and Free Church laymen played in the movement shows. The faith of most Canadian abolitionists taught them that all men were their brothers, and a predominantly evangelical outlook dictated the necessity of actively striving to meet the spiritual and physical needs of their brothers. For evangelicals to have evaded these responsibilities would have been to disregard the demands of the Christian gospel, to endanger social stability, and to commit personal sin. This was the root of their antislavery and other benevolent activity, and in all likelihood it was an important factor in their involvement in politics and local offices.

Professionals made up more than one-half of the leadership and about one-quarter of the membership; they possessed the skills and superior education that was so useful in managing a public organization. Businessmen, primarily merchants, constituted about 25 per cent of both categories; but more than 40 per cent of the rank and file came from the skilled, unskilled, and agricultural levels of society, and this shows unmistakably that there was large-scale involvement by the working classes in Canadian antislavery.

Blacks conducted their own antislavery activities in the province, but clearly they also participated in considerable numbers in British North America's white antislavery movement. A judicious estimate of the number of blacks in the Canadas in the 1860s is that they were about 3–4 per cent of the population. Since they were 9.4 per cent of the leadership and 22.2 per cent of the Elgin Association stockholders, they clearly occupied a position in Canadian antislavery that far exceeded what might have been expected, given their proportion of the population.[2]

While the foregoing analysis reveals the presence of many working-class Canadians and blacks in the antislavery movement and provides a general profile of the rank and file and leadership, it sheds little light on the role of women. Since they were neither office holders nor committee members in the three associations, and since they were not Elgin Association stockholders, it is apparent that Canadian antislavery, while admitting blacks, abided by the mid-nineteenth-century mores that excluded women from joint participation with men in public affairs. This leaves the false impression that women were absent from the movement. In fact, as was noted in chapter 6, women were very much involved with Canadian antislavery through their own committee. They carried on most of the relief work of the ASC, and, until Ward's tour in Britain filled the society's treasury, they raised their own funds.[3]

# 9 Ontario and the Freedman

When the Anti-Slavery Society of Canada (ASC) met in February 1863 to celebrate the progress towards ending slavery that had been made during the previous two years and that had culminated in Lincoln's Emancipation Proclamation, there was no indication that this would be its final meeting. The society elected a new slate of officers, and although the executive offered no new programs, it seemed that the organization would soldier on until the victory over American slavery was complete. However, the ASC never met again. Within two years the North prevailed in the American Civil War, and together with the ratification of the Thirteenth Amendment to the Constitution, this sealed the fate of slavery in the United States.

Ironically, these two events – the Northern victory and the Thirteenth Amendment – did not signal the end of the antislavery movement in the United States. For, as Americans laboured to reincorporate the seceded states into the Union, they also had to find a role in American society for the 4 million former slaves. These two issues were the central themes of the Reconstruction era. Abolitionists, who had campaigned for three decades to liberate the slaves, were determined not to let the opportunity to secure a large measure of political and social equality for their clients – won so dearly on the Civil War's battlefields – slip through their hands in the postwar period. This final phase in the long antislavery campaign saw the radical Republicans (the remnant of the abolitionists) wage a vigorous struggle in Congress to secure rights for the freedmen.

It ended only when the compromise of 1877 left the South free to deal with the freedmen on its own.[1]

Despite the demise of the ASC, Ontarians showed considerable interest in this terminal stage of the antislavery struggle. Their long concern for abolition – extending from the UCAS of the late 1830s, through the Elgin Association, to the ASC – and the participation of some British North Americans in the Civil War made it unlikely that they would ignore the welfare of the former slaves who were now relishing their first sweet taste of freedom. No new organizations were formed to assist the freedmen or to appeal to public opinion on their behalf. Instead, the residents of the province voiced their concern through the commentary of newspapers, whose editors kept a close eye on the American effort to define the role of the freedmen in the United States. An analysis of their comments shows that many were pessimistic about the future of the freedmen in American society. It also reveals a deep-seated racism among British North Americans, which in retrospect casts a new light on the reluctance of many to support antislavery before the Civil War.[2]

IN 1865 THE AMERICANS FACED THE AWESOME task of recreating a peaceful union from a nation torn by civil war. Demobilizing armies, managing towering public debts, and rebuilding physical devastation are the usual tasks of postwar leaders. For the American statesmen of the 1860s, these problems were compounded by the need to restore the seceded states to the Union and to determine the role that the freedmen would play in society. Americans quickly discovered that the solutions to these problems were different phases of a single process.

The long journey to freedom for nearly 4 million slaves ended with the ratification of the Thirteenth Amendment in 1865. Although constitutional revision was a necessity to end slavery formally, most Americans knew that the institution was doomed, and consequently the amendment's ratification aroused little interest. But there was great discussion of the freedman's future. This turned on several broad questions. Would Congress assist the freedmen during their transition to liberty, or must they rely on their own resources bolstered by private philanthropy? Would individual states determine their policies with respect to the freedmen, or would Congress reserve that task? Would the freedmen advance to full citizenship and its associated rights at once, or must they remain suspended somewhere between bondage and citizenship?

Like Americans, Canadian editors paid slight attention to the Thirteenth Amendment in 1865. Rather, they speculated about the freedman's prospects for success as he stood on the threshold of a new era. Predictably, the Toronto *Globe*, long a defender of the former slaves, saw hopeful signs in a recent parade of freedmen in Charleston, South Carolina. A black regiment and band, numerous tradesmen, and nearly 1800 schoolchildren had paraded in an "orderly" celebration of liberty. Undeniably, some freedmen were degraded and dissolute, admitted the editor, but the liberated marchers promisingly symbolized the industrious inclinations of many, and the schoolchildren's presence showed that black parents valued education. Equipped with books and land, the paper declared, the freedman's transition to learning and civilization would be easier than many had predicted.[3]

Such optimism contrasted starkly with the gloomy predictions of most newspapers. One supposed obstacle to the freedman's advance was the incurable laziness that many editors attributed to blacks. "If they work at all, they will do just enough to secure themselves from starvation," one paper claimed. The freedmen, asserted another, thought that emancipation had released them from Adam's curse of physical labour; liberty to them meant "revellings, idleness and every wickedness." Blacks were believed to be especially prone to dissipation in tropical regions like the American South, for wherever "luscious fruits" provided ready food with little exertion, they would rather "dance by the light ob de moon" than work. The reason for this lethargy, implied the London *Free Press*, was that black labourers, unlike white workers, lacked the energy that was needed for regular work. Once freed, they would labour for only a short time "from mere habit" and then lapse into increasing indolence. Without the drive to compete with other labourers, the freedman would become the "restless child of change and accident."[4]

Journalists found other flaws in the character of the African American. Some claimed that he possessed a superstitious, "easily wrought imagination" that rendered him easy prey to those wishing to manipulate him. Others believed that whites could readily mould the ideas of the "impressionable" blacks, whom they depicted as being like clay in the potter's hand. Frequently, newspapers portrayed them as a "docile" people, the "tools of fad men and fanatics," meekly accepting the directions of others. Blacks, it seemed, were destined to became nothing more than "good servants" for whites, who were viewed as their "natural leaders and guides."[5]

While freedmen were often pictured as "timid," "kindly" people, they were also said to be unreliable and dangerously erratic; given the right circumstances, these volatile elements in their personalities, which were said to be only very thinly concealed by a veneer of domestication, could trigger outbreaks of "savage ferocity." The Toronto *Leader* claimed that recent racial strife in Texas showed that blacks were "merciless monsters when they [found] the whites helplessly in their power." Driven by the "animal passions of a half brute," the freedmen occasionally vented their wild urges in aggressive sexual behaviour and "savage outbursts of almost demoniacal rage and lust." This behaviour was said to be most apparent in the South. There, according to one editor, the freedmen had avenged themselves for the social exclusiveness of white males by widespread "violation of white womanhood," which supposedly had been the "ruling passion" of blacks during the previous six months.[6]

Certain traits that journalists found in the black character were less undesirable but were hardly complimentary. For example, many believed that blacks were uniquely suited by nature and habit for life in warm climates and that they could not flourish in northern latitudes. The London *Free Press* saw an "irrepressible joyousness" among blacks, while a visitor to the South condescendingly reported the "broad grin, so peculiar to the negro." Another paper described the freedman's voice pattern as an amalgam of rasping "hisses and groans such as can come from Darkies only." Some characteristics attributed to blacks even bordered on the exotic. One account claimed that the natural skill of black dancers was superior to the disciplined artistry of trained white performers; it was "all that a breakdown [could] be, in its mechanical energy, its humorous vagaries, and those intricacies of heel and toe which [drove] the legitimate dancing masters nearly crazy with jealousy." All these attributes were not necessarily regarded as liabilities, but in the popular mind they unflatteringly differentiated blacks from the surrounding white majority.[7]

Incorrigibly lazy, explosively passionate, pliable and credulous, and possessing certain bizarre qualities that bemused whites – these were the salient features of the African-American character as seen by the Ontario editors who were pondering the freedman's future. Blacks, they concluded, were poor candidates for success in postslavery America. Moreover, as the press scrutinized the long-awaited Reconstruction program in relation to blacks, this erroneous negative characterization was expanded.

Before the war ended, Congress had implemented a program to aid the freedmen, since many were destitute in the wake of the collapsed plantation system. A Bureau of Refugees, Freedmen, and

Abandoned Lands, usually called the Freedmen's Bureau, was created. It channelled food, clothing, and medical supplies to the needy, assisted them in finding shelter and employment, and helped settle them on available land. Although the bureau was initially chartered for a single year, its life was extended by Congress in 1866. Furthermore, since the new state governments in the South had passed laws enabling them to regiment and exploit the former slaves, Congress broadened the bureau's authority to counteract this evil. It permitted the bureau to supervise the freedmen's labour contracts and to establish special courts for blacks who were unable to receive fair treatment in the regular courts. This strengthened agency monitored the freedmen's perilous journey to freedom until Congress terminated its mandate in 1869.[8]

A few Ontario newspapers applauded the strengthened Freedmen's Bureau. They agreed with the *Globe* that the agency had contributed significantly to the education of the freedmen who, if left to themselves, would have fared badly at the hands of their former masters. But most papers praised President Andrew Johnson's veto of the bureau's extension, even though Congress soon mustered enough votes to overturn it. Like the *Leader*, they believed that the bureau was a necessary device to help the slave take the first step into freedom. But they felt that after that objective had been achieved, it would be a mistake to give further aid, for the improvident freedmen would then conclude that the government was paternalistic, bound to care even for those who would not exercise the "degree of industry by which alone the great mass of mankind can procure sustenance and the comforts of a home." Such unjust burdening of industrious whites would be unnecessary when "negroes were willing to perform an ordinary share of labor." If the freedmen could not take care of themselves in their newly won liberty, declared one editor, it would prove that emancipation had been a "great mistake" and a "gross injustice."[9]

Since the Freedmen's Bureau was a temporary agency, Congress attempted to secure more permanent rights for the freedmen with the 1866 civil rights bill. This bill declared that citizens of all races and colours had equal rights before the courts in all states to make contracts and to exchange property, while enjoying the full benefit of all laws and legal proceedings affecting person and property. To protect the bill from hostile courts in the future, Congress included its provisions in the first section of the Fourteenth Amendment, which was ratified in 1868.[10]

Canadian newspapers that commented on the civil rights bill usually supported the goal of securing for the freedmen a large measure of personal liberty, but they disagreed over the means. One editor reasoned that since the federal government had freed the slaves, it should therefore protect them, because to leave the freedmen dependent on the justice they could hope to receive from their former owners would be to forgo one of the main fruits of victory. By contrast, the Toronto *Leader* (reflecting the disregard for black interests whenever they conflicted with white interests – an attitude that so often marked the Ontario press) felt that black rights should be left in state hands. Other papers complained that the measure unfairly elevated blacks over whites by legislating in their favour and warned that the bill failed to protect society adequately against the "foolish and emotional excesses" of the freedmen. But, generally, Ontario newspapers paid little attention to the first section of the Fourteenth Amendment. Instead, they concentrated on what they believed to be the central issue: the enfranchisement of the freedmen. [11]

Congress approached this delicate matter cautiously, for recent state elections had revealed that there was strong opposition to giving the vote to blacks. When the radical wing of the Republican party gained control of Congress in 1866, it took up the issue, albeit timidly. The radicals first enfranchised blacks in the District of Columbia, where the constitution empowered Congress to determine voter qualification. Next, Congress required black suffrage to be included in the new state constitutions that Southern conventions were drafting. Since the U.S. constitution lodged responsibility for defining voter qualifications with the states, the continuing opposition to black suffrage in some Northern areas made constitutional amendment necessary if African Americans were to vote everywhere in the nation. Still treading warily, the radicals addressed the issue indirectly in the second section of the Fourteenth Amendment; this penalized states for denying the vote to any male citizen, except in cases of rebellious or criminal behaviour, by reducing their congressional delegations. Only after winning the presidential election in 1868 did the Republicans venture to carry the Fifteenth Amendment, which unequivocally prevented the suffrage from being denied on account of race, colour, or previous servitude.

Eighteen of the twenty-one journals that were examined for this study commented on the suffrage question. Five favoured enfranchising adult black males immediately; three viewed black suffrage as a risky experiment at best and supported restricted enfranchisement by applying to freedmen voter qualification criteria that were not required of whites. The remaining ten opposed black suffrage for at least a generation, if not permanently. Those in the first cat-

Table 33

An Analysis of the Attitudes of 21 Ontario Newspapers (1865–77) towards Measures to Enhance the Social and Civil Rights of Freedmen during Reconstruction

| Paper | Extension of Freedmen's Bureau | | Civil rights bill of 1866 | | Black suffrage | | | Social equality & civil rights bill of 1875 | |
|---|---|---|---|---|---|---|---|---|---|
| | For | Against | For | Against | Immediately | For qualified blacks only | Not at present | For | Against |
| Kingston British Whig | | | | | | | | | X |
| Canada Christian Advocate | | | | | X | | | | X |
| Canadian Freeman | | X | | | | | X | | X |
| Ottawa Citizen | | X | | X | | X | | | |
| Christian Guardian | | | X | | | X | | X | |
| Kingston Daily News | | X | | | | X | | | |
| Newmarket Era | X | | X | | | | | | |
| Evangelical Witness | | | | | | | X | | |
| Peterborough Examiner | | X | | X | | | X | | |
| London Free Press | | X | | X | | | X | | X |
| Toronto Globe | X | | X | | X | | | X | |
| Toronto Leader | | X | | X | | | X | | |
| Barrie Northern Advance | | X | | | | | | | |
| Sarnia Observer | | | X | | X | | | | |
| Chatham Planet | | | X | | X | | | | |
| Goderich Signal | | X | | | | | X | | |
| Hamilton Spectator | | X | X | | X | | | | X |
| Hamilton Times | | X | | X | | | X | | X |
| Ottawa Times | X | | | X | | | X | | X |
| Oshawa Vindicator | X | | | | | | X | | |
| London Western Advertiser | | | | | | | X | | |
| Total | 4 | 10 | 6 | 6 | 5 | 3 | 10 | 2 | 7 |

egory characteristically asserted that denying the vote to the freedmen would be unjust when so many of them had fought to save
the Union. In addition, they protested the shortsightedness of freeing
the slaves without guaranteeing them the political means of protecting themselves. The *Globe* predicted that if the perceptive blacks
won the vote, they would learn, despite their lack of education and
political experience, how to use it for their own interest while serving
the good of the nation (table 33). [13]

Among the three newspapers which felt that enfranchising only
qualified freedmen would be justified, the views of the Ottawa *Citizen* were representative. It opposed enfranchising all blacks, among
whom "education and learning" were so limited, when some whites
who constituted the "superior class" could not vote. Nevertheless,
the paper believed that the suffrage could safely be conceded to
those who had fought in the Union army, who owned property,
who were literate, or who had belonged to a religious organization
for the previous five years. Admittedly, this might thrust "ignorant,
excitable, easily led" blacks into power, but such men would be
unable to maintain it. "Three or four years at the most," the paper
assured its readers, "will see them in their proper position, as the
free servants and labourers of the whites, guarded by them from
the evils to which they have been exposed by their sudden trans-
ference from servitude to liberty. [14]

The ten newspapers that opposed black suffrage altogether justified their stand in a variety of ways. Several feared that the destitute
"nigger," as some journalists named him, would soon discover the
salability of his vote and would offer it to the highest bidder, thereby
degrading American political institutions even further. Another argument was that the pliable freedmen's votes would be manipulated
too easily by their former owners, thereby restoring the planter class
monopoly of political power. [15] Frequently, papers asserted that the
question was best left in the hands of the states or to the wisdom
of the time. [16] The *Canadian Freeman*, a paper sensitive to the honour
of Irish immigrants, indignantly opined that the radical Republicans
intended to use black votes to offset the ballots of Irish Americans,
who ordinarily voted for Democrats. [17] Virtually all opponents of
black suffrage agreed that the freedmen should not vote because
they were unprepared to do so. Characteristically, the Hamilton
*Times* editor wrote:

If intelligence and virtue are necessary to discharge their duties as citizens
in a proper manner, then it must be certain that the emancipated slaves of
the South are utterly unfit to be entrusted with the elective franchise, and

moreover they never will be until better educated and trained to the discharge of their duties as citizens.[18]

Many believed that the illiterate freedmen, "degraded" by two centuries of slavery, which had schooled them in white society's worst features, were "incapable" of understanding the suffrage. Perhaps, one paper grudgingly admitted, their descendants "might be fitted for civilized usages and habits."[19] These considerations, it was said, made the cry for black suffrage nothing but the "wildest fanaticism."[20] The idea of giving blacks the franchise carried "nigger-anthropy" too far. Only when blacks generally had "proved" that they were not "unworthy" of freedom by developing "habits of industry and self-reliance" should they be permitted to vote.[21] Until then, it would be humiliating to the "intelligent whites" of the South to be disfranchised while a million "semi-barbarous" Negroes voted.[22]

The argument against Negro suffrage was also rooted in the belief that the black race was intellectually inferior to the white race. One writer scorned the notion that the "African race [was] equal to our own," saying that blacks did not possess the same "natural capabilities" or "powers of reasoning" as whites; accordingly, the black's role in governing must be limited to an extent that was commensurate with the "apparent inferiority of his mental status." Citing the English novelist Anthony Trollope, another editor claimed that the defective "gifts and nature" of the freedmen disqualified them altogether from participating in the political institutions of white society, for they were "naturally subservient to the White man's greater power of mind." Newspapers of this persuasion had little hope that education would prepare the freedman for a higher status in society, for they believed that, unlike whites, whose natural state was civilization, the normal condition of blacks was barbarism. The record showed, one editorial bluntly stated, that

[blacks] are savage by nature, and utterly incapable of self-sustained civilization. Four thousand years ago, they lived side by side with Egyptian and Arabic civilization, and were just as savage then as in Africa they are now. More pains have been taken, more money and labor extended to civilize the negro than any other race. Yet, in his native wilds he is still a savage, and is reverting rapidly to the savage state wherever relieved from slavery and left to cultivate a civilization of his own. There never was found a nation, tribe, or society, however small, of white savages. The civilization of the whites is indigenous – part of their natures congenial with their race. The savage state is natural to the negro. He never was found with an

indigenous civilization, nor any civilization at all, after he had lived in a society composed only of negroes for five generations.

Thus, since they lacked education, were said to have serious character flaws and to be fatally crippled by their alleged intellectual inferiority, the freedmen, in the eyes of most of the Ontario press, were far from ready to participate fully in American political life. Journalists consigned them to a status well below full citizenship.[23]

In 1875, Congress completed its postwar efforts to define the role of the freedmen in American society by passing a second civil rights bill. The bill guaranteed to all people, regardless of race or creed, equal access to public places of accommodation and entertainment, as well as to transportation facilities, and it barred discrimination, because of race, colour, or previous servitude, in the selection of juries.[24]

This first step towards social equality for freedmen could not expect a warm reception in Ontario, where, well before 1875, many newspapers had frowned on the interracial mingling that social equality implied. Their opposition rested partially on the belief that interracial social contact generated racial friction by violating the "instinctive feelings of repugnance" that whites supposedly harboured against blacks. This allegedly "deep seated" and "natural" sentiment made "society" resent the "mixing and even association" of whites and blacks, the Ottawa Citizen asserted. Some editors warned that forcing interracial social intercourse, as the civil rights bill purportedly did, was dangerous, as events in the South showed. There, the elevation of the freedmen had aroused the "innate antipathy" of their former owners, and race war was imminent. The conflict, said the press, would inevitably destroy blacks, because Northern whites would inevitably close ranks with their Southern brethren; for, as the Hamilton Times explained, people of similar racial background naturally attracted each other, especially when threatened by a group of another racial origin, while people of dissimilar origins repelled each other.[25]

The opponents of social mingling also argued that it would open the forbidden door of intermarriage. Supposedly, once blacks had won citizenship, they would quickly claim social equality and would demand admission to "general society." If they were successful, one paper predicted, "miscegenation and gradual transformation [of North Americans] into a mixed race, by the infusion of negro blood," would be sure to follow. White supremacy must be maintained to prevent this frightening prospect, declared the Freeman, for "hybridism" was a destructive social force. Ordinarily, explained the

Hamilton *Evening Times*, only "kindred races" intermarried, and their offspring were sturdy people with the potential to become "great nations" like England; but when opposites, such as the black and white races were alleged to be, violated nature's edict, their progeny were backward people who gradually degenerated and died out. American society, it seemed, was at a critical juncture and should heed the warning, for "mongrelism" was an evil to be "crushed out at all hazards." The Kingston *British Whig* bolstered these ideas by publishing an invitation from a New Yorker, signed "Caucasian," to join the Anti-Negro Amalgamation Association. This organization proclaimed that blacks were inferior to whites, who had the paternal duty to civilize and protect them. It saw interracial marriage as a violation of the divine will, which had created blacks and whites distinct people. Even the pro-black *Christian Guardian* shared this aversion to social intimacy.[26]

Having already proclaimed the dangers of social mingling, many newspapers doubtless would have opposed the second civil rights bill had they bothered to discuss it. But by 1875 the antislavery and Negro questions were nearly half a century old, and many editors ignored the bill. Few commentators were as forthright in their criticism as the editor of the Ottawa *Times*; while he was misinformed about the provisions of the bill, his condemnation of it, for implementing a policy of "educational miscegenation" that forced black and white school children to mingle for the "purpose of thoroughly erasing any idea of physical or social superiority from the minds of whites," reveals a deep hostility. The views of the Toronto *Globe*, long a defender of blacks, were especially noteworthy. The *Globe* supported the equality of blacks and whites *de jure* in the areas the bill covered; nevertheless, by advising the opponents of racial mingling on how to circumvent the bill without violating it, the newspaper revealed the shallowness of its commitment to social equality. Barbers, hotelkeepers, theatre managers, and cab drivers in the United States, the *Globe* declared, unrealistically feared that compliance with the law would ruin their business by driving away white customers. The bill was necessary to protect blacks from rude public insults, the editor admitted, but its sponsors never intended to obliterate "all social distinctions, or fancied that it would enable any man to secure a position in places and among people when he was not welcome." No one, the paper continued,

will persist in going where he finds himself not welcome, when he finds others glad to see him and to afford him accommodation. It is very easy for a hotel clerk, or a barber, or a theatre manager to obey the law by giving the accommodation required, and yet do it all in such a way that the customer will never trouble him again. Let people kick against the law, and it becomes a fretting sore. Let them acquiesce in its provisions and the grievance is gone, and yet their company in ordinary cases remains as select as ever it was. Ten years hence our friends in the states will wonder why they ever thought the Civil Rights Act a grievance.

Thus, even Canada's staunchest friend of African Americans, as the *Globe* was reputed to be, preferred a system that appeared to achieve a measure of social equality by law but which permitted *de facto* segregation.[27]

By the time that Congress had completed its efforts to fix the status of the freedmen, Ontario journalists had unwittingly penned sketches of the former slaves in rough detail. A small minority had drawn an optimistic picture, tinted in bright hues, that pointed hopefully to the future. They saw the freedmen as industrious people who were eager to take advantage of the economic opportunities that surrounded them. Anxious for education, especially for their children, the freedmen would soon advance in American society; for, in the eyes of these editors, blacks were untrammelled by intellectual weakness or character defects. They believed that the freedmen's natural kindliness and timidity equipped them potentially to be conscientious, orderly citizens, who would use the franchise wisely. They also believed that the former slaves merited a large, if not full, measure of social equality, and these journalists were not alarmed at the prospect of the racial amalgamation that might ensue.

The characteristic image of the freedmen, however, was etched in the darker tones of racial thought that was so representative of the nineteenth-century English-speaking world. Blacks were reputed to be lazy, improvident, docile, and too easily moulded in others' hands for their own or society's good. Yet this placid exterior was said to mask a passionate fury buried deep in the black personality which might burst forth unpredictably in a frenzied orgy of destruction and in aggressive sexual behaviour towards white women. Because the freedman was thought to be uniquely suited to living in warm climates, few people believed that he would migrate in significant numbers to the cool Northern states, let alone to the Dominion of Canada. Tractability and intellectual weakness marked him as an ideal servant for whites, who were his natural guides and benefactors. Moreover, the freedman was unfit to participate in the political responsibilities of citizenship, then or in the future, given his tendency to revert to a state of nature. Nor should he be elevated to full social equality, for, in the view of most journalists, miscegenation and racial degeneracy would inevitably result.

These fragmentary and contrasting depictions of the former slaves contain insufficient evidence to permit a full reconstruction of Canadian racial thought about blacks. Yet they shed considerable light on the nature of racial thought and the influences that shaped it in mid-nineteenth-century Ontario; and incidentally they help to explain the reluctance of some British North Americans to support antislavery. In some instances, there is an apparent correlation between the political loyalty of the newspaper and its attitude towards the freedmen. Most Conservative journals, for example, opposed measures that would enhance the civil and social rights of the freedmen, and they generally portrayed blacks negatively. But this antifreedman predisposition did not clearly distinguish Conservative from Liberal journals, for the latter did not uniformly take the opposite position. In fact, only the *Globe*, the chief Liberal daily, consistently approved of more political and social rights for the freedmen and characterized them in a positive light. The Hamilton *Times*, although advocating the extension of the Freedmen's Bureau and the 1866 civil rights bill, condemned black suffrage and described blacks disparagingly. However, a third Liberal daily, the London *Western Advertiser*, supported black suffrage and drew a hopeful picture of the freedmen. Thus, while Conservative journals were more likely to be ill-disposed towards blacks than their Liberal opponents were, political loyalties do not satisfactorily account for the attitudes of Ontario editors (tables 34 and 35).[28]

A mixed picture also emerges when the religious affiliations of the editors are analysed in relation to their treatment of the freedmen. In the period 1865–77, the twenty-one papers had twenty-four editors; among these, there were six Anglicans, seven Methodists, six Presbyterians, and one each from the Baptist, Disciples of Christ, and Roman Catholic churches, while the religious connections of two could not be determined. Except for the issue of black enfranchisement where their response was mixed, Anglican editors generally opposed Reconstruction measures that enhanced the social and civil rights of the freedmen, characterized them personally and as labourers in negative terms, and drew a bleak picture of their future in the United States. Methodist and Presbyterian editors, on the other hand, had no clear-cut position on these issues. One Presbyterian editor opposed and four supported immediate black suffrage (although one did so only because the U.S. constitution rested on universal manhood suffrage, and despite the editor's belief that enfranchising blacks was unwise); one Methodist editor supported

Table 34

A Comparison of the Attitudes of 19 Liberal and Conservative Newspapers in Ontario (1865–77) on Measures to Enhance the Social and Civil Rights of Freedmen during Reconstruction

| | Extension of Freedmen's Bureau | | Civil rights bill of 1866 | | Black suffrage | | | Social equality & civil rights bill of 1875 | |
|---|---|---|---|---|---|---|---|---|---|
| | For | Against | For | Against | Immediately | For qualified blacks only | Not at present | For | Against |
| **LIBERAL PAPERS** | | | | | | | | | |
| Newmarket Era | X | | X | | | | | | |
| Peterborough Examiner | | X | | X | | | X | | |
| Toronto Globe | X | | X | | X | | | X | |
| Sarnia Observer | | | X | | X | | | | |
| Goderich Signal | | X | | | | | X | | |
| Hamilton Times | X | | X | | | | X | | |
| Ottawa Times (1874–76) | | | | | | | X | | |
| London Western Advertiser | | | | | | | | | X |
| Total | 3 | 2 | 4 | 1 | 2 | 0 | 4 | 1 | 1 |
| **CONSERVATIVE PAPERS** | | | | | | | | | |
| Kingston British Whig | | | | | | | | | X |
| Toronto Canadian Freeman | | X | | | | | | | X |
| Ottawa Citizen | | X | | X | | | X | | X |
| Kingston Daily News | | X | | | | X | | | |
| London Free Press | | X | | X | | X | X | | |
| Toronto Leader | | X | | X | | | X | | X |
| Barrie Northern Advance | | X | | | | | | | |
| Chatham Planet | | | X | | X | | | | |
| Hamilton Spectator | | X | | X | X | | | | X |
| Ottawa Times (1865–74) | | X | | X | | | X | | |
| Oshawa Vindicator | X | | | | | | X | | |
| Total | 1 | 8 | 1 | 5 | 2 | 2 | 5 | 0 | 5 |

Table 35
A Comparison of the Freedman's Image in 19 Liberal and Conservative Newspapers in Ontario (1865–77) with Respect to their Qualities as Labourers, their General Personal Characteristics, and Their Chances of Success in the United States

| | Qualities as labourers | | General personal characteristics | | Future prospects in United States | |
|---|---|---|---|---|---|---|
| | Undesirable[1] | Desirable | Negative | Positive | Pessimistic | Optimistic |
| LIBERAL PAPERS | | | | | | |
| Newmarket Era | | | | | | |
| Peterborough Examiner | | | | | | |
| Toronto Globe | | X | | X | | X |
| Sarnia Observer | | | | | | |
| Goderich Signal | X | | X | | | |
| Hamilton Times | | | X | | X | |
| Ottawa Times (1874–76) | | | X | | | |
| London Western Advertiser | | X | | X | | X |
| Total | 1 | 2 | 3 | 2 | 1 | 2 |
| CONSERVATIVE PAPERS | | | | | | |
| Kingston British Whig | X | | X | | X | |
| Toronto Canadian Freeman | X | | X | | X | |
| Ottawa Citizen | X | | X | | X | |
| Kingston Daily News | X | | X | | | |
| London Free Press | X | | X | | X | |
| Toronto Leader | X | | X | | X | |
| Barrie Northern Advance | | | | | | |
| Chatham Planet | | | | | | |
| Hamilton Spectator (1865–70, 1868–73) | X | | X | | X | X |
| Ottawa Times (1865–74) | X | | X | | X | |
| Oshawa Vindicator | | | | | | |
| Total | 8 | 0 | 8 | 0 | 7 | 1 |

[1]See note 28 of this chapter for an explanation of these terms.

black suffrage, three opposed it, and one advocated immediate suffrage for qualified blacks only. Two of the former as well as two of the latter described the black character in positive terms, and one editor in each group disparaged it. Three editors in each group were optimistic about the freedman's future in the United States, while two Presbyterian editors believed that blacks had generally desirable characteristics as labourers, and one Methodist editor thought they did not. Thus, while the attitude of newspapers towards the freedman and his interests are fairly predictable on the basis of religious affiliation in the case of Anglican editors, the religious identification of Methodist and Presbyterian editors does not appear to have determined their image of the freedmen (tables 36 and 37).[29]

The proximity of the United States, where the antislavery struggle had raged for years, suggests that American racial thought might have shaped the views of Ontario editors on the freedmen. At the beginning of the nineteenth century, the monogenists had dominated American racial thinking. Like the Princeton president, Samuel Stanhope Smith, they accepted the Genesis account that all men sprang from Adam. Physical differences between the races, as well as their allegedly unique mental and moral characteristics, were attributed by such writers either to environmental causes or to contrasting lifestyles. But these differences were assumed to be temporary and reversible. Smith believed that if blacks were removed from the degrading influences of slavery and the degenerative lifestyle of barbarism, education and Christianity could transform them. By this means, with the passage of time, blacks might return to their original white condition.[30]

In the prewar decades, two theories competed for acceptance in American racial thought: the view of the American School of Ethnology and the concepts of the Romantic Racialists. The former, which emerged in the 1840s, accepted polygenesis and was strongly influenced by the scientific work of Samuel G. Morton of the Academy of Natural Sciences of Philadelphia. Relying heavily on craniology, Morton based his main conclusions on a study that compared the skulls of ancient blacks, Indians, and Caucasians with their modern counterparts. He noted that within each racial group there were no appreciable variations in the dimensions of the skull over great periods of time. The physical differences – and, by implication, the alleged mental and moral traits – that separated the races, he concluded, were permanent. They were not the result of contrasting environments or lifestyles, as the monogenists contended. In Morton's view, the races had been created at different times with unique characteristics which suited them to inhabit the

Table 36
An Analysis of the Attitudes of 21 Ontario Newspapers (1865–77) towards Measures to Enhance the Social and Civil Rights of Freedmen during Reconstruction, in Relation to the Religious Affiliation of the Editors/Proprietors

| Paper | Editor/proprietor | Religious affiliation | Extension of Freedmen's Bureau | | Civil rights bill of 1866 | | Black suffrage | | | Social equality & civil rights bill of 1875 | |
|---|---|---|---|---|---|---|---|---|---|---|---|
| | | | | | | | For | | | | |
| | | | For | Against | For | Against | Imme-diately | qualified blacks only | Not at present | For | Against |
| Kingston British Whig | E. Barker | Anglican | | | | | | | | | X |
| Canada Christian Advocate | G. Abbs | Methodist | | | | | X | | | | X |
| Canadian Freeman | J. Moylan | Catholic | | X | | X | | | X | | X |
| Ottawa Citizen | I. Taylor | Anglican | | X | | X | | X | | | |
| Christian Guardian | W. Jeffers (1865–69) | Methodist | | | X | | | X | | X | |
| | E. Dewart (1869–77) | Methodist | | | | | | | | | |
| Kingston Daily News | J. Rowlands | Anglican | | X | | | | X | | | |
| Newmarket Era | E. Jackson | Methodist | X | | X | | | | X | | |
| Evangelical Witness | D. Savage | Methodist | | | | | | | X | | |
| Peterborough Examiner | J. Stratton | Baptist | | X | | X | | | X | | |
| London Free Press | J. Blackburn | Protestant | | X | | X | | | X | | X |
| Toronto Globe | G. Brown | Presbyterian | X | | X | | X | | | | |
| Toronto Leader | J. Beatty | Disciples of Christ | | X | | X | | | X | X | |
| Barrie Northern Advance | D. Crew | Anglican | | X | | | | | | | |
| Sarnia Observer | J. Gemmill | Presbyterian | | | X | | X | | | | |
| Chatham Planet | R. Stephenson | Presbyterian | | | X | | X | | | | |
| Goderich Signal | W. Cox | Methodist | X | | | | | | X | | |

| Newspaper | Editor | Religion | | | | | | | | | |
|---|---|---|---|---|---|---|---|---|---|---|---|
| Hamilton *Spectator* | T. White (1865–70) | Anglican | | | | X | | X | | | X |
| | D. McCulloch (1868–73) | Presbyterian | | | | | | X | | | |
| | J. MacLean | ? | | X | | | | | | X | X |
| Hamilton *Times* | J. Cotton (1865–73) | Anglican | | | X | | X | | | X | X |
| Ottawa *Times* | A.M. Burgess (1874–76) | Presbyterian | | | | | X | | | | |
| Oshawa *Vindicator* | S. Luke | Methodist | | | | | | | X | X | |
| London *Western Advertiser* | J. Cameron | Presbyterian | | | | | | | X | | |
| Summary | | Anglican | 0 | 5 | 0 | 3 | 1 | 2 | 1 | 0 | 2 |
| | | Methodist | 2 | 1 | 2 | 0 | 1 | 1 | 3 | 1 | 0 |
| | | Presbyterian | 1 | 0 | 3 | 0 | 4 | 0 | 1 | 1 | 2 |

Table 37
An Analysis of the Freedman's Image in 21 Ontario Newspapers (1865–77) with Respect to their Qualities as Labourers, General Personal Characteristics, and Chances of Success in the United States, in Relation to the Religious Affiliation of the Editors/Proprietors

| Paper | Editor/ proprietor | Religious affiliation | Qualities as labourers | | General personal characteristics | | Future prospects in United States | |
|---|---|---|---|---|---|---|---|---|
| | | | Undesirable[1] | Desirable | Negative | Positive | Pessimistic | Optimistic |
| Kingston British Whig | E. Barker | Anglican | X | | X | | X | |
| Canada Christian Advocate | G. Abbs | Methodist | | | | X | X | X |
| Canadian Freeman | J. Moylan | Catholic | X | | X | | X | |
| Ottawa Citizen | I. Taylor | Anglican | X | | X | | X | |
| Christian Guardian | W. Jeffers (1865–69) | Methodist | | | | X | | X |
| | E. Dewart (1869–77) | Methodist | | | | | | X |
| Kingston Daily News | J. Rowlands | Anglican | X | | X | | | |
| Newmarket Era | E. Jackson | Methodist | | | | | | |
| Evangelical Witness | D. Savage | Methodist | | | | | | |
| Peterborough Examiner | J. Stratton | Baptist | | | | | | |
| London Free Press | J. Blackburn | Protestant | X | | X | | X | |
| Toronto Globe | G. Brown | Presbyterian | | X | | X | | X |
| Toronto Leader | J. Beatty | Disciples of Christ | X | | X | | X | |
| Barrie Northern Advance | D. Crew | Anglican | | | | | | |
| Sarnia Observer | J. Gemmill | Presbyterian | | | | | | |
| Chatham Planet | R. Stephenson | Presbyterian | | | | | | |
| Goderich Signal | W. Cox | Methodist | X | | X | | | |
| Hamilton Spectator | T. White (1865–70) | Anglican | X | | X | | X | |
| | D. McCulloch (1868–73) | Presbyterian | | | | | | X |
| Hamilton Times | J. MacLean | ? | | | X | | X | |

| | | | | | | | | |
|---|---|---|---|---|---|---|---|---|
| Ottawa *Times* | J. Cotton (1865–73) | Anglican | X | | | | X | |
| Oshawa *Vindicator* | A.M. Burgess (1874–76) | Presbyterian | | | X | | | |
| | S. Luke | Methodist | | | X | | | X |
| London *Western Advertiser* | J. Cameron | Presbyterian | | X | | X | | |
| | | | | | | | | |
| Summary | | Anglican | 5 | 0 | 5 | 0 | 4 | 0 |
| | | Methodist | 1 | 0 | 1 | 2 | 0 | 3 |
| | | Presbyterian | 0 | 2 | 1 | 2 | 0 | 3 |

¹See note 28 of this chapter for an explanation of these terms.

differing geographical provinces of the earth's surface. The American School asserted that the races were separate species of the genus *homo*, with widely varying intellectual capacities and moral sensitivities, though it was taken for granted that whites were at the top and blacks were at the bottom of the racial hierarchy. Some exponents of this school of thought contended that blacks achieved civilization only under white tutelage and quickly reached their maximum cultural development within two generations; and that if white supervision ended, African Americans would quickly revert to their natural backward state.

The American School frowned on miscegenation, especially between blacks and whites, which were classed as "remote" races. Their mulatto progeny would be weaker physically, mentally, and morally than the white parent, and through interbreeding might weaken the white race in the course of time; mixed offspring also would be less fertile than either parent, causing the new bloodline to die out rapidly. On the other hand, Caucasians and Celts might reproduce without harmful results to their children, for they were "proximate" races. These ideas attained widespread recognition when Dr Josiah C. Nott and George A. Gliddon, two ethnologist disciplines of Morton, collaborated to edit and publish the findings of other scholars who had reached similar conclusions under the titles *Types of Mankind* and *Indigenous Races of the Earth*.[31]

Ontario newspapers harbouring negative views of the freedmen reflected several racial concepts that resembled these theories. They readily agreed that the respective races had unique character traits. Their black stereotypes were virtually indistinguishable from those that the American School attributed to African Americans, and in accord with the latter they accepted a racial hierarchy of intellect. Like some adherents of the American School, this portion of the Ontario press believed that blacks had shed barbarism only through white assistance, the effect of which, if withdrawn, would soon dissipate. The Ontario press's aversion to amalgamation, which the American School shared, arose from a mutual belief that racially mixed unions produced weak and infertile progeny, dooming mulatto bloodlines to early extinction. The editors' view that blacks could not flourish in cold climates was akin to the American School's idea that races had been created with differing characteristics so that they might inhabit different geographical zones.

In contrast to the American School of Ethnology, the Romantic Racialists sidestepped the problem of the origin of different races. Like the Cincinnati-based writer and lecturer Alexander Kinmont, they began with the assumption that each race had distinctive character traits that were permanent. But they did not believe that this separated races into a hierarchy based on differing intellectual and moral capacities. Rather, they believed that a general balance of natural gifts existed which ensured to all races a roughly equal quota of desirable and undesirable traits. The Boston Unitarian Romantic Racialist, William Ellery Channing, characteristically asserted that Anglo-Saxons were inventive and enterprising but warlike and domineering, and that this predisposed them against Christianity; on the other hand, although blacks lacked initiative, they were gentle, kindly, and loyal, with an inherent receptivity to Christianity. Some Romantic Racialists believed that if educated and Christianized blacks were returned to Africa, they would soon transform their untutored brethren, who would then raise up a great humanitarian civilization, ensuring a millennial future for the continent. A few representatives of this school of thought advocated amalgamation as a desirable social policy, on the theory that it would produce an ideal racial type as mild black traits tempered harsh Anglo-Saxon features and as the latter invigorated the former. But most Romantic Racialists preferred cultural amalgamation to outright intermarriage.[32]

Traces of these beliefs surfaced in those newspapers that saw a promising future for the freedmen (though the parallels were less numerous than the body of racial ideas shared by the majority of journals and the American School of Ethnology). Like the Romantic Racialists, these newspapers ignored the question of racial origin; and they attributed a unique character to blacks that closely paralleled the African-American stereotype of the Romantic Racialists, who, like them, maintained that each race possessed distinctive traits. Neither group recognized an intellectual hierarchy among races. Moreover, like most Romantic Racialists, this portion of the Ontario press favoured cultural amalgamation over intermarriage but did not condemn the latter.

Clearly, there were similarities between the racial ideas of Ontario editors and the two schools of racial thought in the United States. However, the frequency with which the racial ideas of editors who were well disposed towards the freedmen intersect with the views of the Romantic Racialists is quite limited. As for the correspondence between the negative portrayal of the freedmen which most editors presented and the concepts of the American School of Ethnology, the parallels are of a secondary nature. The heart of the American School's theory – that different races were created with unique characteristics that enabled them to inhabit different quadrants of the earth's surface – is absent from the Ontario press. Thus, despite some similarities, there is only tenuous evidence that the Ontario editors' views of the freedmen were influenced mainly by the ethnological assumptions of the Romantic Racialists and the American School of Ethnology.

It is conceivable that sources in Britain were the chief influences that shaped the racial attitudes of the province's editors, for British-born men dominated the Ontario press at midcentury. Seventeen of the twenty-four editors whose columns were examined for this study were born in the British Isles. Moreover, among the thirteen for whom data was available, the average age at immigration was nineteen years. Typically, they came to British North America as young adults who had been socialized in British society. Their social thought had been moulded in a setting where the antislavery struggle was still a current issue. Even those who came as young children would have been surrounded by families steeped in ideas brought from the homeland. For example, Wellington Jeffers, the editor of the *Christian Guardian* who had come to Canada with his family at age six, had attended a school where his father was the teacher. Only four of the editors were born in British North America, and only two were born in the United States (table 38).

REGARDLESS OF WHAT MAY EVENTUALLY be learned about the roots of nineteenth-century Canadian racial thought, it is clear that British North Americans were cool to the efforts of the radical Republicans to secure civil rights and a measure of social equality for the freedmen. This response rested on a low view of the former slaves. As dark-skinned people, they were presumed to be lazy, pliable, timid, overly passionate, and too gullible for their own or society's good. According to this view, any civilized behaviour they exhibited resulted from contact with whites and was no more than a thin façade that was certain to disappear without constant reinforcement, since blacks soon reverted to a state of nature if left on their own. The root cause of their backwardness was an intellectual inferiority to whites. Such people were poor candidates for full citizenship. In all likelihood, either they would disappear completely from American society because they would be unable to compete with their more gifted neighbours, or at best, they would permanently occupy menial positions. Holding these views, many British North Americans were pessimistic about the freedmen's future in the United States and were critical of radical Reconstruction.

These highly racist assessments of the liberated slaves were not the sudden product of the Reconstruction process. What seems more

Table 38

An Analysis of Country of Origin and Age at Immigration of 24 Editors of Ontario Newspapers that Commented on the Role of the Freedmen in American Society during the Era of Reconstruction

| Paper | Editor/proprietor | National origin | | | Age at immigration |
| --- | --- | --- | --- | --- | --- |
| | | British North America | British Isles | United States | |
| Kingston British Whig | E. Barker | | X | | 33 |
| Canada Christian Advocate | G. Abbs | | X | | 13 |
| Canadian Freeman | J. Moylan | | X | | 30[1] |
| Ottawa Citizen | I. Taylor | | X | | ? |
| Christian Guardian | W. Jeffers (1865–69) | | X | | ? early school age |
| | E. Dewart (1869–77) | | X | | 6 |
| Kingston Daily News | J. Rowlands | X | | | – |
| Newmarket Era | E. Jackson | X | | | – |
| Evangelical Witness | D. Savage | | X | | 11 |
| Peterborough Examiner | J. Stratton | | X | | 15 |
| London Free Press | J. Blackburn | | X | | 27 |
| Toronto Globe | G. Brown | | X | | 25[1] |
| Toronto Leader | J. Beatty | | X | | 20 |
| Barrie Northern Advance | D. Crew | | X | | ? |
| Sarnia Observer | J. Gemmill | | X | | 13 |
| Chatham Planet | R. Stephenson | | | X | ? early age |
| Goderich Signal | W. Cox | | | X | ? |
| Hamilton Spectator | T. White (1865–70) | X | | | – |
| | D. McCulloch (1868–73) | | X | | 7 |
| Hamilton Times | J. MacLean | | X | | 10 |
| Ottawa Times | J. Cotton (1865–73) | | X | | ? |
| | A.M. Burgess (1874–76) | | X | | 21 |
| Oshawa Vindicator | S. Luke | ? | ? | | infant[2] |
| London Western Advertiser | J. Cameron | X | | | – |
| Total | 24 | 4 | 17 | 2 | |

[1]Both men spent five years in the United States after leaving the British Isles before moving to British North America.

[2]Luke was born of English parents in 1834, the same year that the family emigrated to Canada.

likely is that these long-held, if seldom expressed, racist views came to the surface when Canadians saw Americans struggling with the reality of what it would mean to incorporate 4 million former slaves into their society. As the people of Ontario considered this situation, they made judgments, based on their own deep-seated prejudices, about the course Americans should follow. There is much evidence that British North Americans held strong antiblack feelings in the decades before the Civil War. Edwin Larwill tapped this sentiment in 1849 when he stirred up the hostility of Chatham residents against the Elgin Association. The American abolitionist Benjamin Drew, who visited Canada in the 1850s to study the condition of fugitive slaves, encountered widespread prejudice, as did Samuel Gridley Howe when he undertook a similar mission for the Freedman's Inquiry Commission a decade later. Jason Silverman's recent work has systematically traced the rise of antiblack sentiment in Canada West before the Civil War. The earlier expression of racism was relatively muted, for to have voiced it openly would have risked being branded as a defender of slavery, which most people wanted to avoid. It was safer to do so once slavery had ended and Americans were facing the grave question of the future of the freedmen. As the ranks of abolitionists in both the United States and central Canada thinned out, and as North Americans generally tired of the seemingly endless "Negro question," there was rising cynicism about the possibility of forcing social revolution on the South and greater sympathy for the South's resistance. Even social scientists were voicing their doubts about the African American's ability.[33]

The existence of this virulent strain of racism in British North America before the Civil War elucidates the reluctance of some Canadians to support the antislavery movement. To people who believed that the slaves would either remain the mudsills of American society or disappear altogether because they lacked the ability to compete, emancipation was not an unqualified humanitarian solution to slavery. Consigning slaves to a life of menial labour cut free from all supports, or to ultimate extinction, was not necessarily a desirable alternative. However, to have expressed such views would have been to invite criticism as a defender of slavery. Instead, therefore, it seems likely that in addition to opposing antislavery because it was meddling in an American matter, some British North Americans remained on the sidelines because their racial beliefs told them that emancipation in the long run would be largely a futile pursuit.

# 10 Retrospect

The first Upper Canadians ended slavery at home comparatively early, but their descendants were slow to see a challenge in neighbouring American slavery. If morality rather than expediency had prompted the Loyalists' action, the outcome might have been different. Inspired by their fathers' example, second-generation Upper Canadians might have joined the swelling chorus of British antislavery in the 1820s and the Garrisonian awakening among Americans in the early 1830s. Instead, the province's antislavery movement stirred into life only in the late 1830s with the formation of the Upper Canada Anti-Slavery Society (UCAS). The new society, however, failed to demonstrate its effectiveness during the Moseby and Happy incidents, and the fledgling movement suffocated in the fear and suspicion that engulfed the Mackenzie rebellion. This left the Upper Canadian antislavery movement leaderless, disorganized, and dependent on the efforts of a few courageous but isolated individuals.

A decade passed before the movement was revived. In the meantime, the trickle of fugitive slaves into the province grew into a stream as a result of the 1850 Fugitive Slave Law. When the people of the province could no longer ignore the destitute newcomers among them and the more fundamental problem of slavery, they formed the Anti-Slavery Society of Canada (ACS). British North Americans finally joined the antislavery movement at midcentury largely, it seems, because their proximity to the United States made it impossible to escape dealing with the fugitive slaves rather than because of any deep-seated concern for the injustice and suffering inflicted on these unfortunates.

This view of the birth of provincial antislavery identifies an important aspect of the process, for Canada West was decidedly complacent about American slavery. However, it overlooks two important factors which must be considered when assessing the nature of provincial antislavery. In the first place, the movement that appeared at midcentury was in fact a rebirth of provincial antislavery. To be sure, the earlier effort had proved abortive, but it had been grounded in the same ideals that characterized the British and American movements. Moreover, in the interval between the collapse of the UCAS and the 1850 Fugitive Slave Law, the province had witnessed not only a marked increase in the number of fugitive slaves but a continuing influx of British immigrants. Among the latter were veterans of the British antislavery campaign. Such men as Peter Brown, Michael Willis, Robert Burns, and John Roaf had not belonged to the first rank of British antislavery, but they had contributed substantially at local and regional levels. They arrived with their antislavery principles intact and used them to rejuvenate the quiescent provincial movement. Despite its lethargic start, therefore, the antislavery movement in Canada West was neither solely the product of proximity to the United States nor devoid of principles.

These men, and those who shared leadership responsibilities as officers and committee members of provincial abolitionist organizations, were from the middle-class business and professional sectors of British society. They were still relatively young and were eager to establish themselves in a new country. In politics they tended to gravitate to the Reform party, and involvement with antislavery was only one of their many social concerns. Both tendencies could be construed as showing that abolitionists were realists at heart, intent on pursuing their own interests; the democratization of an antiquated and preference-ridden political system would eventually open the doors of opportunity to the newcomers, while vigorous philanthropy could advance their careers as a result of the attendant publicity and broadened contact with influential business and professional people.

Nevertheless, on balance, the evidence indicates that more idealistic considerations were predominant in inspiring the leaders of antislavery. In Britain, evangelicals were generally identified with political reform, even though they were not recent immigrants in a new land trying to get ahead. Michael Willis had risked his position in the church in Scotland rather than compromise his antislavery convictions. Most had emigrated when British concern over ending Southern slavery was at high tide, and they shared the sense of urgency. A majority of the leaders came from Scotland, where the

Scottish enlightenment had nurtured among intellectuals a deep respect for natural law; that slavery was a gross violation of the slave's natural rights was a cardinal doctrine of Scottish abolition, and it was central to both Willis's and Burns's antislavery thought. Moreover, Canadian abolitionists were overwhelmingly evangelicals, intent on obedience to their understanding of the scripture's teaching. In their view, as they so often repeated, God had made all men of one blood. To ignore the circumstances of their brother slaves, who were enduring grave injustice and grinding pain, was to deny the Bible's injunction to help those in need and was therefore sinful. In Canada West, just as in Edinburgh and Glasgow, the principles of the Scottish enlightenment and evangelical religion combined to energize the antislavery movement.

Like the leadership, the rank and file also were predominantly from British backgrounds and also were members of evangelical churches. However, unlike the leaders, a majority of the ordinary members were skilled and unskilled labourers and farmers; and in the Elgin Association, nearly one-quarter of them were black. Canada West's antislavery movement, therefore, was not an exclusively middle-class phenomenon; it saw large-scale participation by the working class and by blacks. In keeping with mid-nineteenth-entury norms, women did not belong to the main organizations; however, they contributed significantly to them by cooperating through a society which they managed and partially funded themselves.

The antislavery movement took two main forms. The first focused on helping fugitive slaves, many of whom arrived with few resources, seeking shelter, safety, and a new life. The other concentrated on arousing public opinion against slavery, in the hope that it would become so reprehensible in the eyes of the world that Southerners would be forced to free their slaves. This was about all that British North Americans could hope to do, since they were outside the American political system.

In the long run, the aiding of slaves proved to be more successful than the struggle for public opinion. The Elgin Association helped upward of twelve hundred African Americans find homes, acquire a modest economic stake and some education, and gain experience in managing their own institutions. Still-to-be-completed research raises questions about whether all of the twelve hundred were in fact former slaves. Nevertheless, the Raleigh Township settlement's unquestioned success seemingly demonstrated to the people of Canada West and elsewhere that liberated slaves would accept the responsibilities of freedom. This strengthened the voice of the abolitionists, who were striving to discredit proslavery arguments that slaves should not be free because they lacked the ability to compete with whites and would become a burden on society.

At first the ASC campaign to capture public opinion for the abolitionist cause was vigorous and successful. Frequent public meetings in Toronto drew large crowds, and Ward's lectures in smaller centres brought about the formation of several auxiliary societies. Yet after 1855 there were hardly any public meetings. Except for Thomas Henning's correspondence with the BFAS and the flourish of activity to prevent Anderson's extradition in 1861, it seemed that the ASC had all but abandoned the effort to educate public opinion.

A possible explanation for this is that friction developed within ASC inner circles during the mid-1850s over whether organizations in Canada West should have dealings with American organizations whose records on slavery were less than spotless. One faction answered with a resounding no, while others were content to be less exacting. It might have seemed wiser, in the circumstances, to avoid meetings and hope for an eventual resolution of the problem, rather than to risk washing dirty linen in public.

The decision to send Ward to Britain rather than retaining him as an agent in the province had much more serious consequences for the ASC's public-education program. The tour succeeded in the immediate sense, for it provided funds and thus enabled the ASC and the Women's Association to continue vital relief activities throughout the 1850s. But it was counterproductive in another respect; by filling the treasury with British sterling, it released the society from having to cultivate the Canada West antislavery vineyard to win new members. There was not the same urgency to keep the public interested and informed by means of antislavery speakers and fund-raising events. As a result, public meetings were very rare after 1855, the auxiliary societies died for lack of support, and the antislavery movement presented only a shadowy profile in the province in the late 1850s.

This was a critical failure, for the continuing apathy and even hostility to abolitionism among some elements in the province meant that antislavery needed constant exposure if the abolitionists were to win the battle for public opinion. The attitude of the churches vividly reflected Canada West's ambivalence on the issue. While all denominations opposed slavery, they were far from being united on abolition. Most evangelicals supported immediate abolition, and some, most notably the Free Church and the Congregationalists, were deeply involved in provincial antislavery. However, mainstream Anglicans, Roman Catholics, and Kirkmen withheld their approval, either by remaining silent or by openly opposing intervention in what they considered to be an American question.

Particularly important in this respect was the role of the Wesleyan Methodists who, in contrast to other provincial Methodists, reverted to neutrality on abolition. Initially, when antislavery had been rising to the surface in the province in the 1830s, the Wesleyans had led the movement. But in the tense atmosphere of the Upper Canadian rebellion, when the establishment needed scapegoats to blame for the outbreak, the Wesleyans felt vulnerable. Accordingly, they sought to avoid jeopardizing their alliance with the ruling constitutionalists by continuing to advocate abolition, which their allies opposed. Furthermore, by pressing the antislavery issue, they would have endangered connexional ties with American Methodists. As a result, the Wesleyans drew back, allowing the nascent UCAS to collapse and decimating the young movement.

The absence of most Anglicans, the Kirk, the Roman Catholics, and the Wesleyan Methodists (the province's largest denomination, with nearly 50,000 members and adherents) seriously weakened the movement, for efforts to influence public opinion were hampered when these churches remained silent or criticized from the sidelines. The churches justified their position by insisting that slavery was a matter for Americans to resolve without British North American interference. But there was another important consideration that influenced provincial reticence on abolition. After the Civil War, many Ontarians accepted the racist belief that the freed slaves lacked the ability to compete successfully with whites and would quickly sink to the bottom of American society and gradually disappear. Such prejudice had by no means been absent from the province before the Civil War; but it had been expressed less openly, possibly for fear of inviting proslavery charges, which most British North Americans would have found distasteful. However, when the people of Ontario saw Americans grappling with the stark reality of absorbing 4 million freedmen into their society, the latent prejudice surfaced freely, and it readily found acceptance in the provincial press. Undoubtedly, many of those who harboured a low view of blacks were apathetic about abolition, and the assertion that slavery was a problem for Americans to settle was a convenient rationale for inaction. This undercurrent of prejudice retarded the germination of antislavery in the province and inhibited the campaign for public opinion.

# Notes

CHAPTER ONE

1 Toronto *Globe*, 5 February 1863.
2 Riddell, "Slavery in Canada," 261–377; Trudel, *L'Esclavage Canada fran-çais*; Winks, *Blacks in Canada*, chs. 1–4. For Winks's assessment of Gar-neau's questionable treatment of slavery in New France, see ibid., 19, n. 45. See also Toronto *Globe*, 21 March 1849.
3 Winks, *Blacks in Canada*, 1–3; Riddell, "Slavery in Canada," 263.
4 Winks, *Blacks in Canada*, 5.
5 Ibid., 5–6, 9–10.
6 Riddell, "Slavery in Canada," 268, 273–5; Winks, *Blacks in Canada*, 24–6; Temperley, *British Antislavery*, 1.
7 Riddell, "Slavery in Canada," 275–83; Winks, *Blacks in Canada*, 26.
8 Riddell, "Slavery in Canada," 359–64; Winks, *Blacks in Canada*, 27–8.
9 Ibid., 29–46.
10 Ibid., 28–9.
11 Mealing, "John Graves Simcoe"; Riddell, "Slavery in Canada," 317; Winks, *Blacks in Canada*, 96–8.
12 Cruikshank, *Simcoe Correspondence*, 1:304; Winks, *Blacks in Canada*, 86–7; Riddell, *Life of Simcoe*, 192–3.
13 See Fraser, *Sixth Report, Bureau of Archives, Ontario*, 32–3, 35–6, 38, to follow the legislation through the legislative assembly; and his *Seventh Report, Bureau of Archives, Ontario*, 25–7, for the legislative council. Riddell, *Life of Simcoe*, 201; Simcoe to Dundas, 16 September 1793, in Cruikshank, *Simcoe Correspondence*, 2:53; Colgate, "Diary of John White," 165.

14 See Fraser, *Sixth Report, Bureau of Archives, Ontario*, 41–3, for Simcoe's speech in the assembly 9 July 1793; see also Ontario Archives, *Upper Canada, Laws, Statutes, etc., 1792–1819*, 60.

15 For the effort to renew slave importation in 1798, see, for the legislative assembly and the legislative council, respectively, Fraser, *Sixth Report, Bureau of Archives, Ontario*, 67, 69, 70–1, 74, and his *Seventh Report, Bureau of Archives, Ontario*, 67–70; Riddell, "Slavery in Canada," 321–39; Winks, *Blacks in Canada*, 98–9.

16 Riddell, "Slavery in Canada," 305; Winks, *Blacks in Canada*, 99–100.

17 Riddell, "Slavery in Canada," 306–9; Winks, *Blacks in Canada*, 100–1.

18 Riddell, "Slavery in Canada," 309–15; Winks, *Blacks in Canada*, 100–2.

19 Riddell, "Slavery in Canada," 359–75; Winks, *Blacks in Canada*, 102–10.

20 Riddell, "Slavery in Canada," 322, 332, 372–3; Winks, *Blacks in Canada*, 110–11.

CHAPTER TWO

1 Howard Temperley, *British Antislavery*, 1.

2 Ibid., 6.

3 Ibid., 6–9.

4 Ibid., 8–10.

5 Mathieson, *British Slavery and Its Abolition*, 119–21.

6 Ibid., 122–4.

7 Ibid., 138–58, 165.

8 Ibid., 166–95.

9 Ibid., 196, 206–7; Barker, *Charles Stuart*, 41–3.

10 Temperley, *British Antislavery*, 16–18; Mathieson, *British Slavery and Its Abolition*, 207–42.

11 Wolverhampton *Chronicle*, 25 January and 2 February 1826.

12 Mander, *Wolverhampton*, 169; Jones, *Congregational Churches of Wolverhampton*, 147; Careless, "John Roaf"; Staffordshire *Advertiser*, 6 October 1832; Wolverhampton *Chronicle*, 13 October 1830, 16 February and 18 May 1831, 10 October 1832, 20 February 1833, 26 February 1834.

13 Burns, *Speech at Anti-Slavery Meeting, Paisley*, 17; Minutes, Synod of Glasgow and Ayr, 12 and 13 October 1830, 5:339–47, Scottish Record Office, CH2/464/5.

14 Edinburgh *Evening Courant*, 7, 9, 16, 21, and 23 October 1830; Thomson, *Speech at Edinburgh Society*; Anderson, *History of Edinburgh*, 405–7; Barker, *Charles Stuart*, 43. Rice, *Scots Abolitionists*, 38.

15 R.F. Burns, *Life and Times of Robert Burns*, 279.

16 Burns, *Speech at Anti-Slavery Meeting, Paisley*, which contains the resolutions and the petition.

17 Minutes, Paisley Presbytery, 1 December 1830, 282–3, Scottish Record Office, CH2/294/14.

18 Barker, *Charles Stuart*, ch. 1, 28–44; Landon, "Charles Stuart, Abolitionist," 2.
19 Ibid., 44.
20 Ibid.
21 Ibid., 43–52.
22 Ibid.
23 Ibid., 53–63.
24 Temperley, *British Antislavery*, 12–16.
25 Barker, *Charles Stuart*, 67, 69, 78–83.
26 Edinburgh *Scotsman*, 26 October 1833; Rice, *Scots Abolitionists*, 36–8.
27 Ibid. For indications of Brown's status in Edinburgh, see *Evening Courant*, 16 July 1829, reporting his election to the board of directors of the Chamber of Commerce and Manufacturers of the City of Edinburgh; and ibid., 5 April 1833, for his appointment to a subcommittee of ward representatives to prepare a petition to Parliament against the pending new police bill; see also Edinburgh *Scotsman*, 2 July 1836, for an announcement that he is taking over the warehouse above his shop; and *Post-Office Annual Directory, and Calendar, for 1836–7*, 289, for his naming as collector of assessments. See also Thompson, *Voice to the United States*, 8, 36; Edinburgh *Scotsman*, 26 October 1833.
28 Rice, *Scots Abolitionists*, 38–41; GES Minute Book, 6 and 12 December 1833, 28 December 1835, 29 February, 3 March, and 16 June 1836, Mitchell Library; GES Cash Book 1833–58, 16 February 1836, Mitchell Library; Bingham, "Glasgow Emancipation Society," 45; *Glasgow Post-Office Annual Directory for 1831–32*, 155.
29 Boyd, "David Buchan." Unfortunately, Boyd's article does not identify Buchan's relatives, nor does he cite sources; from the following material, however, it is clear that his maternal uncle, the powerful James Ewing, was the most likely candidate. See *Glasgow Past and Present by J.B.*, 2; Mackay, *Memoir of James Ewing*; and *Glasgow Post-Office Annual Directory for 1833–34*, 39.
30 Glasgow *Evening Post*, 1 October 1836; Paisley *Advertiser*, 8 October 1836, 17 February, 5 May, and 4 August 1838, 1 and 22 August 1840.
31 *Edinburgh Christian Instructor*, New Series, 2 (July 1839); GES Minute Book, 1 August 1839, 14 October 1842, and 1 August 1843, Mitchell Library.
32 Willis's education and his decision to enter the ministry is discussed in Nicholson, "Michael Willis," 9–13. The organization of the Renfield Street church is described in ibid., 13–15, and in *St. John's – Renfield Church 1819–1969*, 14–17. A copy of this congregational history was kindly provided by the Rev. Colin G. McIntosh, the current minister, who stated that it had been prepared by the late Mr John Montgomery, a local historian who was a member of the church; McIntosh to author, 2 October 1984.

33 Nicholson, "Michael Willis," 15–19, 24–7; *St. John's – Renfield Church 1819–1969*, 17–20. The minutes of the Renfield Street church for 1839–47 are held by the Scottish Record Office, Edinburgh (CH3/1166/1), and were graciously examined for the author by Dr B.L.H. Horn, assistant keeper of the records, for evidence of the congregation's social concern under Willis; Horn to author, 2 August 1984.

34 "Autobiography," 13, 18–19, William King Papers, NAC. For Willis's early interest in the slavery question, see the anonymous pamphlet "Renfield Church," 7, Glasgow Collection, Mitchell Library.

35 Committee members who attended meetings were often named in the minutes, but sometimes the record merely stated "and others." Thus, the absence of Willis's name from the minutes is inconclusive evidence. The record, however, clearly substantiates Bingham's statement (40, 50–3) that Willis was an active member of the committee 1843–47.

36 For Willis's role in the union of the Original Associate Synod with the Church of Scotland, see Nicholson, "Michael Willis," 30–6. On the "Great Disruption" and the deputation to the United States, see ibid., 36–9; also Rice, *Scots Abolitionists*, ch. 5 and 124–6; Bingham, "Glasgow Emancipation Society," 171–4; and two articles by George Shepperson, "The Free Church and American Slavery" and "Thomas Chalmers, the Free Church of Scotland, and the South."

37 GES Minute Book, 14 and 25 March and 1 July 1844, Mitchell Library; Bingham, "Glasgow Emancipation Society," 175–6; Free Church of Scotland, *Acts and Proceedings of the General Assembly*, 20 and 25 May 1844.

38 GES Minute Book, 1 July and 1 August 1844, Mitchell Library; Bingham, "Glasgow Emancipation Society," 66–8.

39 GES Minute Book, 1 August and 17 October 1844, Mitchell Library; *Free Church Magazine* 2 (June 1845): 219–20; *Proceedings, Commission of the General Assembly of the Free Church of Scotland 1844–45*, 11 September 1844; Chalmers to Smythe, 25 September 1844, quoted in Shepperson, "Thomas Chalmers, the Free Church of Scotland, and the South," 521.

40 Space precludes a recounting of the details of the tortuous course of events during the conflict between the Free Church and GES over fellowshipping, but the controversy and Willis's role in it may be traced in the following: GES Minute Book, 17 October and 18 November 1844, 10 February and 17 March 1845, Mitchell Library; Rice, *Scots Abolitionists*, 129, 140–1; Bingham, "Glasgow Emancipation Society," 177, 182–3; Willis's overture in Glasgow Free Church Presbytery, 4 December 1844, cited in ibid., 179; *Free Church Magazine* 2 (June 1845): 219–20; Free Church of Scotland, *Acts and Proceedings of the General Assem-*

*bly,* 2 June 1845; GES Minute Book, 1 August 1845, 10 and 21 April 1846, Mitchell Library. The actions of the general assembly are re- ported in the Toronto *Banner,* 26 June and 3 July 1846; and a full re- view of the general assembly's treatment of the slavery issue 1844–46, including numerous motions, speeches, and letters, appears in Free Church of Scotland, *Report of the General Assembly on May 30 and June 1, 1846.*

41 Presbyterian Church in Canada, *Minutes of Synod* 1 (1844): 26, (1845): 42 and (1846): 86. See also Nicholson, "Michael Willis," 39–41.

42 *Minutes of Synod* 1 (1845): 44–5.

43 Toronto *Banner,* 17 April and 22 and 29 May 1846. Winks, *Blacks in Canada,* 254, states that Willis attended the 1846 American Anti- Slavery Society's annual meeting, but the *Banner* claimed to have had correspondence with him showing that he did not.

44 GES Minute Book, 10 June 1846, Mitchell Library. The text of the letter is given in the Toronto *Banner,* 10 July 1846.

45 GES Minute Book, 30 September and 18 October 1846, 12 May 1847, Mitchell Library; Committee of the Free Church Anti-Slavery Society, *An Address to the Office-Bearers and Members of the Free Church of Scot- land,* in John Bishop Estlin Papers, microfilm 1, nos. 16, 12, 23.

46 For notices of the seven lectures with the speakers and their topics, see Edinburgh *Witness,* 2, 10, 12, and 23 December 1846, 6 and 30 Jan- uary, 10 February, 17 March, and 3 April 1847. Willis's lecture was published in pamphlet form as *Slavery Indefensible.*

47 Rice, *Scots Abolitionists,* 24–7. Willis, *Slavery Indefensible,* 6, 10.

48 Ibid., 6–10.

49 Ibid., 10–12.

50 Ibid., 13–15.

51 Ibid.

52 For the list of publications, see Committee of the Free Church Anti- Slavery Society, *Strictures on the Proceedings of the Last General Assembly.*

53 Ibid., 6–9.

54 Committee of the Free Church Anti-Slavery Society, *Strictures on the Proceedings of the Last General Assembly.* Willis's speech and his motion in the Glasgow presbytery appear in *Slavery Indefensible,* 16–23; the opposing speeches and the vote were noted by the Toronto *Banner,* 3 and 30 November 1846.

55 It is clear that the Free Church, like Willis, opposed slavery mainly because slavery disregarded man's natural rights and violated biblical teachings. See Henry Grey, the Free Church moderator in 1844, to John Murray and William Smeal, secretaries of GES, 21 June 1844, in GES Minute Book, 1 July 1844, Mitchell Library; see also the report of the general assembly's committee on slavery to the Free Church Com-

mission, 11 September 1844, in Free Church of Scotland, *Report of the General Assembly on May 30 and June 1, 1846*, 4; James Cunningham's speech on slavery at the 1846 general assembly, ibid., 36; and the draft of a letter, approved 2 June 1846, from the general assembly to the general assembly of the Presbyterian Church in the US, ibid., 50–2.

56 Presbyterian Church in Canada, *Minutes of Synod* 1 (1847): 26–7; see also the call to Willis from the Colonial Committee in an undated letter, John Bonar to Willis, and Willis's speech to Glasgow presbytery, 3 November 1847, both cited in Toronto *Banner*, 31 December 1847.

57 Ibid.; *St. John's – Renfield Church*, 20; Fladeland, *Men and Brothers*, 296–7.

58 Toronto *Banner*, 17 April, 1 and 22 May, 5 and 26 June, 3, 10 and 17 July, 18 September, 3 and 26 November, and 11 December 1846, 12 March 1847; the Toronto *Ecclesiastical and Missionary Record* 4 (June 1848): 34–5.

59 William McClure, *Life and Labours*, 6, 47, 144–5, 177. In a meeting of the Canadian Anti-Slavery Society in Toronto in early February 1863, McClure mentioned having attended antislavery meetings like that in Toronto "many years ago," presumably in Ireland; see Toronto *Globe*, 5 February 1863. The Rev. Samuel J. May identified McClure as a man whose acquaintance William L. Garrison had made in Belfast during an antislavery tour; see May to Garrison, letters dates 2 and 4 April 1851, cited in the *Liberator*, 11 April 1851.

CHAPTER THREE

1 British and American abolitionism for this important period is examined in Taylor, *British and American Abolitionists*; Temperley, *British Antislavery*; Walvin, *Slavery and British Society*; Rice, *Scots Abolitionists*; Filler, *Crusade against Slavery*; Dillon, *The Abolitionists*; Fladeland, *Men and Brothers*; Friedman, *Gregarious Saints*; Kraditor, *Means and Ends in American Abolitionism*; Stewart, *Holy Warriors*; McKivigan, *War against Proslavery Religion*.

2 Toronto *Patriot*, 17 May 1833; Toronto *Christian Guardian*, 13 May 1831, 8 May, 5 and 19 June, 10 and 17 July, 7 and 21 August 1833; Kingston *Chronicle and Gazette*, 27 July and 3, 17, and 31 August 1833; Kingston *Upper Canada Herald*, 19 June, 10, 17, and 31 July 1833, 14 August 1834; Toronto *Correspondent*, 26 March, 18 May, 4 July, and 4 August 1833; Niagara *Reporter*, 1 August 1833; Niagara *Gleaner*, 6, 13, 20, and 27 July, and 19 October 1833; Hamilton *Western Mercury*, 18 July and 1 and 8 August 1833; St Catharines *British Colonial Argus*, 2 November 1833.

3 Niagara *Gleaner*, 19 October 1833; St Catharines *British Colonial Argus*, 2 November 1833; Toronto *Christian Guardian*, 7 August 1833, 6 August 1834.

4 Niagara *Reporter*, 1 August 1833; Toronto *Patriot*, 2 December 1834.

5 Niagara *Gleaner*, 19 October 1833.

6 Barker, *Captain Charles Stuart*, 20–37, 64–73; Filler, *Crusade against Slavery*, 67–9.

7 Toronto *Patriot*, 15 September 1835.

8 The 1835 Wesleyan Methodist annual conference appointed Evans. See *Christian Guardian*, 17 July, 7 and 21 August 1833, 14 May and 6 August 1834; *New York Christian Advocate and Journal*, 18 July 1834, cited in *Christian Guardian*, 30 July 1834; *New England Christian Herald*, 29 July 1834, cited in *Christian Guardian*, 20 August 1834; ibid., 4 January 1834. On Wesleyan influences in Evans's early life, see Carroll, *Case and His Contemporaries*, 3: 203. The circulation of the *Guardian* in the 1830s is described in Sissons, *Egerton Ryerson*, 1: 129–30, 335.

9 AAS, *1834 Annual Report*, 17–18; Matlack, *American Slavery and Methodism*, 74–5; *Christian Guardian*, 16 September and 16 December 1835; Mathews, *Slavery and Methodism*, chs. 5, 6.

10 Matlack, *American Slavery and Methodism*, 154–79; AAS, *1837 Annual Report*, 62–4; *Christian Guardian*, 17 August 1836.

11 Ibid., 9 November and 7 December 1836, 4 January 1837; Toronto *Constitution*, 31 August 1836.

12 *Christian Guardian*, 4 January 1837.

13 Winks, *Blacks in Canada*, 484–96.

14 Silverman, *Unwelcome Guests*, chs. 4–6.

15 Ripley, *Black Abolitionist Papers*, 2: 11–18.

16 Turner, "Thomas Rolph." See also Toronto *Patriot*, 4 July 1834, 22 July and 2 September 1836, 3 and 17 February and 8 August 1837; Rolph to Lord John Russell, 31 August 1836, cited in ibid., 8 November 1836; Rolph, *Observations on West Indies*, 12–13. Writing in 1844, Rolph claimed that he had been elected an agent for blacks in Upper Canada in 1834, a statement that cannot be confirmed. He probably meant 1837, when a meeting of Toronto blacks asked him to intervene with the British government on their behalf to prevent fugitive slaves from being returned from Canada to the United States. See Rolph, *Emigration and Colonization*, 313–14; and 59 below.

17 Rolph, *Observations on West Indies*, chs. 1–6, especially 56–7.

18 On Hiram Wilson's activities, see Winks, *Blacks in Canada*, 179–81, 197–200, 224–6; Pease and Pease, *Bound with Them in Chains*, 115–39; "Commission," dated 3 October 1836, in Hiram Wilson Papers, Oberlin College Archives; Wilson to Gillett, 10 April 1837, ibid.,

7/1/5 Box 3; AAS, *1836 Annual Report*, 34–5; Philadelphia *National Enquirer*, 24 August 1837.

19 On Dunlop, see Stewart, "Robert Graham Dunlop"; *Christian Guardian*, 11 January 1837; Philadelphia *National Enquirer*, 24 August 1837.

20 Unfortunately, no minutes, annual reports, or other documents of the UCAS have been located, and its activities must be pieced together from a few newspaper accounts of the founding meeting and a later one in November 1837; see *Christian Guardian*, 4 and 11 January and 15 November 1837, and Hiram Wilson's letter of 16 January 1837 in *Emancipator*, 22 February 1837. On James Johnston, see GES Minute Book, 12 December 1833, 28 December 1835, 29 February, 1 and 3 March, and 16 June 1836, Mitchell Library; Bingham, "Glasgow Emancipation Society," 45, who states that Johnston started an antislavery society in Canada; Rice, *Scots Abolitionists*, table, 208; Murray, "Canada and Anglo-American Anti-Slavery," 3, who credits Wilson with founding the society; Winks, *Blacks in Canada*, 253–4, who names Evans.

21 *Christian Guardian*, 11 January 1837.

22 Ibid., 11 January, 8 and 15 February, 8 March, and 5 April 1837; Kingston *Upper Canada Herald*, 17 January 1837; Quebec *Gazette*, 25 January and 24 February 1837.

23 Winks, *Blacks in Canada*, 168–9.

24 The Moseby affair can be traced from accounts in the Niagara *Reporter*, 14 September 1837, St Catharines *Journal*, 21 and 28 September, 5 October, and 9 November 1837, and *Christian Guardian*, 27 September 1837. Relevant government documents are in NAC RG1/E1/49, 217–35, which contains Hagerman's advice to the executive council and its recommendation to Head dated 6 and 7 September 1837; Alexander Stewart, counsel for Moseby, to John Joseph, 5 September 1837; affidavits from Kentuckians Daniel Kelly and David Castleman; and petitions from both black and white residents of Niagara.

25 The Happy case can be pieced together from NAC RG1/E3/35, 204–37, which contains Happy's memorial to Head from the Hamilton jail, 26 September 1837; Hagerman's opinion; the Hamilton petitions; Kentucky Governor James Clark's request for extradition, 19 August 1837; and the actions of the executive council, 9 September and 12 October 1837. Head's actions and the responses of the British government are evident from Head to Glenelg, no. 112, 8 October 1837, with enclosures, NAC MG/11/Q398/1; Glenelg to Head, no. 255, 4 December 1837, NAC RG7/G1/83; and Glenelg to Arthur, no. 38, 9 March 1838, NAC RG7/G1/84.

26 Winks, *Blacks in Canada*, 175–6.

27 *Christian Guardian*, 15 November 1837.

28 Stewart, "Robert Graham Dunlop"; Graham, *Tiger Dunlop*, 200–3; Careless, "John Roaf."
29 On the Upper Canada rebellion, see Careless, *Canada*, 164–74.
30 Sissons, *Egerton Ryerson*, 1, chs. 9–12, follows the Methodist involvement in Upper Canadian reform from Ryerson's perspective.
31 Careless, *Canada*, 193; Sissons, *Egerton Ryerson*, 1:453–4; Rea, *Bishop Alexander Macdonell*, 119–20, 183.
32 Carroll, *Case and His Contemporaries*, 4:152, 184–90; Matlack, *American Slavery and Methodism*, 184–5; Thomas, *Ryerson of Upper Canada*, 85–7; *Zion's Watchman and Wesleyan Observor*, 13 October 1840; Toronto *Patriot*, 9, 13, and 16 October 1840. On the desire of Canadian Methodists to retain good ties with American Methodists, and on the abolitionists' criticism of Ryerson, see below, 83, 157–8.
33 For Rolph's effort to place the petition before the Queen and the ensuing controversy with the British government, see below, 59–60. See also the letters from Rolph to Russell, chap. 4, notes 5–7 below.

CHAPTER FOUR

1 For the count which blacks took themselves and which was not quite complete at the time the report was made, see Toronto *British Colonist*, 8 April 1840; and see ibid., 5 June 1839, for the request for schools and teachers made by the black residents of Hamilton in September 1838. For Hiram Wilson's reference to the meeting of Toronto blacks that must have been in December 1837, see the reference to his letter of 15 January 1838 to James G. Birney, editor of the *Emancipator*, cited in the *Emancipator*, 8 February 1838. For the July 1838 meeting of Toronto blacks, see Toronto *Patriot*, 24 July 1838; for Durham's promise, see Governor General's secretary (name illegible) to Rolph, 20 July 1838, NAC CO42/468; and for Rolph's public letter to the blacks of the province, 17 November 1838, see St Catharines *Journal*, 6 December 1838. See also Murray, "Canada and Anglo-American Anti-Slavery," 133–41.
2 For Rolph's letter to Arthur, see "Thos. Rolph, Secretary, and in behalf of Messrs. Dunlop, St. Remy and Gallego" to Arthur, undated but certainly 11 May 1839, in Arthur to Russell, 23 May 1839, NAC CO42/459. See also W. Macaulay to Rolph, 17 May 1839, NAC CO42/468.
3 Ibid., Rolph to Yorke, 23 August 1839; Rolph to Russell, 10 September 1839; Yorke to Rolph, 11 September 1839; Harrison to Rolph, 20 September 1839. On Rolph's mission to Britain with Macdonell, see Shepperson, *British Emigration to North America* 40–6.

4 For the opinions of the law officers and the concurrence of the government, see NAC CO42/468, a memo initialled by Russell on 19 September 1839, entitled "Dr. Rolph's letter respecting Negro Petition from Upper Canada 23 August."

5 Ibid., Rolph to Russell, 24 September 1839.

6 Ibid., Rolph to Russell, 3 November 1839.

7 Ibid., Rolph to Russell, 10 December 1839. See also NAC CO42/474: Rolph to Russell, 19 January 1840; draft to Rolph, 6 February 1840; draft to Rolph, 4 March 1840; Rolph to Russell, 4 March 1840; Rolph to Russell, 12 March 1840; Russell to Rolph, 19 March 1840; Rolph to Russell, 7 April 1840; Rolph to Russell, 20 April 1840; and Russell to Rolph, 29 April 1840.

8 Toronto *British Colonist*, 8 April 1840.

9 *Emancipator*, 6 August 1840; *British and Foreign Anti-Slavery Reporter*, 1 and 29 July, 12 August 1840, and 14 June 1843; "Minute Book, General Anti-Slavery Convention 1840," 48, 50, 95–7, Rhodes House Library; Murray, "Canada and Anglo-American Anti-Slavery," 142.

10 The previous extradition agreement was article 27 of Jay's Treaty; see Corey, *Crisis of 1832–1842*, 169–79, and Murray, "Canada and Anglo-American Anti-Slavery," 136–40, for a detailed treatment of the extradition clauses in the 1842 Webster-Ashburton Treaty.

11 Toronto *Patriot*, 14 September 1840; St Catharines *Journal*, 1 October 1840; Gallego to Rolph, 1 November 1841, cited in Murray, "Canada and Anglo-American Anti-Slavery," 143.

12 Rolph, *Emigration and Colonization*, 313; Woodward, *Trinidad in Transition*, 65–72; Williams, *The People of Trinidad and Tobago*, ch. 8.

13 Russell to Sydenham, 9 February 1841, enclosures, Rolph to MacLeod, 31 August 1840, and Arthur White to Rolph, 14 November 1840, NAC RG7/G2/1/303.

14 MacLeod to Russell, 14 November 1840, and Frederick Elliot and Edward E. Villiers to James Stephen, 2 January 1841, NAC RG7/G2/1/93; Sydenham to Russell, 23 April 1841, NAC CO42/478/51; Russell to Sydenham, 20 May 1841, NAC RG7/G1/95/379.

15 Rolph, *Emigration and Colonization*, 275, 309–19.

16 Wilson's "Commission," dated 15 October 1836, and Wilson to Gillett, 10 April 1837, in Hiram Wilson Papers, Oberlin College Archives. See also Wilson to Wright, 19 November 1836, cited in *Emancipator*, 22 December 1836.

17 *Emancipator*, 23 February, 6 April, and 21 September 1837; see also AAS *Fourth Annual Report*, 19, 32, 34–5.

18 *Emancipator*, 22 December 1836, 6 April 1837, 8 February 1838, 16 May 1839, 16 December 1841.

19 Ibid., 8 February 1838, 10 December 1841; *National Anti-Slavery Standard*, 11 June 1840; *Liberator*, 14 May 1841; *British and Foreign Anti-Slavery Reporter*, 29 July 1840, 136; General Anti-Slavery Convention 1840, Minute Book, 48. Charles E. Lester, a minister from Utica, New York, was one of the delegates who spoke on behalf of Upper Canadian blacks at the London convention in 1840 and served with Rolph on the committee. Before returning, Lester raised $650 among English supporters for the Canada Mission.

20 "The Oberlin Institute," *London and Westminster Review*, cited in *British and Foreign Anti-Slavery Reporter*, 26 February 1840, 36; *National Anti-Slavery Standard*, 24 June 1841; *Emancipator*, 16 December 1841.

21 *National Anti-Slavery Standard*, 14 and 28 January, 4 and 11 February, and 24 June 1841, 26 January 1843; *Liberator*, 16 April and 14 May 1841; *Emancipator*, 16 December 1841.

22 *National Anti-Slavery Standard*, 14 and 24 June and 28 December 1841, 26 January 1843; Fuller to "Friend of Man," 12 March 1841, cited in *Emancipator*, 16 December 1841; *Liberator*, 11 November 1842; Murray, "Canada and Anglo-American Anti-Slavery," 80.

23 Wilson to Hamilton Hill, 25 April 1843, Hiram Wilson Papers, Oberlin College Archives; *British and Foreign Anti-Slavery Reporter*, 21 and 28 June 1843; *Emancipator*, 25 January and 11 September 1844, 8 October 1845; *National Anti-Slavery Standard*, 11 November 1847; Murray, "Canada and Anglo-American Anti-Slavery," 86–90.

24 *Emancipator*, 5 May and 9 June 1847.

25 Murray, "Canada and Anglo-American Anti-Slavery," 90–7; Winks, *Blacks in Canada*, 178–81, 197–204; *Liberator*, 17 October 1848, 1 March 1850.

26 *National Anti-Slavery Standard*, 26 January 1843; Murray, "Canada and Anglo-American Anti-Slavery," 69–70; *Emancipator*, 25 January 1844; *Liberator*, 27 October 1848, 1 March, 2 August, 25 October, and 13 December 1850.

27 *Emancipator*, 16 December 1841.

28 Leavitt to Scoble, 9 March 1843, cited in Murray, "Canada and Anglo-American Anti-Slavery," 82; James Fairchild to Mary Kellogg, 19 July 1841, Hiram Wilson Papers, Oberlin College Archives.

29 Careless, "Peter Brown" and *Brown of the Globe*, 1, ch. 1.

30 Peter Brown, *Fame and Glory of England Vindicated*, 10, 198, 199–200, 237–40, 243–4, 260–306.

31 Toronto *Banner*, 1 January 1847, 25 August 1843.

32 Ibid., 3 November 1843, 12 January, 15 March, and 5 April 1844, 21 February, 11 July, 5 September, and 26 December 1845, 9 and 19 January and 19 June 1846, 5 March 1847.

33 Ibid., 9 May, 6 June, and 7 November 1845, 5 June 1846, 26 February 1847. On slavery and the Old School Presbyterians, see McKivigan, *War against Proslavery Religion*, 83, 165–6.

34 Toronto *Banner*, 2, 16, and 23 May 1845.

35 Ibid., 3 April 1846.

36 Ibid., 26 June and 3, 10, and 24 July 1846.

37 Ibid., 10 July, 18 September, 3 and 20 November, and 11 December 1846.

38 Ibid., 12 March 1847; Edinburgh *Scotsman*, 2 June 1847.

39 Roaf to Scobie, 17 April 1843, Anti-Slavery Papers, Rhodes House Library, c21/47; see also Toronto *Banner*, 3, 17 April, 1, 29 May 1847.

CHAPTER FIVE

1 I am indebted to Professor Michael Wayne, of the University of Toronto history department, who generously shared the preliminary results of his research on the character of the black population in Canada West in 1861 based on provincial census data. His work was incomplete at the time of writing.

2 Silverman, *Unwelcome Guests*, ch. 3; Winks, *Blacks in Canada*, 143, 148–9, 248–52.

3 Ripley, *Black Abolitionist Papers*, 2:4, 11, 14–15.

4 "Autobiography," 4, 6, William King Papers, NAC.

5 Ibid., 11–38.

6 Ibid., 42–3.

7 Ibid., 43–4.

8 Ibid., 47–63.

9 Minute Book, Presbytery of Toronto, 1(1844–61), 14 and 21 January, 18 March, and 28 April 1847, United Church Archives; King to clerk of Toronto presbytery, 21 June 1848, William King Papers, NAC.

10 "Autobiography," 63–72, ibid.

11 King to clerk of Toronto presbytery, 21 June 1848, ibid. Minute Book, Presbytery of Toronto, 1 (1844–61), 23 June 1848, United Church Archives.

12 Presbyterian Church in Canada, *Minutes of Synod* 1 (1844–56), 26 and 28 June 1848.

13 "Autobiography," 73–4, William King Papers, NAC. King to Elgin, 29 August 1848, ibid.; "Scheme for Improving the Coloured People of Canada," ibid. See also "Prospectus of a Scheme for the Social and Religious Improvement of the Coloured People of Canada," *Ecclesiastical and Missionary Record* 5 (January 1849): 29–30.

14 Toronto *Globe*, 21 March and 7 June 1849.

15 The memorial is cited in the Detroit *Tribune*, 17 April 1892; Pease and Pease, "Opposition to Founding of Elgin Association," 202–18.

16 Chatham *Chronicle*, 21 August 1849.

17 Ibid., 4, 11, and 18 September 1849.

18 Pease and Pease, "Opposition to Founding of Elgin Association," 208, 212–15; Toronto *Globe*, 13 September 1849; Chatham *Chronicle*, 18 September and 16 October 1849, 5 February and 30 April 1850; Ogden, "George Skeffington Connor"; Beyea, "James Scott Howard"; Bailey, "John Fisher"; Houston, "Andrew Taylor McCord"; Belleville *Daily Intelligencer*, 30 March 1876; Carnochan, *History of Niagara*, 252; St Catharines *Constitutional*, 19 and 26 January 1860; "Lieut.-Col. Alexander David Ferrier," Morgan, *Canadian Parliamentary Companion*, 196.

19 "Second Annual Report of the Elgin Association," Sandwich *Voice of the Fugitive*, 5 November 1851.

20 "Third Annual Report of the Elgin Association," ibid., 23 September 1852; "Autobiography," 94, William King Papers, NAC.

21 Jamieson, *William King*, 158; Elgin Association, *Tenth and Eleventh Annual Reports*, 1–7.

22 Detroit *Tribune*, 12 June 1892; *Voice of the Fugitive*, 6 May 1852; "The Elgin Settlement, Canada West," *British Anti-Slavery Reporter*, 1 February 1860, 36–8; Elgin Association, *Sixth Annual Report*, 5, *Seventh Annual Report*, 6, *Ninth Annual Report*, 5–7, and *Tenth and Eleventh Annual Reports*, 5–7.

23 Robbins, *Legacy to Buxton*, 62; Detroit *Tribune*, 19 June 1892; Elgin Association, *Ninth Annual Report*, 5–7, *Tenth and Eleventh Annual Reports*, 5–7.

24 "Autobiography," 117–8, and Lord Alfred Churchill, African Aid Society Executive Committee chairman, to King, 17 March 1861, in William King Papers, NAC. Detroit *Tribune*, 10 July 1892.

25 May to editor, 3, 20, and 31 August 1852, *National Anti-Slavery Standard*, 19 August, 2 and 9 September 1852.

26 Henning, "The Coloured Population in Canada," *British Anti-Slavery Reporter*, 1 December 1855, 271–2.

27 "The Colony at Buxton," by a commissioner of the New York *Tribune*, cited in the *National Anti-Slavery Standard*, 7 and 14 November 1857.

28 Detroit *Tribune*, 12 June 1892; Henry Christy to King, 18 January 1860, and Spencer, Probyn, and Christy to King, 19 January 1860, cited in *British Anti-Slavery Reporter*, 1 February 1860; "Autobiography," 124, William King Papers, NAC.

29 Ibid., 118–20.

30 Ibid., 121–3.

31 Ibid.

32 King stated that "for a few years there was a large exodus from Buxton," and Professor Winks puts the number at 700; Jonathan William
Walton, in a recent study that relies heavily on census and tax data,
offers no specific figure but sees the outflow less dramatically in the
form of small groups and individuals moving away. See "Autobiography," 125, William King Papers, NAC; Winks, *Blacks in Canada*, 289;
Walton, "Blacks in Buxton and Chatham," 164–74.

33 The final report of the association to the Ontario legislature, dated
13 March 1873 and prepared by Thomas Henning and William Reid, is
found in 36 Victoria, *Sessional Papers* 1873, nos. 61, 63. See also "Autobiography," 124–5, William King Papers, NAC; Detroit *Tribune*, 10 July
1892; Robbins, *Legacy to Buxton*, 62; Ripley, *Black Abolitionist Papers*,
2:43–4.

CHAPTER SIX

1 Toronto *Globe*, 10 June 1852; Murray, "Canada and Anglo-American
Anti-Slavery," 293–7; Ripley, *Black Abolitionist Papers*, 2:9–10; Campbell, *Slave Catchers*, chs. 1, 3, 6.

2 Murray, "Canada and Anglo-American Anti-Slavery," 203–4; Toronto
*British Colonist*, 4 and 15 October 1850; Toronto *Globe*, 19 September
and 4 October 1850.

3 McClure, *Life and Labours*, 201–2; *Globe*, 25 February 1851.

4 Ibid., 27 February and 1 March 1851; ASC, *Constitution and Bye-Laws*;
Pemberton, "The Anti-Slavery Society of Canada," ch. 2.

5 Toronto *British Colonist*, 4 March 1851; *Church*, 10 April 1851; Toronto
*Mirror*, 28 February 1851; *Globe*, 6 March 1851.

6 *St. Lawrence Hall*, 41, 72–3. Murray states in "Canada and Anglo-
American Anti-Slavery," 209, that St Lawrence Hall seated "over
two thousand," but the *Globe*, 3 April 1851, claimed its capacity was
1200.

7 Toronto *Globe*, 3 April 1851.

8 Ibid., May to Garrison, 2 and 4 April 1851; *Liberator*, 11 April 1851.

9 Toronto *Globe*, 5 April 1851; Rochester *North Star*, 10 April 1851.

10 Toronto *Globe*, 10 April 1851.

11 Ibid., 18 March and 10 April 1851.

12 Filler, *Crusade against Slavery*, ch. 6.

13 Rochester *North Star*, 10 April 1851; *Ecclesiastical and Missionary Record*,
7, no. 8 (June 1851): 118–9; Henning to May, 5 May 1851, cited in *National Anti-Slavery Standard*, 15 May 1851.

14 Executive Committee of ASC, *First Annual Report*, 12–13, and *Second
Annual Report*, 28; Toronto *Globe*, 4, 9, 13, 16, 18, and 20 September

1851; Toronto *Examiner*, 24 September 1851; *National Anti-Slavery Standard*, 9 October 1851.

15 Peter Brown and Andrew Hamilton to J. Leslie, provincial secretary, 25 August 1851, cited in Toronto *Globe*, 18 September 1851.

16 *Globe*, 1 and 17 May, 3 and 10 June 1851; Sandwich *Voice of the Fugitive*, 21 May 1851; *Liberator*, 18 May 1852; Toronto *Examiner*, 28 April 1852; Executive Committee of ASC, *First Annual Report*, 11–12. For a report of the second concert on 7 January 1852, addressed by Willis, Henning, and Ward, see Port Hope *Echo and Protestant Episcopal Recorder*, 21 January 1852.

17 Ward, *Autobiography of a Fugitive Negro*, 136; Burke, "Samuel Ringgold Ward," 61–78; Winks, "Samuel Ringgold Ward"; Murray, "Canada and Anglo-American Anti-Slavery," 215–18; Sandwich *Voice of the Fugitive*, 5 November 1851.

18 Ibid., 19 November and 17 December 1851, 26 February and 11 March 1852; Toronto *Globe*, 17 December 1851.

19 Executive Committee of ASC, *First Annual Report*, v, vi; Toronto *Examiner*, 31 March and 28 April 1852; *Liberator*, 28 May 1852; Sandwich *Voice of the Fugitive*, 20 May 1852.

20 Ibid., 26 August 1852; Bremner, *City of London, Ontario*, 89; *History of the County of Middlesex*, 356–7; McClure, *Life and Labours*, 209; London *Canadian Free Press*, 9 September 1852; Hamilton *Daily Spectator*, 23 March 1853; Hamilton *Canada Christian Advocate*, 23 March 1853; Toronto *Globe*, 18 December 1852; Executive Committee of ASC, *Second Annual Report*, 8.

21 Sandwich *Voice of the Fugitive*, 21 October and 18 November 1852.

22 McClure, *Life and Labours*, 210; London *Canadian Free Press*, 9 September 1852; Montreal *Register*, 12 October 1843 and 7 November 1844; Fitch, *Baptists of Canada*, 107; Brock, *History of the County of Middlesex*, 167, 222, 314–19, 356–7; Miller, "London, Ontario Pioneer Welfare Planner," 15 November 1960, 249–56, "Scrapbook," 47, London Public Library; *Railton's Directory, London*, 14, 16, 17, 144, 155. Rev. John Scott, minister of St Andrews Free Church, Congregationalist Rev. William F. Clarke, and several important community figures (the surgeon-druggist and social reformer John Salter, the Edinburgh-trained physician John Wanless, John Fraser, William Rowland, and black merchant and banker A.B. Jones) made up the board of directors.

23 Toronto *Globe*, 22 March 1853; Hamilton *Daily Spectator*, 2, 16, and 18 March 1853; see also Hamilton *Canada Christian Advocate*, 23 March 1853, in which the officers of the Hamilton society are listed as Tristram Bickle, president, Hugh Cochran, secretary, Robert Hopkins,

treasurer, and the committee members as Revs J. Hogg, J. Caroll,
G. Shephard, A. Boaker, T. Goldsmith, E. Ebbs, and Mr Robert
Brown. For a brief report on the Grey County society, see Toronto
*Globe*, 21 June 1853, which lists the officers as Heman Hurlburt, presi-
dent, Thomas Holdship, secretary, George Holdship, treasurer, and
the committee members as Jehiel Hurd, Wesley Burchill, and John
MacKey. See also Port Hope *Echo*, 31 March 1852; Murray, "Canada
and Anglo-American Anti-Slavery," 213.

24 *Liberator*, 30 July 1852; *National Anti-Slavery Standard*, 17 August 1852.
   The ASC's *Second Annual Report* claimed that the statement appeared in
   the British *Banner*.

25 Executive Committee of ASC, *Second Annual Report*, 9–10; Toronto
   *Globe*, 29 March 1853.

26 Executive Committee of ASC, *Second Annual Report*, 11–12. For the Ladies' Association's "Appeal from Canada," see Toronto *Globe*, 11 January 1853; *National Anti-Slavery Standard*, 20 January 1853; and *Canadian
   Churchman*, 20 January 1853.

27 Executive Committee of ASC, *Second Annual Report*; Murray, "Canada
   and Anglo-American Anti-Slavery," 228–30.

28 Burke, "Samuel Ringgold Ward," 79–83; *British and Foreign Anti-Slavery
   Reporter*, 1 June and 1 July 1853, 1 May 1854; Rochester *Frederick
   Douglass' Paper*, 14 July 1854.

29 Toronto *Provincial Freeman*, 28 June 1854; Toronto *Globe*, 24 June 1854;
   Rochester *Frederick Douglass' Paper*, 30 June, 6 and 14 July 1854.

30 Rochester *Frederick Douglass' Paper*, 25 May 1855.

31 Ibid.

32 Henning to Chamerovzow, 10 December 1855 and 17 January 1856,
   Anti-Slavery Papers, Rhodes House Library, C32/38–46; Murray,
   "Canada and Anglo-American Anti-Slavery," 274–7; Burke, "Samuel
   Ringgold Ward," 82–6.

33 An outline of Henning's activities in Canada prior to his affiliation
   with the *Globe* may be pieced together from Quebec *Gazette*, 28 September 1842, 3 February 1843; *Abstract of the Minutes of the Synod of the
   Presbyterian Church, Canada, Session XII*, 17; Hawkins, *Quebec Directory
   and Stranger's Guide*, 108; Toronto Academy Minute Book, 2 and
   10 September 1846, 8 October 1849, 2 July and 11 August 1852, Presbyterian Church Archives; Toronto *Telegram*, 13 December 1888, 19
   January 1889; Toronto *Globe*, 29 December 1888. For Henning's articles
   (not all signed but certainly his), see "The Coloured Population in
   Canada," "The Dawn Institute," "The Coloured Population of Canada," and "The Coloured Population of Canada: The Settlement
   of St. Catharines," *British Anti-Slavery Reporter*, 1 December 1885, 1
   May, 1 June, 1 October 1856, respectively.

34 See transcript of the fourth annual meeting in Rochester *Frederick Douglass' Paper*, 25 May 1855.

35 The *Globe* articles were reprinted, with comments, as a pamphlet in Henning and Linton, *Slavery in the Churches*. On Linton's activities, see Murray, "Canada and Anglo-American Anti-Slavery," 245–67.

36 Upper Canada Tract Society, *Colportage in Canada*, 3–14, 21–30; Henning and Linton, *Slavery in the Churches*, 7; Murray, "Canada and Anglo-American Anti-Slavery," 245–7.

37 *Brown's Toronto General Directory 1856*, xlvi.

38 Executive Committee of ASC, *Sixth Annual Report*; this report is mistitled, since it was actually the fifth report. See also Toronto *Globe*, 2 May 1857.

39 On the Anderson case, see Brode, *John Anderson*; and Reinders, "The John Anderson Case" and "Anglo-Canadian Abolitionism." See also the committee's statement dated 4 December 1860, entitled "The Extradition Case," in Toronto *Globe*, 5 December 1860.

40 Henning to Chamerovzow, 17 December 1860, Anti-Slavery Papers, Rhodes House Library, c32/42; Henning to Chamerovzow, 20 December 1860, ibid., c32/43. See also Toronto *Globe*, 20 December 1860.

41 Murray, "Canada and Anglo-American Anti-Slavery," 555–6.

42 Newcastle to Williams, 9 January 1861, and no. 34, 16 January 1861, cited in ibid., 557.

43 Murray, "Canada and Anglo-American Anti-Slavery," 557–8; Henning to Chamerovzow, 4 February 1861, Anti-Slavery Papers, Rhodes House Library, s18 c32/44. The writ appears in ibid., c32/46. Murray states that the barrister was Frederick S. Flood, but the *Globe*, 30 January 1861, names him Edwin Jones; however, Brode, *John Anderson*, 71, authoritatively identifies him as Edwin John James.

44 Murray, "Canada and Anglo-American Anti-Slavery," 565–7; Toronto *Globe*, 17, 18, and 20 December 1860, 16, 17, 22, 28, and 30 January, and 7, 11, and 12 February 1861; Henning to Chamerovzow, 4 February 1861, Anti-Slavery Papers, Rhodes House Library, s18 c32/44.

45 *British Anti-Slavery Reporter*, 1 February, 1 March, and 1 April 1861; Murray, "Canada and Anglo-American Anti-Slavery," 573.

46 Toronto *Globe*, 5 February 1863.

CHAPTER SEVEN

1 On the churches and antislavery, see Landon, "Relation of Canada to Anti-Slavery and Abolition in the U.S.," 55–60; Murray, "Canada and Anglo-American Anti-Slavery," 238–62; Pemberton, "Anti-Slavery Society of Canada," 100–12; and Winks, *Blacks in Canada*, 219–24.

2 On Rolph, see above, 48, 56, 58–66. See also Toronto *Mirror*, 11 October 1850; *Voice of the Fugitive*, 26 February 1852.
3 Ibid., 28 February 1851.
4 Ibid., 4 April 1851.
5 Carrington, *Anglican Church in Canada*, chs. 7–9; Diocese of Toronto, *Proceedings of Synod, 1851–65*; Church Society of Diocese of Toronto, *Constitution and Objects*, 6–10; Flint, *John Strachan*, 31; Winks, *Blacks in Canada*, 169; Church Society of Diocese of Toronto, *Annual Report*, 1843–65.
6 *Church*, 3 January 1850.
7 Ibid., 20 December 1849.
8 Ibid., 10 April 1850.
9 *Canadian Churchman*, 19 August and 16 September 1852.
10 On the Canadian women's letter, see above, 125–6. See also *Canadian Churchman*, 20 January 1853.
11 On Linton's activities, see above, 132, 147, and Murray, "Canada and Anglo-American Anti-Slavery," 245–67. See also *Canadian Churchman*, 25 January 1856.
12 Elliott, "Black Education in Canada West," 25–9, chs. 2, 3; Murray, "Canada and Anglo-American Anti-Slavery," 486–518; Colonial Church and School Society, *17th Annual Report*, 20, 39–42, and *Annual Report, 1854–55*, 42–3, NAC MG17/B4; *Provincial Freeman*, 9, 16, 23 September and 25 November 1854.
13 Colonial Church and School Society, *Annual Report, 1854–55*, 44–8, and *Annual Report, 1855–56*, 52–4, NAC MG17/B4.
14 Ibid., 51–9; Elliott, "Black Education in Canada West," ch. 4; Murray, "Canada and Anglo-American Anti-Slavery," 502–6; London *Free Press*, 30 and 31 May 1856. For the later activities of the mission, see Colonial Church and School Society Reports for 1856–57, 1859, and 1866.
15 *Echo and Protestant Episcopal Recorder*, 2 December 1851, 21 January, 11 February, 31 March, 5 May, and 16 June 1852, 10 August 1853, 25 September 1857; Carverhill, *Toronto Directory 1859–60*, 256.
16 Niagara *Christian Examiner*, November 1840, 343–6; Presbyterian Church in Canada in Connection with the Church of Scotland, *Acts and Proceedings of Synod, 1831–1865*.
17 *Minutes of the Missionary Presbytery of the Canadas*, 1:1, 141, 147; 2:213.
18 *Minutes of Synod of the United Presbyterian Church in Canada*, 3:97–8; "Colportage in Canada West," *United Presbyterian Magazine* 1, no. 10 (October 1854).
19 "Slavery and its Christian Advocates," ibid. 8, no. 4 (April 1861).
20 Ibid.
21 For the impact of the "Great Disruption" in Canada, see Moir, *Enduring Witness*, 101–6. On the *Banner*, see above, 75–80. See also United

Church Archives, *Minute Book of the Presbytery of Toronto* 1 (3 June 1845):21; Presbyterian Church in Canada, *Minutes of Synod* 1 (6 June 1845):44–5.

22 Ibid. 4 (11 June 1851):24.

23 Ibid. 1 (8–14 June 1853):19; 2 (17 June 1857):34.

24 Ibid. 1 (27 June 1849):22, (5–13 June 1850), and (4–11 June 1851):23; *Ecclesiastical and Missionary Record* 4 (March 1850):66–7, 7 (January 1851):33–4, 7 (July 1851):131–2, 8 (July 1852):130, 9 (December 1853):25.

25 Presbyterian Church in Canada, *Minutes of Synod* 1 (4–11 June 1851):23; *Ecclesiastical and Missionary Record* 7 (January 1851):33–4, 8 (March 1852):68, 9 (July 1853):132, 10 (August 1854):146–7; Elgin Association, *Ninth Annual Report*, 7.

26 On the development of the various branches of Methodism in Canada, see Grant, "Canada," in Harmon, *Encyclopedia of World Methodism*, 1:385–401; Cornish, *Cyclopedia of Methodism in Canada*, 32.

27 Toronto *Christian Guardian*, 13 August 1831, 8 May, 5 and 19 June, 10 July, and 7 August 1833.

28 On the Wesleyan Methodists and the Mackenzie rebellion, see above, 54–5.

29 Carroll, *Case and His Contemporaries*, 4:188; Matlack, *American Slavery and Methodism*, ch. 10; see above, 55–6.

30 See above, 55–6; *Zion's Watchman and Wesleyan Observor*, 31 October 1840; *British and Foreign Anti-Slavery Reporter*, 26 August 1840, 209–10.

31 *Christian Guardian*, 5 March and 6 April 1851.

32 Ibid., 12 and 26 December 1855, 9 and 16 January and 5 March 1856.

33 Ibid., 9 January 1856.

34 Ibid., 28 September 1859, 23 January 1861.

35 Ibid., 3 April 1861, 1 June 1864.

36 *Canada Christian Advocate*, 27 March, 5 and 26 June 1845, 2 November 1847, 4 March and 8 April 1851; Webster, *Methodist Episcopal Church in Canada*; Methodist Episcopal Church in Canada, *Minutes of Niagara and Bay Quinte Conferences*, 1864, 6, 18.

37 *Canada Christian Advocate*, 19 October 1853, 29 February, 3 September, 8 October, and 3 December 1856.

38 Methodist Episcopal Church in Canada, *Year Book 1836–1865*; *Minutes of Bay of Quinte Conference*, 17 June 1863, 52–4; *Minutes of Ontario Conference*, May 1863, 34–5; *Minutes of Niagara and Bay of Quinte Conferences*, 1864.

39 On the Methodist New Connexion Church, see Grant, "Canada," in Harmon, *Encyclopedia of World Methodism*, 1:391–2, and Cornish, *Cyclopedia of Methodism in Canada*, 455.

40 Canadian Wesleyan Methodist New Connection Church, *Minutes*, 23d Conference, 4–9 June 1851, 12; *Minutes*, 26th Conference,

7–14 June 1854, 12; *Minutes*, 27th Conference, 6–13 June 1855; *Minutes*, 28th Conference, 4–10 June 1856, 16.

41 On the early history of Congregationalism in Upper Canada, see Eddy, "Congregationalism in the Early Canadas," i–xxi, 209–80. The petition Lillie signed is found in NAC RG1/E3/35, 216–216B; for his early work at Brantford, see above, ch. 4, n. 17. Peter Freeland was a partner in Freeland and Taylor, a Toronto soap and candle manufacturing firm; his son Patrick was a Toronto lawyer; John F. Marling was a Toronto resident of independent means and, like the Freelands, a prominent Congregationalist; see *Brown's Toronto General Directory, 1856*, 20, 36, 39. Thomas Ellerby pastored Zion Congregational Church from the mid-1850s, and Francis H. Marling held the pulpit at the Congregational church on Yonge Street; see Caverhill, *Toronto Directory, 1859–60*, 256; "Summary of Statistics – 1858–59," *Canadian Independent*, no. 1, July 1859, 17.

42 *Canadian Independent*, 18 September 1854 [36] and 25 June 1855 [110]; see also Winks, *Blacks in Canada*, 222.

43 *Canadian Independent*, 16 April [156], 1 May [164–5], 21 May [173–4], and 29 May [178–9] 1855.

44 Winks, *Blacks in Canada*, 219; Niagara Baptist Association, *Minutes of the Thirty-Seventh Anniversary Meeting*, June 1856, 6, cited in Murray, "Canada and Anglo-American Anti-Slavery," 242–3; Canada Baptist Union, *2nd Annual Report, 1845*, 9, *4th Annual Report, 1847*, 10; Toronto *Gospel Tribune* 1 (June 1854):55; 2 (September 1855):141–2, (October 1855):166–7, (January 1856):229–30, (February 1856):257–61, (April 1856):334; 3 (June 1856):46–51. On Robert Dick, see Dyster, "Robert Dick."

45 Dorland, *Society of Friends*, 281–4. See also Ontario Archives, MS303, "Proceedings and Minutes of Canada Meetings 1810–1955, Canada Half Year's Meeting of Friends Held at Yonge Street 2nd of 9th Month 1835," "Yonge Street Monthly Meeting 13th of 9th month 1849," and "West Lake Monthly Meetings 1849–1876," 14 December 1854. No Quakers, Mennonites, or Jews surfaced in the analysis of the office holders of the UCAS, the ASC, or the Elgin Association, or, with the exception of two Jews, among the stockholders of the latter. See tables 18 and 32. See also Moir, *Enduring Witness*, 126.

46 Moir, *Church in the British Era*, 165.

47 Ibid.

CHAPTER EIGHT

1 Gathering the information for the nearly four hundred people on which the tables in this chapter are based took several years. The sources are so numerous that citing them individually would be im-

practicable. In some cases the people themselves kept diaries and journals or wrote autobiographical accounts of their lives; in a few cases there were published book-length biographies. Often, however, the information had to be ferreted out piece by piece. The *Dictionary of American Biography*, like the *Dictionary of National Biography*, was helpful, and vols. 9–11 of the *Dictionary of Canadian Biography* (DCB) were indispensable. Other frequently used standard sources of nineteenth-century Canadian biography included Morgan's *Bibliotheca Canadensis* and *Canadian Men and Women of the Time*, Rose's *Cyclopedia of Canadian Biography*, Cochrane's *Canadian Album*, and Wallace's *Macmillan Dictionary of Canadian Biography*. City and county directories were a rich source of information on individuals, as were the files of published obituaries held at many public libraries throughout the province. Especially productive in the case of church leaders were the biographical files of the Presbyterian Church in Canada Archives at Knox College and the United Church of Canada Archives at Victoria University, both in Toronto. The Canada West census for 1842, 1851, and 1861 often provided bits of information that were not available in obituaries and that frequently confirmed material obtained elsewhere.

A computer greatly facilitated the analysis of the data on the 132 antislavery leaders, and I owe a great debt of gratitude to my friend and colleague at St Francis Xavier University, Professor Muhammad Fiaz, then chairman of the Department of Sociology, who generously spent many hours patiently guiding me through the unfamiliar territory of the SPSSX format. A detailed code book comprising 115 categories of information was prepared; it proved to be more elaborate than was necessary, for sufficient information was found in only about half the areas. The device was modelled on an instrument that Professor John McKivigan, associate editor of the Frederick Douglass Papers at Yale University, used in a paper entitled "Schism: The Non-Ideological Factors Underlying the Factionalization of the American Anti-Slavery Movement," which he presented at the annual meeting of the Society for the History of the Early American Republic in July 1985 at Gunston Hall, Lortonville, Virginia. I am grateful to Professor McKivigan for allowing me to use his code book, which was modified substantially to meet the needs of this study.

As the data on the Elgin Association stockholders was much smaller in volume, it was analysed manually.

2 On Black abolition in Canada, see Ripley, *Black Abolitionist Papers*, 2:3–46. The precise number of blacks in Canada in the 1860s or at any other time is uncertain. The percent used here originates with Professor Winks, who made a careful assessment of the question. See his essay "How Many Negroes in Canada?" in *Blacks in Canada*, 484–96.

3 See above, 119–20, 125–6, 127–8.

CHAPTER NINE

Substantial portions of this chapter were published previously in "A Restless Child of Change and Accident."

1 Three authoritative studies of Reconstruction are Randall and Donald, *Civil War and Reconstruction*, 2d ed., Franklin, *Reconstruction after the Civil War*, and Stampp, *Era of Reconstruction*.

2 The editorial pages, excluding telegraphic borrowings, of twenty-one newspapers published in Ontario between 1865 and 1877 were the main sources for this chapter. The list was compiled to ensure an adequate geographic distribution while maintaining a balance among the various political and sectarian perspectives in the region. In most cases titles were read issue by issue, though in some instances this was not possible since the title did not span the entire period.

3 Toronto *Globe*, 6 April and 6 June 1865; *Christian Guardian*, 12 April 1875.

4 Hamilton *Daily Spectator*, 27 November 1865, 24 January 1866; Toronto *Leader*, 18 May 1865, 2 February 1867; London *Free Press*, 20 June 1865, 30 October 1869, 18 February 1874; Toronto *Canadian Freeman*, 6 June 1865. For other revealing comments, see Ottawa *Times*, 2 May 1866, which stated that the freedmen would work only "under the driver's lash"; the London *Free Press*, 13 January 1866, which predicted that the planters would soon seek other labourers, leaving the mass of blacks unemployed; and the Goderich *Semi-Weekly Signal*, 23 April 1868, which warned that under such conditions the blacks who were "too lazy to work" would "rob, pillage, murder and ravish on every hand."

5 London *Western Advertiser*, 28 February and 10 April 1868; Toronto *Leader*, 28 March 1867, 4 April 1870; Hamilton *Daily Spectator*, 18 November 1865; Kingston *Daily News*, 26 March 1867; Ottawa *Times*, 4 September 1869; Toronto *Globe*, 8 November 1867; Ottawa *Citizen*, 18 December 1868, 8 July 1869.

6 London *Free Press*, 29 July 1868; Toronto *Globe*, 7 August 1874; Toronto *Leader*, 6 April 1866, 21 July 1868; Kingston *British Whig*, 27 August 1868; *Canadian Monthly and National Review*, November 1876, 449–50; Hamilton *Daily Spectator*, 1 September 1865; Ottawa *Times*, 7 September 1874.

7 Hamilton *Daily Spectator*, 24 January 1866; Hamilton *Evening Times*, 5 February 1867; Ottawa *Citizen*, 24 February, 6 December 1866; London *Free Press*, 20 June 1865; *Canadian Christian Advocate*, 5 June 1867.

8 Stampp, *Era of Reconstruction*, 131–5.

9 Toronto *Globe*, 5 February 1866, 9 November 1867; Toronto *Leader*, 22 February 1866; Peterborough *Examiner*, 5 April 1866; Hamilton *Daily Spectator*, 2 June 1866; London *Free Press*, 13 January, 20 March

1866; Goderich *Semi-Weekly Signal*,
23 February 1866; Ottawa *Times*, 23 February 1866; Toronto *Canadian Freeman*, 1 March 1866.

10 Stampp, *Era of Reconstruction*, 135–40.

11 Newmarket *Era*, 6 April 1866; Toronto *Globe*, 28, 31 March 1866; Toronto *Leader*, 21 and 29 March 1866; Peterborough *Examiner*, 5 April 1866; *Christian Guardian*, 4 April 1866; London *Free Press*, 30 March and 11 April 1866.

12 Stampp, *Era of Reconstruction*, 141–3.

13 Toronto *Globe*, 5 and 8 May, 22 June, and 3 July 1865, 12 October 1875; Chatham *Weekly Planet*, 6 July 1865, 12 April 1866; *Canadian Christian Advocate*, 31 May, 26 July, and 18 October 1865; Sarnia *Observer*, 28 April and 4 August 1865; Hamilton *Daily Spectator*, 3 July 1865, 6 and 31 January, 18, 25, and 31 August 1866, 31 August 1868.

14 Ottawa *Citizen*, 21 and 24 June 1865, 8 July 1869; Kingston *Daily News*, 23 January 1866; *Christian Guardian* 5 July 1865.

15 Ottawa *Times*, 23 February 1866; Toronto *Leader*, 6 October 1865; London *Free Press*, 24 September 1866.

16 Toronto *Leader*, 6 December 1865, 31 January and 16 February 1866; London *Free Press*, 14 September 1865, 13 January and 24 September 1866.

17 Toronto *Canadian Freeman*, 6 September 1866.

18 Hamilton *Evening Times*, 22 July 1865.

19 Toronto *Leader*, 11 November 1865.

20 Ibid., 14 October 1867, 28 June 1865. See also Oshawa *Vindicator*, 28 February 1866; Peterborough *Examiner*, 27 April 1865; Hamilton *Evening Times*, 14 March 1872; London *Western Advertiser*, 10 January 1873; London *Free Press*, 13 January and 12 May 1866, 18 October 1867; Ottawa *Times*, 23 February and 31 May 1866; *Evangelical Witness*, 15 January 1873, 16 September 1874.

21 London *Free Press*, 12 May 1866; Toronto *Leader*, 6 October 1865; Ottawa *Times*, 8 December 1866.

22 Toronto *Leader*, 7 September and 9 November 1868; Hamilton *Daily Spectator*, 31 August 1868.

23 Ibid., 18 November, 7 December 1875, 27 March 1866; Toronto *Leader*, 30 and 31 March 1866; London *Free Press*, 29 July 1868; Kingston *British Whig*, 6 October 1866; Toronto *Canadian Freeman*, 6 June 1865.

24 Stampp, *Era of Reconstruction*, 138–41.

25 Toronto *Canadian Freeman*, 6 June 1865; Kingston *British Whig*, 21 August 1876; Hamilton *Evening Times*, 29 October 1867.

26 Ottawa *Citizen*, 9 December 1868; Toronto *Canadian Freeman*, 6 June 1865; Hamilton *Evening Times*, 6 November 1867; Kingston *British Whig*, 5 October 1866, 27 August 1868; *Christian Guardian*, 12 July 1865, 17 April 1867, 19 February 1868.

27 Ottawa *Times*, 28 May 1874. See also Hamilton *Daily Spectator*, 20 February 1875, which stated that Congress should have concentrated on repealing the laws that differentiated between blacks and whites, instead of forcing social intercourse; London *Free Press*, 10 March 1875, which believed that forcing social contact would merely exacerbate social feelings and which applauded the efforts of some states to circumvent the bill and agreed that either the black man must be put in his "proper place" or the races must separate; *Canadian Monthly and National Review*, October 1874, 380; Toronto, *Globe*, 17 March 1875.

28 In tables 35 and 37 the following explanation of terms should be noted:
   *Undesirable labourer*   Lazy; must be forced to work; would work only enough to survive; could not compete successfully with other labourers.
   *Desirable labourer*   Good worker; eager to work; reliable; could compete successfully with other labourers.
   *Negative general personal character*   Indolent; childlike; brutish; docile; sensual; slow to learn; revert to state of nature without white supervision; inferior to whites.
   *Positive general personal character*   Gentle; loving; trustworthy; eager to learn; not lazy; do not revert to state of nature if left to themselves.
   *Pessimistic about future prospects in United States*   Will die out in America; will remain at lower levels of society; will be objects of scorn and social outcasts.
   *Optimistic about future prospects in United States*   Will not die out in United States; will increase in numbers; will prosper in time; will become good citizens.

29 See above.

30 See Frederickson, *Black Image in the White Mind*, 71–2.

31 On the American School of Ethnology, see Morton, *Crania Americana*, especially 1–7, 62–94, 260–1, and 269–91, an essay by George Combe on the relationship of craniology to contemporary ethnological thought; Nott and Gliddon, *Types of Mankind* and *Indigenous Races*. Frederickson provides a good introduction to the American School of Ethnology in *Black Image in the White Mind*, ch. 3.

32 Frederickson develops the ideas of the Romantic Racialists in *Black Image in the White Mind*, ch. 4.

33 See Drew, *North-Side View of Slavery*, 94–5, 118–19, 234–5, and 341 for Drew's own comments on prejudice in Canada West; and 121, 130, 137, 159, 173, 279, 313, and 371 for the comments of former slaves; see also Howe, *Refugees from Slavery in Canada West*. The theme of Canadian prejudice recurs throughout the report. See also Silverman, *Unwelcome Guests*.

# Bibliography

PRIMARY SOURCES

*Manuscript Collections*

CANADIAN BAPTIST ARCHIVES, HAMILTON, ONTARIO
Canada Baptist Union. 2nd Annual Report, 1845.
– 4th Annual Report, 1847.

LONDON PUBLIC LIBRARY, LONDON, ONTARIO. LONDON ROOM
Scrapbook.

METROPOLITAN TORONTO CENTRAL LIBRARY. BALDWIN ROOM
Toronto Mechanics' Institute. Board Minutes, 1840–48.

MITCHELL LIBRARY, GLASGOW. SMEAL COLLECTION
Glasgow Emancipation Society. Cash Book, 1833–58.
– Minute Books, 1833–47.
– Miscellaneous Papers, 1.

NATIONAL ARCHIVES OF CANADA
Canada West Census, 1842, 1851, 1861.
Manuscript Group 11, Public Record Office, London: Colonial Office.
    Q Series, Correspondence and Enclosures from Governors, Administra-
    tors, and Interdepartmental Correspondence, vols. 398, 403.
Public Record Office, London: CO42. Canada Original Correspondence,
    vols. 459, 468, 474, 478.

Record Group 1, State Records of the Executive Council.
  E1, Minute Books, 1764–1867, vols. 49, 54.
  E3, Upper Canada State Papers, 1791–1841, vols. 35, 49.
Record Group 7, Records of the Governor General's Office.
  G1, Despatches from the Colonial Office, 1784–1909, vols. 83, 84, 95.
  G2, Despatches from the Colonial Office, 1794–1909.
Rev. William King Papers, MG24/J14.


OBERLIN COLLEGE ARCHIVES, OBERLIN, OHIO
Hiram Wilson Papers.


ONTARIO ARCHIVES, TORONTO
MS303, Records of the Orthodox Friends and Associated Meetings.


PRESBYTERIAN CHURCH IN CANADA ARCHIVES, TORONTO
Toronto Academy Minute Book.
Bryan, T.G.M., compiler. "Biographical Directory of Graduates and Students
  of Knox College, Toronto, 1845–1945."


RHODES HOUSE LIBRARY, OXFORD
Papers of the British and Foreign Anti-Slavery Society and Aborigines Protection Society.


SCOTTISH RECORD OFFICE, EDINBURGH
Minutes. Paisley Presbytery, 1830.
Minutes of Session. Free St George's, Paisley, 1845.
Minutes. Synod of Glasgow and Ayr, 1830.
Minutes of Renfield Street Church, 1839–47.


STAFFORD COUNTY RECORD OFFICE
Queen Street Congregational Church Minute Book from September 1809 to
  27 July 1854.


UNITED CHURCH OF CANADA ARCHIVES, TORONTO
John Street Church, Belleville, Ontario. Communion Roll, 1847–87.
Minute Book of the Congregational Church Hamilton, Gore District, Upper
  Canada, 1835–51.
Minute Book of the Presbytery of Toronto in Connexion with the Presby-
  terian Church of Canada ... 1844–61.
St James–Bond Street Congregational Church, Toronto, Minute Book, 1849–
  57.
Zion Church. Congregational. Toronto. Church Book of Record.

WILLIAM L. CLEMENTS LIBRARY, UNIVERSITY OF MICHIGAN, ANN ARBOR
Weld-Grimke Papers

## Published Reports

Abstract of the Minutes of the Synod of the Presbyterian Church of Canada in Connection with the Church of Scotland. Session XII. Holden at Montreal, 7th–12th July, 1842. Toronto: Hugh Scobie, 1842.

Alexander, William Lindsay. Memoirs of the Life and Writings of Ralph Wardlaw, D.D. 2d ed. Edinburgh: Adam and Charles Black, 1856.

American Anti-Slavery Society. Annual Report. New York, 1834–40.

Anti-Slavery Society of Canada. Constitution and Bye-Laws of the Anti-Slavery Society of Canada. Toronto: George Brown, Globe Office, 1851.

Armstrong, J., ed. Rowsell's City of Toronto and County of York Directory for 1850–1 ... Toronto: Henry Rowsell, 1850.

Barnes, Gilbert H., and Dwight L. Dummond, eds. Letters of Theodore Dwight Weld, Angelina Grimke Weld, and Sarah Grimke, 1822–1844. 2 vols. New York: D. Appelton Century Company, Inc., 1934.

Brown, Peter. The Fame and Glory of England Vindicated Being an Answer to "The Glory and Shame of England." By Veritas. New York and London: Wiley and Putnam, 1842.

Brown's Toronto City and Home District Directory 1846–7 ... Toronto: George Brown, 1846.

Brown, W.R., compiler, Brown's Toronto General Directory 1856 ... Toronto: MacLear and Co., 1856.

– Brown's Toronto General Directory 1861 ... Toronto: W.C. Chewett and Co., 1861.

Burns, Rev. Dr. Speech Delivered at the Anti-Slavery Meeting, Held at Paisley, on the 1st November, 1830. Paisley: Alex. Gardner, 1830.

Burns, Rev. Robert F., ed. The Life and Times of the Rev. Robert Burns, D.D., F.A.S., F.R.S.E. Toronto. Including an Unfinished Autobiography. Toronto: James Campbell and Son, 1872.

Campbell, C.T. Pioneer Days in London: Some Account of Men and Things in London Before It Became a City. London: Advertiser Job Printing Company, 1921.

Canadian Wesleyan Methodist New Connexion Church. Minutes of the Annual Conferences of the Canadian Wesleyan Methodist New Connexion Church, 1836–65.

Canniff, William. The Medical Profession in Upper Canada 1783–1850: An Historical Narrative, with Original Documents Relating to the Profession Including Some Brief Biographies. Toronto: William Briggs, 1894.

Caverhill, W.C.F. Caverhill's Toronto City Directory 1859–60. Toronto: W.C.F. Caverhill, 1859.

*Censuses of Canada, 1665 to 1871. Statistics of Canada.* Vol. 4. Ottawa: I.B. Taylor, 1876.

*The Christian's Manual; Select Pamphlets and Tracts.* Toronto: Lowell and Gibson for Andrew Hamilton, 1861.

Church Society of the Diocese of Toronto. *Annual Report.* Toronto: Anglican Church House, 1843–65.

– *The Constitution and Objects of the Church Society of the Diocese of Toronto.* Toronto: Diocesan Press, 1852.

*City of Hamilton Directory ...* Hamilton: Spectator Office for C.W. Cooke, 1853.

*City of Hamilton Directory ... 1858.* Hamilton: William A. Shepherd, 1858.

Colgate, William, ed. "The Diary of John White." *Ontario History* 47, no. 4 (1955–56): 147–70.

Colonial Church and School Society. *The Annual Report of the Colonial Church and School Society for the Year 1853–1854 ...* London: Society's Offices, 1854.

– *The Annual Report of the Colonial Church and School Society for the Year 1854–55 ...* London: Society's Offices, 1855.

– *The Annual Report of the Colonial Church and School Society for the Year 1855–56.* London: Society's Offices, 1856.

– *The Annual Report, for the Year 1856–57, of the Colonial Church and School Society ...* London: Society's Offices, 1857.

– *Seventeenth Annual Report of the Colonial Church and School Society ...* London: Society's Offices, 1853.

Committee of the Free Church Anti-Slavery Society. *An Address to the Office-Bearers and Members of the Free Church of Scotland on Her Present Connexion with the Slave-Holding Churches of America from the Committee of the Free Church Anti-Slavery Society.* Edinburgh: Charles Ziegler, 1847.

– *Strictures on the Proceedings of the Last General Assembly of the Free Church of Scotland, Regarding Communion with the Slave-Holding Churches of America, Respectfully Addressed to the Office-Bearers and Members of That Church.* Edinburgh: Charles Ziegler, 1847.

*County of Perth Gazetteer and General Business Directory for 1863–4 ...* Ingersoll: Sutherland Bros., 1863.

Cruikshank, E.A., ed. *The Correspondence of Lieutenant Governor John Graves Simcoe, with Allied Documents ... 1789–1793.* Toronto: Ontario Historical Society, 1923.

Diocese of Toronto. *Proceedings of Synod, Diocese of Toronto, 1851–1865.* Toronto: Anglican Church House, n.d.

– *Journal of the Incorporated Synod of the Church of England in the Diocese of Toronto. Fortieth Session, 1892.* Toronto: Rowsell and Hutchison, 1892.

*Directory of the County of Hastings ... 1860–61.* Belleville: Mackenzie Bowell, 1860.

Drew, Benjamin. *A North-Side View of Slavery. The Refugee: Or the Narrative of Fugitive Slaves in Canada. Related by Themselves, with an Account of the History and Condition of the Colored Population of Upper Canada.* Boston: John Jewett and Company, 1856.

Elgin Association. *Third Annual Report of the Directors of the Elgin Association. Presented at the Annual Meeting, Held on the First Day of September, 1852.* Toronto: John Carter, printer, 1853.

– *Fifth Annual Report of the Directors of the Elgin Association. Presented at the Annual Meeting, Held on the Seventh Day of September, 1854.* Toronto: Globe Book and Job Office, 1854.

– *Sixth Annual Report of the Directors of the Elgin Association. Presented at the Annual Meeting, Held on the Fifth Day of September, 1855.* Toronto: Globe Book and Job Office, 1855.

– *Seventh Annual Report of the Directors of the Elgin Association. Presented at the Annual Meeting, Held on the Third Day of September, 1856.* Toronto: Globe Book and Job Office, 1856.

– *Ninth Annual Report of the Directors of the Elgin Association. Presented at the Annual Meeting, Held on the First Day of September, 1858.* Toronto: Globe Book and Job Office, 1858.

– *Tenth and Eleventh Annual Reports of the Directors of the Elgin Association, for the Years 1859 to 1860.* Toronto: Globe Book and Job Office, 1861.

Executive Committee of the Anti-Slavery Society of Canada. *First Annual Report, Presented to the Anti-Slavery Society of Canada, by its Executive Committee, March 24th, 1852.* Toronto: Brown's Printing Establishment, 1852.

– *Second Annual Report Presented to the Anti-Slavery Society of Canada, by its Executive Committee, March 23rd, 1853.* Toronto: Brown's Printing Establishment, 1853.

– *Sixth Annual Report of the Anti-Slavery Society of Canada, Presented at the Annual Meeting, Held on the 29th April, 1857.* Toronto: Globe Book and Job Office, 1857.

Ferrier, A.D. *Reminiscences of Canada and the Early Days of Guelph.* 2d ed. Fergus: Fergus New Record, 1923.

Fraser, Alexander. *Sixth Report of the Bureau of Archives for the Province of Ontario, 67–74.* Toronto: L.K. Cameron, 1909.

– *Sixth Report of the Bureau of Archives for the Province of Ontario, 32–43.* Toronto: L.K. Cameron, 1911.

– *Seventh Report of the Bureau of Archives for the Province of Ontario 1910, 25–7, 67–70.* Toronto: L.K. Cameron, 1911.

Free Church of Scotland. *Acts and Proceedings of the General Assembly of the Free Church of Scotland, 1844–47.*

– *Report of the Proceedings of the General Assembly on Saturday, May 30, and Monday, June 1, 1846 Regarding the Relations of the Free Church of Scotland*

*and the Presbyterian Churches of America*. Rev. ed. Edinburgh: John Johnstone, 1846.

*Gazetteer and Directory of the County of Perth, 1867*. Toronto: Irwin and Bunham, 1867.

General Anti-Slavery Convention. *Minute Book. General Anti-Slavery Convention 1840*. Oxford: Rhodes House Library, 1840.

Gilfillan, George. *The Debasing and Demoralizing Influence of Slavery, on All and Everything Connected with It. A Lecture by the Reverend George Gilfillan, Dundee. Delivered at the Request of the Free Church Anti-Slavery Society*. Edinburgh: Charles Ziegler, 1847.

*Glasgow Post-Office Annual Directory for 1830–31* ... Glasgow: John Graham, 1830.

*Glasgow Post-Office Annual Directory for 1831–32* ... Glasgow: John Graham, 1831.

*Glasgow Post-Office Annual Directory for 1833–34* ... Glasgow: John Graham, 1833.

Glasgow Emancipation Society. *2nd Annual Report*. Glasgow: Aird and Russell, 1836.

– *Fifth Annual Report*. Glasgow: Aird and Russell, 1839.

– *Sixth Annual Report*. Glasgow: Aird and Russell, 1840.

– *Ninth Annual Report*. Glasgow: David Russell, 1843.

– *Tenth Annual Report*. Glasgow: David Russell, 1844.

– *Twelfth Annual Report*. Glasgow: David Russell, 1847.

*Gray's Annual Directory. 1833–34*. Edinburgh: John Gray, 1833.

Hawkins, Alfred. *The Quebec Directory and Stranger's Guide, to the City and Environs 1844–5*. Quebec: W. Cowan and Son, 1844.

Henning, Thomas. "The Coloured Population in Canada." *British and Foreign Anti-Slavery Reporter* 3 (1 December 1855): 271–2.

– "The Coloured Population of Canada. Amherstburgh and Malden." *British and Foreign Anti-Slavery Reporter* 4 (2 June 1856): 134–6.

– "The Coloured Population of Canada. Settlement of St. Catharine's." *British and Foreign Anti-Slavery Reporter* 4 (1 October 1856): 229–30.

– "The Dawn Institute. Canada West." *British and Foreign Anti-Slavery Reporter* 4 (1 May 1856): 110–13.

Henning, Thomas, and J.J.E. Linton. *Slavery in the Churches, Religious Societies, etc. A Review: By Thomas Henning, with Prefatory Remarks by J.J.E. Linton*. Toronto: Globe Book and Job Office, 1856.

Henning, Thomas, and William Reid. "Report of the Elgin Association," 18 March 1873. In *Ontario Legislature. 36 Victoria. Sessional Papers*, 1873, 61, 63.

*Historical Atlas of Wellington County, 1906*. Reprinted as *Illustrated Historical Atlas of Wellington County, Ontario*. Belleville: Mika Press, 1972.

Howe, Samuel Gridley. *The Refugees from Slavery in Canada West. Report of the Freedmen's Inquiry Commission.* Boston: Wright and Potter, 1864.

Hutchinson, Thomas. *Hutchinson's Hamilton Directory for 1862–63 ...* Hamilton, C.W.: John Eastwood and Company, 1862.

Lewis, Francis, compiler. *Toronto Directory and Street Guide for 1843–44.* Toronto: H. and H. Rowsell, 1843.

– *MacLear and Company's Canadian Almanac, and Depository of Useful Knowledge, for the Year 1856 ...* Toronto: MacLear and Co., n.d.

Mackay, Rev. MacIntosh, LL.D. *Memoir of James Ewing Esq., of Strathleven, Formerly Lord Provost of Glasgow, and M.P. for that City, LL.D. of the University of Glasgow.* Glasgow: Joseph MacLehose, 1866.

McClure, William. *Life and Labours of the Rev. Wm. McClure, for More than Forty Years a Minister of the Methodist New Connexion,* ed. by David Savage. Toronto: James Campbell and Son, 1872.

McEvoy, Henry. *C.E. Anderson and Company's Toronto City Directory for 1868–9 ...* Toronto: C.E. Anderson and Co., 1868.

Methodist Episcopal Church in Canada. *Methodist Episcopal Year Book 1836–1857.* N.p., n.d.

– *Minutes of the Bay of Quinte Conference 1844–1865.* N.p., n.d.

– *Minutes of the Niagara Conference 1844–1865.* N.p., n.d.

– *Minutes of the Ontario Conference 1863–1865.* N.p., n.d.

*Minutes of Missionary Presbytery of the Canadas in Connexion with the United Associate Synod of the Secession Church in Scotland.* N.p., n.d.

*Mitchell and Company's General Directory for the City of Toronto, and Gazetteer of the Counties of York and Peel for 1866.* Toronto: Mitchell and Company, 1866.

Morton, Samuel George. *Crania Americana; or a Comparative View of the Skulls of Various Aboriginal Nations of North and South America to Which is Prefixed an Essay on the Varieties of the Human Species.* Philadelphia: J. Dobson, 1839.

Nelson, Isaac. *Slavery Supported by the American Churches, and Countenanced by Recent Proceedings in the Free Church of Scotland. A Lecture by the Reverend Isaac Nelson, Belfast. Delivered at the Request of Free Church Anti-Slavery Society.* Edinburgh: Charles Ziegler, 1847.

Nott, J.C., and George R. Gliddon. *Indigenous Races of the Earth; or, New Chapters of Ethnological Inquiry; Including Monographs on Special Departments of Philology, Iconography, Cranioscopy, Paleontology, Pathology, Archaeology, Comparative Geography, and Natural History ...* Philadelphia: J.B. Lippincott and Company, 1857.

– *Types of Mankind: or, Ethnological Researches, Based upon the Ancient Monuments, Paintings, Sculptures, and Crania of Races, and upon their Natural, Geographical, and Biblical History ...* Philadelphia: Lippincott, Gramb, and Company, 1854.

Ontario Archives. *Upper Canada. Laws, Statutes, etc., 1792–1819.* N.p., n.d.

Paisley Philosophical Institution. *Rules of the Paisley Philosophical Institution.* Paisley: Wm. M'Intyre, 1857.

*Post Office Annual Directory for 1830–31 ... in Edinburgh ...* Edinburgh: Ballantyne and Co., 1830.

*Post Office Annual Directory, and Calendar, for 1836–37.* Edinburgh: Ballantyne and Co., 1836.

Presbyterian Church in Canada. *Minutes of the Synod of the Presbyterian Church in Canada, 1844–56.* Toronto: Presbyterian Church in Canada Archives, n.d.

Presbyterian Church in Canada in Connection with the Church of Scotland. *Acts and Proceedings of the Presbyterian Church in Canada in Connection with the Church of Scotland, 1831–65.* Montreal: n.d.

*Railton's Directory for the City of London, C.W. ... 1856–1857.* London, C.W.: Geo. Railton, 1856.

Rolph, Thomas. *A Brief Account, Together with Observations, Made during a Visit in the West Indies, and a Tour through the United States of America, in Parts of the Years 1832–3; Together with Statistical Account of Upper Canada.* Dundas, U.C.: Hayworth Hackstaff, 1836.

– *Emigration and Colonization; Embodying the Results of a Mission to Great Britain and Ireland, During the Years 1839, 1841, and 1842.* London: John Mortimer, 1844.

Stuart, Charles. *A Memoir of Granville Sharp ...* New York: American Anti-Slavery Society, 1836.

– *Liberia; or, The American Colonization Scheme Examined and Exposed.* Glasgow: W.R. M'Phun and George Gallie, 1833.

– "On the Abolition of Slavery by Great Britain." *Quarterly Anti-Slavery Magazine* 1 (October 1835): 3–21.

– "On the Coloured People of the United States." *Quarterly Anti-Slavery Magazine* 2 (October 1836): 11–22.

– "On the Use of Slave Produce." *Quarterly Anti-Slavery Magazine* 2 (January 1837): 153–72.

– *Prejudice Vincible, etc. ...* Boston: Garrison and Knapp, 1833.

– *Remarks on the Colony of Liberia and the American Colonization Society. With Some Account of the Settlement of Coloured People at Wilberforce, Upper Canada.* London: J. Messeder, 1832.

– *The American Colonization Scheme Further Unravelled.* Bath: John and James Keene, n.d.

– *The West India Question ...* New Haven: Hezekiah Homes and Company, 1833.

Sutherland, James, compiler. *City of Toronto Directory for 1867–8 ...* Toronto: W.C. Chewett and Co., 1867.

Thomas, Edward. *Irish Methodist Reminiscences; Being Mainly Memorials of the Life and Labours of the Rev. S. Nicholson.* London: J.C. Watts, 1889.

Thompson, George. *A Voice to the United States of America from the Metropolis of Scotland. Being an Account of Various Meetings Held in Edinburgh on the Subject of American Slavery, Upon the Return of Mr. George Thompson, from his Mission to that Country* ... Edinburgh: William Oliphant and Son, 1836.

Thomson, Andrew. *Substance of the Speech Delivered at the Meeting of the Edinburgh Society for the Abolition of Slavery, on October 19, 1830.* Edinburgh: William Whyte and Co., 1830.

Upper Canada Tract Society. *Colportage in Canada. An Address of the Committee of the Upper Canada Tract Society.* Toronto: Globe Book and Job Office, 1854.

Walton, George. *City of Toronto and Home District Commercial Directory for 1837.* Toronto: T. Dalton and W.J. Coates, n.d.

Ward, Samuel Ringgold. *Autobiography of a Fugitive Negro: His Anti-Slavery Labours in the United States, Canada, and England.* London: John Snow, 1855.

Willis, Michael. *Death Made Tributary to the Glory of God: A Sermon Preached in Gould Street Presbyterian Church, Toronto, on Sabbath, 22nd August, 1869: On the Occasion of the Death of the Rev. Dr. Robert Burns* ... Toronto: Adam, Stevenson and Co., 1869.

– *Slavery Indefensible: Showing that the Relation of Slave and Slaveholder Has No Foundation either in the Law of Nature or of Christianity with Remarks on Communion with Pro-Slavery Churches.* Glasgow: Maurice Ogle and Son, 1847.

Young, David. *Slavery Forbidden by the Word of God. A Lecture by the Rev. David Young, D.D. Perth. Delivered at the Request of the Free Church Anti-Slavery Society.* Edinburgh: Charles Ziegler, 1847.

Zion Congregational Church Toronto. *Annual Report for the Year 1872.* Toronto: Copp, Clark, and Company, 1873.

## Newspapers and Periodicals

AMERICAN

*Emancipator.* Boston, 1833–50.

*Frederick Douglass' Paper.* Rochester, 1851–55.

*Liberator.* Boston, 1836–59.

*National Anti-Slavery Standard.* New York, 1840–59.

*National Enquirer and Constitutional Advocate of Universal Liberty.* Philadelphia, 1837.

*North Star.* Rochester, 1847–51.

*Tribune.* Detroit, 1892.

*Zion's Watchman and Wesleyan Observor.* New York, 1840.

BRITISH

*Advertiser.* Paisley, 1836–40.

*Advertiser.* Staffordshire, 1830–33.

*Aris's Birmingham Gazette.* Birmingham, 1831.

*British and Foreign Anti-Slavery Reporter.* London, 1840–61.

*Chronicle.* Wolverhampton, 1826–37.

*Edinburgh Christian Instructor and Colonial Religious Register.* Edinburgh, 1839–43.

*Evening Courant.* Edinburgh, 1829–32.

*Evening Post.* Glasgow, 1836.

*Free Church Magazine.* Edinburgh, 1845.

*Herald.* Paisley, 1869.

*Scotsman.* Edinburgh, 1833–36, 1847–48.

*Witness.* Edinburgh, 1847–48.

CANADIAN

*Banner.* Toronto, 1843–48.

*British Colonial Argus.* St Catharines, 1833–35.

*British Colonist.* Toronto, 1838–54.

*British Whig.* Kingston, 1865–77.

*Canada Christian Advocate.* Hamilton, 1853, 1865–76.

*Canadian Christian Examiner and Presbyterian Review.* Niagara, 1837–40.

*Canadian Free Press.* London, 1852, 1856, 1865–77.

*Canadian Freeman.* Toronto, 1865–68.

*Canadian Independent.* London, 1854–55, 1858–65.

*Canadian Monthly and National Review.* Toronto, 1872–76.

*Canadian United Presbyterian Magazine.* Toronto, 1854–61.

*Christian Guardian.* Toronto, 1830–77.

*Chronicle.* Chatham, 1849–50.

*Chronicle and Gazette.* Kingston, 1831–35.

*Churchman.* Toronto, 1837–56.

*Citizen.* Ottawa, 1865–77.

*Constitution.* Toronto, 1836–37.

*Constitutional.* St Catharines, 1860.

*Correspondent.* Toronto, 1833.

*Daily Herald.* Stratford, 1889.

*Daily News.* Kingston, 1865–74.

*Daily Spectator.* Hamilton, 1853, 1865–75.

*Ecclesiastical and Missionary Record for the Presbyterian Church of Canada.* Toronto, 1847–61.

*Echo and Protestant Episcopal Recorder.* Port Hope, 1851–53.

*Evangelical Witness.* London, 1873–74.

*Evening Telegram.* Toronto, 1888.

*Evening Times.* Hamilton, 1865–77.

*Examiner*. Peterborough, 1865–77.
*Examiner*. Toronto, 1846–55.
*Gazette*. Quebec, 1834–38.
*Gleaner*. Niagara, 1824–36.
*Globe*. Toronto, 1844–77.
*Gospel Tribune*. Toronto, 1854–57.
*Journal*. St Catharines, 1836–43.
*Leader*. Toronto, 1865–77.
*Mirror*. Toronto, 1846–57.
*North Ontario Observor*. Port Perry, 1909.
*Observer*. Sarnia, 1865–77.
*Patriot*. Toronto, 1825–41.
*Provincial Freeman*. Windsor and Toronto, 1853–57.
*Reporter*. Niagara, 1830–40.
*Semi-Weekly Signal*. Goderich, 1865–73.
*Times*. Ottawa, 1865–77.
*Upper Canada Herald*. Kingston, 1833–37.
*Vindicator*. Oshawa, 1865–71.
*Voice of the Fugitive*. Sandwich, 1851–52.
*Weekly Planet*. Chatham, 1865–75.
*Western Advertiser*. London, 1866–76.
*Western Mercury*. Hamilton, 1831–34.

## SECONDARY SOURCES

Armstrong, Frederick H. "John Birrell." DCB 10.
Anderson, John. *A History of Edinburgh from the Earliest Period to the Completion of the Half Century 1850*. Edinburgh and London: A. Fullerton and Co., 1856.
Bailey, Thomas M., ed. "John Fisher." *Dictionary of Hamilton Biography*, vol. 1. Hamilton: W.L. Griffin, 1981.
Barker, Anthony J. *Captain Charles Stuart: Anglo-American Abolitionist*. Baton Rouge: Louisiana State University Press, 1986.
Bearden, Jim and Linda Jean Butler. *Shadd: The Life and Times of Mary Shadd Cary*. Toronto: NC Press, 1977.
Beyea, Marion. "James Scott Howard." DCB 9.
Bingham, Robert LeBaron. "The Glasgow Emancipation Society, 1833–1876." M. Litt. thesis, University of Edinburgh, 1973.
Boyd, John A. "David Buchan." *McMaster University Monthly* (February 1897): 194–203.
Bremner, Archie. *City of London, Ontario, Canada. The Pioneer Period and the London of Today*. 2d ed. London: London Printing and Lithographing Co., 1900. Reprint. London Public Library Board, 1967.

Bridgman, H.J. "Robert Burns." DCB 9.
- "Three Scots Presbyterians in Upper Canada: A Study in Emigration, Nationalism, and Religion." Ph.D. dissertation, Queen's University, 1978.
Brock, Daniel. *History of the County of Middlesex, Canada*. New ed. Belleville: Mika Studio, 1972.
Brode, Patrick. *The Odyssey of John Anderson*. Toronto: University of Toronto Press for the Osgoode Society, 1989.
Burke, Kevin Ronald. "Samuel Ringgold Ward: Christian Abolitionist." Ph.D. dissertation, Syracuse University, 1975.
Campbell, Stanley W. *The Slave Catchers: Enforcement of the Fugitive Slave Law, 1850–1860*. Chapel Hill: University of North Carolina Press, 1970.
*Canadian Baptist Register for 1858, The*. Toronto: Globe Book and Job Office, 1857.
Careless, J.M.S. *Brown of the Globe*. 2 vols. Toronto: Macmillan Company of Canada Limited, 1959, 1963.
- *Canada: A Story of Challenge*. 3rd ed. Toronto: Macmillan, 1974.
- "James Lesslie." DCB 11.
- "John Roaf." DCB 9.
- "Peter Brown." DCB 9.
Carnochan, Janet. *History of Niagara*. Toronto: William Briggs, 1914.
Carrington, Philip. *The Anglican Church in Canada: A History*. Toronto: Collins, 1963.
Carroll, John. *Case and his Contemporaries; or Canadian Itinerants Memorial: Constituting a Biographical History of Methodism in Canada, from its Introduction into the Province till the Death of the Rev. Wm. Case in 1855*. 5 vols. Toronto: Wesleyan Printing Establishment, 1867.
Caven, William. "The Rev. Michael Willis, D.D., LL.D." *Knox College Monthly* 4, no. 3 (January 1886): 97–101.
Champion, Thomas Edward, ed. *The Methodist Churches of Toronto: A History of the Methodist Denomination and Its Churches in York and Toronto, with Biographical Sketches of Many of the Clergy and Laity*. Toronto: G.M. Rose and Sons, Company Ltd, 1899.
Cobb, W. Montague. "Alexander Thomas Augusta." *Journal of the National Medical Association* 44, no. 4 (1952): 327–9.
Cochrane, Rev. William, D.D., ed. *The Canadian Album. Men of Canada; or Success by Example, in Religion, Patriotism, Business, Law, Medicine, Education and Agriculture* ... 4 vols. Brantford: Bradley, Garretson and Company, 1891.
*Commemorative Biographical Record of the County of York, Ontario. Containing Biographical Sketches of Prominent and Representative Citizens of Many of the Early Families*. Toronto: J.H. Beers and Co., 1907.
Cooper, J.I. "The Mission to the Fugitive Slaves at London." Ontario Historical Society. *Papers and Records* 66 (1954): 133–9.

Corey, Albert B. *The Crisis of 1830–1842 in Canadian-American Relations*. New Haven: Yale University Press, 1941.

Cornish, George H. *Cyclopedia of Methodism in Canada* ... Toronto: Methodist Book and Publishing House, 1881.

*Dictionary of American Biography*. 20 vols. New York: Charles Scribner's Sons, 1928–33.

*Dictionary of Canadian Biography*, ed. George W. Brown et al. 12 vols. to date Toronto: University of Toronto Press, 1965–.

*Dictionary of National Biography*, ed. Sir Leslie Stephen and Sir Sydney Lee. 21 vols. London: Oxford University Press, 1917.

Dillon, Merton L. *The Abolitionists: The Growth of a Dissenting Minority*. DeKalb: Northern Illinois University Press, 1974.

Dorland, Arthur Garratt. *A History of the Society of Friends (Quakers) in Canada*. Toronto: Macmillan Company of Canada, 1927.

Duberman, Martin, ed. *The Antislavery Vanguard: New Essays on the Abolitionists*. Princeton, New Jersey: Princeton University Press, 1965.

Dyster, Barrie. "Robert Dick." DCB 11.

Eddy, Earl B. "The Beginnings of Congregationalism in the Early Canadas." Th.D. thesis, Emmanuel College, 1957.

Elliott, Christopher Bruce. "Black Education in Canada West: A Parochial Solution to a Secular Problem, Rev. M.M. Dillon and the Colonial Church and School Society." M.A. thesis, Wilfrid Laurier University, 1989.

Farrell, John K.A. "Schemes for the Transplanting of Refugee American Negroes from Upper Canada in the 1840's." *Ontario History* 52 (1960): 245–9.

– "The History of the Negro Community in Chatham Ontario, 1787–1865." Ph.D. dissertation, University of Ottawa, 1955.

Farris, Allan L. "Michael Willis." DCB 10.

Filler, Louis. *The Crusade against Slavery 1830–1860*. New York, Evanston, and London: Harper and Row, 1960.

Fitch, E.R. *The Baptists of Canada: A History of Their Progress and Achievements*. Toronto: Standard Publishing Co. Ltd., 1911.

Fladeland, Betty. *Men and Brothers: Anglo-American Antislavery Cooperation*. Urbana: University of Illinois Press, 1972.

– *Abolitionists and Working-Class Problems in the Age of Industrialization*. Baton Rouge: Louisiana State University Press, 1984.

Flint, David. *John Strachan: Pastor and Politician*. Toronto: University of Toronto Press, 1971.

Forman, Debora, ed. *Legislators and Legislatures of Ontario: A Reference Guide*. 3 vols. Toronto: Legislative Library, Research and Information Services, 1984.

Franklin, John Hope. *Reconstruction after the Civil War*. Chicago: University of Chicago Press, 1961.

Frederickson, George M. *The Black Image in the White Mind: The Debate on Afro-American Character and Destiny, 1817–1914*. New York: Harper and Row, 1971.

Friedman, Lawrence J. *Gregarious Saints: Self and Community in American Abolitionism, 1830–1870*. Cambridge: Cambridge University Press, 1982.

French, G.S. "James Richardson." DCB 10.

Gates, Lillian Francis. "John Doel." DCB 10.

*Glasgow Past and Present Embracing Loose Memorabilia on Glasgow … by J.B.* 3 vols. Glasgow: David Robertson and Co., 1884.

Graham, W.H. *Tiger Dunlop*. London: Hutchinson, 1962.

Grant, John Webster. "Canada. British North America, 1765 to 1883." In *The Encyclopedia of World Methodism*, ed. Nolan B. Harmon, vol. 1, 385–401. Nashville, Tenn.: United Methodist Publishing House, 1974.

– *The Church in the Canadian Era: The First Century of Confederation*. Toronto: McGraw-Hill Ryerson, 1972.

Gregg, William D. *History of the Presbyterian Church in the Dominion of Canada …* Toronto: Presbyterian Printing and Publishing Company, 1885.

– "The Late Rev. William Reid, D.D." *Knox College Monthly* (March 1896): 473–8.

Hill, Daniel Grafton, Jr "Negroes in Toronto: A Sociological Study of a Minority Group." Ph.D. dissertation, University of Toronto, 1960.

– *The Freedom-Seekers: Blacks in Early Canada*. Agincourt, Ont.: Book Society, 1981.

*Historical Sketch of Markham Township 1793–1950*, compiled under supervision of Historical Committee: Alex. D. Bruce, chairman, Wesley C. Gohn, secretary. Markham: Economist and Sun, n.d.

*History of the County of Middlesex …* Toronto and London: W.A. and C.L. Goodspeed, n.d.

Hite, Roger W. "Voice of a Fugitive: Henry Bibb and Ante-bellum Black Separatism." *Journal of Black Studies* 4, no. 3 (March 1974): 269–84.

Hopper, R.P. *Old-Time Primitive Methodism in Canada 1829–1884*. Toronto: William Briggs, 1904.

Houston, Susan E. "Andrew Taylor McCord." DCB 11.

Jamieson, Annie Straith. *William King: Friend and Champion of Slaves*. Toronto: Missions of Evangelism, 1925.

Jarvis, Eric. "Charles Albert Berczy." Typescript, 1985, provided by Professor Jarvis, Department of History and Political Science, King's College, University of Western Ontario.

Jones, Alderman W.H., J.P. *History of the Congregational Churches of Wolverhampton from the Year 1662 to 1894*. London: Alexander and Shepheard, 1894.

Jones, Elwood. "John Scoble." DCB 9.

Kraditor, Aileen S. *Means and Ends in American Abolitionism: Garrison and His Critics on Strategy and Tactics 1834–1850*. New York: Pantheon Books, 1967.

Landon, Fred. "Abolitionist Interest in Upper Canada." *Ontario History* 44 (1952): 165–72.

– "Canada's Part in Freeing the Slave." Ontario Historical Society, *Papers and Records* 17 (1919): 74–84.

– "Captain Charles Stuart, Abolitionist." *Western Ontario History Nuggets*, no. 24 (1956).

– "The Anderson Fugitive Slave Case." *Journal of Negro History* 7, no. 3 (July 1922): 233–42.

– "The Anti-Slavery Society in Canada." *Journal of Negro History* 4 (January 1919): 33–44.

– "The Relation of Canada to the Anti-slavery and Abolition Movements in the United States." M.A. thesis, University of Western Ontario, 1919.

Leitch, Adelaide. *Floodtides of Fortune: The Story of Stratford and the Progress of the City through Two Centuries*. Stratford: Corporation of the City of Stratford, 1980.

Lindsay, Arnett G. "Diplomatic Relations between the United States and Great Britain Bearing upon the Return of Negro Slaves." *Journal of Negro History* 5, no. 4 (October 1920): 391–419.

Logan, Rayford W., and Michael R. Winston, eds. *Dictionary of American Negro Biography*. New York and London: W.W. Norton and Company, 1982.

London Chamber of Commerce. *Seventy Years of Service in Community Building. London, Canada, 1857–1934*. N.p., n.d.

McCalla, Douglas. "George Percival Ridout." DCB 10.

– "John McMurrich." DCB 11.

McDougall, Elizabeth Anne Kerr. "William Rintoul." DCB 8.

MacGregor, George. *The History of Glasgow from the Earliest Period to the Present Time*. Glasgow: Thomas D. Morison, 1881.

McKivigan, John R. "Schism: The Non-Ideological Factors Underlying the Factionalization of the American Antislavery Movement." Unpublished paper presented at the annual meeting of the Society for the History of the Early American Republic, July 1985, Gunston Hall, Lortonville, Virginia.

– *The War against Proslavery Religion: Abolitionism and the Northern Churches, 1830–1865*. Ithaca: Cornell University Press, 1984.

Magdol, Edward. *The Antislavery Rank and File: A Social Profile of the Abolitionists' Constituency*. New York: Greenwood Press, 1986.

Mander, Gerald P. *A History of Wolverhampton to the Early Nineteenth Century*, edited and completed by Norman W. Tildesley. Wolverhampton: Wolverhampton C.B. Corporation, 1960.

Mathews, Donald G. *Slavery and Methodism: A Chapter in American Morality*. Princeton: Princeton University Press, 1965.

Matlack, Lucius C. *The History of American Slavery and Methodism, from 1780 to 1849; and History of the Wesleyan Methodist Connection in America* ... New York: privately printed, 1849.

Mathieson, William Law. *British Slavery and Its Abolition 1823–1838*. 1926. Reprint. New York: Octagon Books, 1967.

May, Arthur Henry. *Queen Street Congregational Church Wolverhampton: The Story of a Hundred Years 1809–1909*. N.p., n.d.

Mealing, S.R. "John Graves Simcoe." DCB 5.

Miller, Floyd J. *The Search for a Black Nationality: Black Emigration and Colonization 1787–1863*. Urbana: University of Illinois Press, 1975.

Miller, Orlo. *Gargoyles and Gentlemen: A History of St. Paul's Cathedral, London, Ontario, 1834–1964*. Toronto: Ryerson Press, 1966.

Moir, John S. *Enduring Witness: A History of the Presbyterian Church in Canada*. Don Mills, Ont.: Presbyterian Publications, 1974.

– *The Church in the British Era, from the British Conquest to Confederation*. Toronto: McGraw-Hill Ryerson, 1972.

Morgan, Henry James. *Bibliotheca Canadensis: or a Manual of Canadian Literature*. Ottawa: G.E. Desbarats, 1867.

– , ed. *Canadian Parliamentary Companion*, 6th ed. Montreal: Gazette Steam Printing House, 1871.

– , ed. *The Canadian Men and Women of the Time: A Handbook of Canadian Biography*. Toronto: William Briggs, 1898.

Murray, Alexander Lovell. "Canada and the Anglo-American Anti-Slavery Movement: A Study in International Philanthropy." Ph.D. dissertation, University of Pennsylvania, 1960.

– "The Extradition of Fugitive Slaves from Canada: A Re-evaluation." *Canadian Historical Review* 43 (December 1962): 298–314.

Nicholson, David. R. "Michael Willis: Missionary Statesman, Social Activist, Christian Educator, and Reformed Theologian." M.Th. thesis, Toronto School of Theology, 1973.

Ogden, R. Lynn. "George Skeffington Connor." DCB 9.

Osofsky, Gilbert, ed. *Puttin' on Ole Massa: The Slave Narratives of Henry Bibb, William Wells Brown, and Solomon Northrup*. New York: Harper and Row, 1969.

Pease, William H. and Jane H. *Black Utopia: Negro Communal Experiments in America*. Madison, Wis.: State Historical Society of Wisconsin, 1963.

– *Bound with Them in Chains: A Biographical History of the Antislavery Movement*. Westport, Conn.: Greenwood Press, 1972.

– "Josiah Henson." DCB 11.

– "Opposition to the Founding of the Elgin Association." *Canadian Historical Review* 38, no. 3 (September 1857): 202–18.

Pemberton, Ian Cleghorn. "The Anti-Slavery Society of Canada." M.A. thesis, University of Toronto, 1967.
- "William McClure." DCB 10.
Randall, James G., and David Donald. *The Civil War and Reconstruction.* 2d ed. Lexington, Mass.: D.C. Heath and Company, 1969.
Rea, J.E. *Bishop Alexander Macdonell and the Politics of Upper Canada.* Toronto: Ontario Historical Society, 1974.
Reinders, Robert C. "Anglo-Canadian Abolitionism: The John Anderson Case, 1860–1861." *Renaissance and Modern Studies* 19 (1975): 72–97.
- "John Anderson." DCB 9.
- "The John Anderson Case, 1860–1: A Study in Anglo-Canadian Imperial Relations." *Canadian Historical Review* 56, no. 4 (December 1975): 393–415.
*Renfield Church: The Story of Its Origins and Its Ministers 1819–1919.* N.p., n.d.
Riach, Douglas. "Ireland and the Campaign against American Slavery, 1830–1860." Ph.D. dissertation, University of Edinburgh, 1975.
Rice, C. Duncan. *The Scots Abolitionists 1833–1861.* London and Baton Rouge: Louisiana State University Press, 1981.
Riddell, William Renwick. "Slavery in Canada." *Journal of Negro History* 5, no. 3 (July 1920): 261–377.
- *The Bar and the Courts of the Province of Upper Canada or Ontario.* Toronto: Macmillan Co., 1928.
- *The Life of John Graves Simcoe, First Lieutenant-Governor of the Province of Upper Canada 1792–96.* Toronto: McClelland and Stewart, 1926.
Ripley, C. Peter, ed. *The Black Abolitionist Papers*, vol. 2, *Canada 1830–1865.* London and Chapel Hill: University of North Carolina Press, 1986.
Robertson, J. Ross. *Landmarks of Toronto.* Toronto: J. Ross Robertson, 1898.
- *The History of Freemasonry in Canada.* Toronto: Morang, 1900.
Robbins, Arlie C. *Legacy to Buxton.* North Buxton, Ont.: A.C. Robbins, 1983.
Rose, George MacLean. *A Cyclopedia of Canadian Biography.* Toronto: Rose Publishing Co., 1886.
Russell, Peter A. "Robert Graham Dunlop." DCB 7.
Russell, Victor Loring. "Angus Morrison." DCB 11.
*St. John's – Renfield Church 1819–1969.* N.p., n.d.
*St. Lawrence Hall.* Toronto and Montreal: Nelson, 1969.
Shepperson, George. "The Free Church and American Slavery." *Scottish Historical Review* 30 (October 1951): 126–43.
- "Thomas Chalmers, the Free Church of Scotland, and the South." *Journal of Southern History* 17 (November 1951): 517–37.
Shepperson, W.G. *British Emigration to North America: Projects and Opinions in the Early Victorian Period.* Minneapolis: University of Minnesota Press, 1957.
Siebert, Wilbur H. *The Underground Railroad from Slavery to Freedom.* New York: Macmillan Co., 1899.

Silverman, Jason H. "Kentucky, Canada, and Extradition: The Jesse Happy Case." *Filson Club History Quarterly* 54 (January 1980): 50–60.

– "The American Fugitive Slave in Canada: Myths and Realities." *Southern Studies* 19 (Fall 1980): 215–27.

– *Unwelcome Guests: Canada West's Response to American Fugitive Slaves, 1800–1865*. Millwood, N.Y.: Associated Faculty Press, Inc., 1985.

– "'WE Shall be Heard!': The Development of the Fugitive Slave Press in Canada." *Canadian Historical Review* 65 (March 1984): 54–69.

Simpson, Donald George. "Blacks in Ontario from Earliest Times to 1870." Ph.D. dissertation, University of Western Ontario, 1971.

– "Charles Stuart." DCB 9.

Sims, Florence K. "Sheriff Davidson." *Waterloo Historical Society Annual Report*, 1928, 84–5.

Sissons, C.B. *Egerton Ryerson: His Life and Letters*. Toronto: Oxford University Press, 1937.

Somers, Hugh Joseph. "The Life and Times of the Hon. and Rt. Rev. Alexander Macdonell, D.D., First Bishop of Upper Canada 1762–1840." Ph.D. dissertation, Catholic University of America, 1931.

Stampp, Kenneth M. *The Era of Reconstruction, 1865–1877*. New York: Knopf, 1965.

Stewart, I. Annette. "Robert Graham Dunlop: A Huron County Anti-Compact Constitutionalist." M.A. thesis, University of Toronto, 1947.

Stewart, James B. *Holy Warriors: The Abolitionists and American Slavery*. New York: Hill and Wang, 1976.

Stouffer, Allen P. "A 'Restless Child of Change and Accident': The Black Image in Nineteenth Century Ontario." *Ontario History* 76 (June 1984): 128–50.

– "Michael Willis and the British Roots of Canadian Antislavery." *Slavery and Abolition* 8 (December 1987): 294–312.

Swainson, Donald. "Robert Wilkes." DCB 10.

Symons, Thomas H.B. "John Ryerson." DCB 10.

Taylor, Clare. *British and American Abolitionists: An Episode in Transatlantic Understanding*. Edinburgh: University of Edinburgh Press, 1974.

Temperley, Howard. *British Antislavery 1833–1870*. Columbia, S.C.: University of South Carolina Press, 1972.

Thomas, Clara. *Ryerson of Upper Canada*. Toronto: Ryerson Press, 1969.

Trudel, Marcel. *Dictionnaire des esclaves et de leur propriétaires au Canada français*. Montreal: Hurtubise HMH, 1990.

– *L'Esclavage Canada français: Histoire et conditions de l'esclavage*. Quebec: Les Presses Universitaires Laval, 1960.

Turner, Wesley B. "Thomas Rolph." DCB 8.

Ullman, Victor. *Look to the North Star: A Life of William King*. Boston: Beacon Press, 1971.

Wallace, W. Stewart. *A History of the University of Toronto 1827–1927*. Toronto: University of Toronto Press, 1927.

– , ed. *The Macmillan Dictionary of Canadian Biography*. 4th ed. Toronto: Macmillan of Canada, 1978.

Walton, Jonathan William. "Blacks in Buxton and Chatham, Ontario, 1830–1890: Did the 49th Parallel Make a Difference?" Ph.D. dissertation, Princeton University, 1979.

Walvin, James, ed. *Slavery and British Society 1776–1846*. London: Macmillan, 1982.

Webster, Thomas. *History of the Methodist Episcopal Church in Canada*. Hamilton: Canada Christian Advocate Office, 1870.

– *Life of Rev. James Richardson, a Bishop of the Methodist Episcopal Church in Canada*. Toronto: J.B. Magurn, 1876.

Williams, Eric. *History of the People of Trinidad and Tobago*. London: Andre Deutsch Ltd, 1964.

Winks, Robin W. "'A Sacred Animosity': Abolitionism in Canada." In *The Anti-Slavery Vanguard: New Essays on the Abolitionists*, ed. Martin Duberman, 301–42. Princeton, N.J.: Princeton University Press, 1965.

– "Samuel Ringgold Ward." DCB 9.

– *The Blacks in Canada: A History*. Montreal, New Haven, and London: Yale University Press, 1971.

– "Wilson Ruffin Abbott." DCB 10.

Woodward, Donald G. *Trinidad in Transition: The Years after Slavery*. London and New York: Oxford University Press, 1968.

# Index